Mastering Design Patterns for Layered Testing

Master Strategic Test Design, Enhance Automation, and Integrate CI/CD Seamlessly Across API and UI Layers with Python

Manish Saini

www.orangeava.com

First Published: April 2025

Published By: Orange Education Pvt Ltd, AVA®

Address: 9, Daryaganj, Delhi, 110002, India

275 New North Road Islington Suite 1314 London,

N1 7AA, United Kingdom

ISBN (PBK): 978-93-48107-49-7
ISBN (E-BOOK): 978-93-48107-16-9

Scan the QR code to explore our entire catalogue

www.orangeava.com

Dedicated To

My Beloved Wife:

Priyanka Bareja

Whose Unwavering Support, Love, and Encouragement
Inspire Me Every Day

About the Author

Manish Saini is a seasoned Lead SDET Consultant with over a decade of expertise in software quality assurance and test automation. His technical prowess spans multiple programming languages including Python, JavaScript, Golang, and Java, which he has leveraged to architect robust automation frameworks and implement sophisticated testing solutions for complex software systems. Through his work with industry leaders such as DigitalOcean and Akamai, he has gained deep expertise in cloud infrastructure, Kubernetes, and API performance testing. He consistently delivers high-impact testing solutions for cloud-based applications and microservices architectures.

As an active leader in the BrowserStack QA Community, Manish is passionate about knowledge sharing and community building. He regularly organizes meetups, bug bash events, and technical sessions, delivering keynote talks on QA strategies, automation best practices, and CI/CD integration. His commitment to mentoring aspiring SDETs has helped numerous professionals transition into automation roles and build successful careers in software testing. Through articles and YouTube podcasts, he continues to share practical insights that help testing professionals stay ahead in this rapidly evolving field.

At the core of his professional approach is a strong foundation in modern testing practices, with a particular focus on feedback-based test execution in CI/CD pipelines. His expertise in performance testing and cloud infrastructure has made him a trusted expert for organizations looking to scale their test automation practices. This book reflects his practical approach to test automation, drawing on real-world experiences and best practices gained from years of working with diverse technologies and teams.

When not immersed in the world of software testing, Manish is an avid FPS (First-Person Shooter) gamer, drawn to the mix of entertainment and strategic thinking that competitive gaming offers. He is also passionate about traveling, exploring new destinations and cultures, which he believes brings fresh perspectives to problem-solving in technology. His belief in continuous learning, combined with his diverse interests, enables him to bring unique insights to the field of test automation, making complex concepts accessible to both newcomers and experienced professionals alike.

About the Technical Reviewer

Vitaly Skadorva is a Quality Assurance Automation Engineer with over 15 years of hands-on experience in software testing. Throughout his career, Vitaly has been dedicated to improving testing processes across various organizations by introducing advanced test automation frameworks and integrating CI/CD practices. He is the author of *Ultimate Web Automation Testing with Cypress*, a widely valued guide for QA professionals aiming to master Cypress. As a consultant, Vitaly significantly reduced regression times and improved test stability by leading the implementation of Cypress for component testing in React and Angular projects. His skill set covers various tools and technologies, including Cypress, Playwright, and Selenium. Vitaly also enjoys mentoring aspiring QA engineers, sharing his knowledge to foster their professional growth. Beyond his technical contributions, he is an active speaker at industry events, where he loves to exchange ideas and experiences with fellow professionals.

Acknowledgements

Writing this book has been an incredible journey, and I could not have completed it without the support and encouragement of several people and communities.

First and foremost, I extend my deepest gratitude to my wife, **Priyanka Bareja,** for her unwavering support, patience, and belief in me. Her encouragement has been my strength throughout this process.

I am immensely grateful to the **QA communities** that continue to push the boundaries of software testing and encourage professionals like me to stay current with the latest advancements. A special thanks to the **BrowserStack QA Community** and **Ministry of Testing** for being vibrant platforms that foster knowledge sharing and innovation in software testing.

I owe a great deal to **LinkedIn,** which has been more than just a professional network–it has connected me with some of the brightest minds in testing and enriched my perspective through insightful discussions and shared experiences.

I would also like to acknowledge all my peers, mentors, and colleagues who have contributed to my learning journey, whether through direct collaboration, thought-provoking discussions, or their own contributions to the testing domain.

Lastly, my heartfelt appreciation to the readers of this book. Your passion for testing and continuous learning is what drives the evolution of this field. I hope this book serves as a valuable resource in your journey.

Preface

This book covers comprehensive aspects of test automation, from fundamental principles to advanced implementation strategies in modern software development. It introduces crucial concepts and practical approaches to test automation, emphasizing its vital role in ensuring software quality and reliability. Through detailed exploration of various testing layers - from unit tests to end-to-end integration - this book demonstrates how effective test automation can significantly enhance software development lifecycles.

The book takes a practical, hands-on approach to test automation, incorporating real-world examples and industry best practices. It covers essential tools and frameworks, with a special focus on Python and its powerful testing ecosystem. Readers will learn how to design and implement robust automation frameworks, integrate tests into CI/CD pipelines, and leverage advanced techniques for API, UI, and contract testing.

This book is divided into 11 chapters that progressively build your understanding of test automation:

Chapter 1 explores test design patterns, their importance in automation, and strategies for implementing them effectively. It covers fundamental principles of test design, different types of patterns, and their practical applications in real-world scenarios.

Chapter 2 delves into test design practices, examining how to create maintainable and scalable test suites. It discusses best practices, common pitfalls, and techniques for writing effective test cases.

Chapter 3 focuses on unit testing strategies, introducing key concepts and frameworks. It explains how to write effective unit tests, manage test dependencies, and achieve comprehensive code coverage.

Chapter 4 covers integration testing approaches, demonstrating how to validate interactions between different components of an application. It explores various integration testing strategies and tools for ensuring reliable component communication.

Chapter 5 addresses API testing techniques, providing detailed guidance on validating REST APIs, handling authentication, and ensuring API reliability. It includes practical examples using popular testing tools and frameworks.

Chapter 6 introduces contract testing, explaining its importance in microservices architectures. It covers consumer-driven contracts, provider verification, and tools for implementing effective contract testing.

Chapter 7 examines strategies for distributing tests across UI, API, and backend layers. It discusses how to maintain test efficiency while ensuring comprehensive coverage across different application layers.

Chapter 8 focuses on integrating tests into CI/CD pipelines, demonstrating how to automate test execution and maintain reliable deployment processes. It covers tools, best practices, and strategies for efficient pipeline integration.

Chapter 9 explores advanced CI/CD strategies, including parallel test execution, test optimization, and pipeline monitoring. It addresses challenges in scaling test automation and maintaining pipeline efficiency.

Chapter 10 looks at the future of test automation, discussing emerging trends like AI-driven testing, self-healing tests, and advanced automation frameworks. It includes a bonus chapter on leveraging Generative AI in testing.

Chapter 11 explores the transformative potential of Generative AI in test automation. This additional chapter delves into how GenAI is revolutionizing testing practices through intelligent test case generation, dynamic test data creation, and enhanced test coverage.

Whether you are new to test automation or an experienced practitioner looking to enhance your skills, this book provides valuable insights and practical guidance. Each chapter includes real-world examples, code samples, and best practices that you can apply immediately in your projects. The book emphasizes not just the "how" but also the "why" of test automation, helping readers make informed decisions about testing strategies in their own environments.

Through this comprehensive guide, readers will gain the knowledge and skills needed to implement effective test automation strategies, ultimately contributing to better software quality and more efficient development processes.

Get a Free eBook

We hope you are enjoying your recently purchased book! Your feedback is incredibly valuable to us, and to all other readers looking for great books.

If you found this book helpful or enjoyable, we would truly appreciate it, if you could take a moment to leave a short review with a 5 star rating on Amazon. It helps us grow, and lets other readers discover our books.

As a thank you, we would love to send you a free digital copy of this book, and a **30%** discount code on your next cart value on our official websites:

www.orangeava.com

www.orangeava.in (For Indian Subcontinent)

☑ **Here's how:**

Leave a review for the book on Amazon.

Take a screenshot of your review, and send an email to **info@orangeava.com** (it can be just the confirmation screen).

Once, we receive your screenshot, we will send you the digital file, within 24 hours.

Thank you so much for your support – it means a lot to us!

Downloading the code bundles and colored images

Please follow the links or scan the QR codes to download the
Code Bundles and Images of the book:

https://github.com/ava-orange-education/Mastering-Design-Patterns-for-Layered-Testing

The code bundles and images of the book are also hosted on
https://rebrand.ly/lfwsgfn

In case there's an update to the code, it will be updated on the existing GitHub repository.

Errata

We take immense pride in our work at **Orange Education Pvt Ltd,** and follow best practices to ensure the accuracy of our content to provide an indulging reading experience to our subscribers. Our readers are our mirrors, and we use their inputs to reflect and improve upon human errors, if any, that may have occurred during the publishing processes involved. To let us maintain the quality and help us reach out to any readers who might be having difficulties due to any unforeseen errors, please write to us at :

errata@orangeava.com

Your support, suggestions, and feedback are highly appreciated.

DID YOU KNOW

Did you know that Orange Education Pvt Ltd offers eBook versions of every book published, with PDF and ePub files available? You can upgrade to the eBook version at **www.orangeava.com** and as a print book customer, you are entitled to a discount on the eBook copy. Get in touch with us at: **info@orangeava.com** for more details.

At **www.orangeava.com**, you can also read a collection of free technical articles, sign up for a range of free newsletters, and receive exclusive discounts and offers on Print Books and eBooks.

PIRACY

If you come across any illegal copies of our works in any form on the internet, we would be grateful if you would provide us with the location address or website name. Please contact us at **info@orangeava.com** with a link to the material.

ARE YOU INTERESTED IN AUTHORING WITH US?

If there is a topic that you have expertise in, and you are interested in either writing or contributing to a book, please write to us at **business@orangeava.com**. We are on a journey to help developers and tech professionals to gain insights on the present technological advancements and innovations happening across the globe and build a community that believes Knowledge is best acquired by sharing and learning with others. Please reach out to us to learn what our audience demands and how you can be part of this educational reform. We also welcome ideas from tech experts and help them build learning and development content for their domains.

REVIEWS

Please leave a review. Once you have read and used this book, why not leave a review on the site that you purchased it from? Potential readers can then see and use your unbiased opinion to make purchase decisions. We at Orange Education would love to know what you think about our products, and our authors can learn from your feedback. Thank you!

For more information about Orange Education, please visit **www.orangeava.com**.

Table of Contents

CHAPTER 1
Introduction to Strategic Test Design

Introduction

In modern software development, the demand for rapid delivery of high-quality applications has never been greater. As companies strive to stay competitive, the need for efficient and reliable testing solutions has become important. Automation has emerged as a critical component in the testing landscape, enabling teams to execute large volumes of tests quickly and accurately. Over the past few years, automation has transitioned from a luxury to a necessity, driven by the complexities of modern software architectures, such as microservices and APIs. The ability to automate repetitive and complex testing tasks not only accelerates the development cycle but also ensures a higher degree of consistency and accuracy, which improves overall product quality.

However, despite the widespread adoption of automation, many teams still struggle to realize its full potential. Through discussions with numerous team leads and managers, it has become evident that the expected value often falls short while significant investments are made in automation. Common issues include poor test design, inadequate test coverage, and maintenance challenges, which undermine the efficiency and effectiveness of automation efforts. This highlights the importance of a well-thought-out test design strategy, which can make the difference between a successful automation initiative and one that fails to deliver the desired outcomes.

By the end of this chapter, you will have a clear picture of the importance of strategic test design and be well-prepared to delve into more detailed and technical topics in the subsequent chapters.

Structure

In this introductory chapter, we aim to help you understand the fundamentals necessary for effective strategic test design. This chapter includes:

- The Importance of Test Design in Test Automation
- Overview of Test Design Principles
- Importance of Strategic Test Planning
- Introduction to Layered Testing
- Overview of APIs and Microservices
- Tools and Technologies
- Best Practices for Test Distribution

The Importance of Test Design in Test Automation

While automation provides the tools to execute tests efficiently, any automated testing effort's success hinges on the test design's quality. Test design is the most critical phase of test automation because it lays the groundwork for creating tests that are not only effective in finding defects but also scalable and maintainable. A well-designed test strategy ensures that all critical aspects of the application are covered, from unit tests that verify individual components to integration tests that ensure seamless interaction between different modules. Poor test design can lead to inadequate coverage, brittle tests, and increased maintenance efforts, ultimately undermining the benefits of automation. Therefore, understanding and applying strategic test design principles is essential for maximizing the value of automated testing.

Let us start by looking at the principles of test design.

Overview of Test Design Principles

The effectiveness of any testing strategy hinges on well-defined principles that guide the design and execution of tests. Test design principles provide the framework for creating tests that are not only comprehensive but also efficient and maintainable. This section explores the core principles that underpin strategic test design, ensuring that our testing efforts yield high-quality results.

Principle 1: Clarity and Precision

Clear and precise tests are essential for identifying issues and ensuring that code changes do not introduce new defects. Tests should be easy to understand and follow, minimizing ambiguity. This clarity is achieved by writing tests with well-defined inputs, expected outputs, and specific conditions under which they are executed. By maintaining clarity and precision, we ensure that our tests are reliable and easy to maintain.

Principle 2: Coverage and Depth

Comprehensive test coverage is crucial for validating the functionality and performance of APIs and microservices. Coverage refers to the extent to which the codebase is tested, while depth pertains to the thoroughness of each individual test. Achieving both high coverage and depth requires a strategic approach, targeting various aspects of the application, from unit tests to integration and end-to-end tests. This layered testing approach helps in identifying defects early and ensures that all components of the application are functioning correctly.

Principle 3: Reusability and Maintainability

In the dynamic world of software development, tests must be reusable and maintainable to keep up with frequent changes. Reusable tests can be leveraged across different parts of the application, reducing redundancy and effort. Maintainability ensures that tests remain relevant and functional as the codebase evolves. Adhering to this principle involves writing modular tests, using fixtures, and following best practices for code organization.

Importance of Strategic Test Planning

Strategic test planning is the cornerstone of effective testing. It involves defining clear objectives, identifying the scope of testing, and allocating resources efficiently. A well-thought-out test strategy ensures that testing efforts are aligned with the overall goals of the project and that potential risks are mitigated early on.

- **Defining Clear Objectives:** Setting clear objectives for testing helps in focusing efforts on the most critical aspects of the application. Objectives should align with the project's goals and user requirements, ensuring that the tests validate the most critical functionalities and performance metrics. Clear objectives provide direction and purpose, making it easier to measure the success of the testing process.
- **Identifying Scope and Coverage**: Determining the scope of testing involves identifying the parts of the application that need to be tested and the extent of testing required. This includes defining the boundaries of what will and will not be tested based on factors such as risk, impact, and priority. By clearly delineating the scope, we can ensure that all critical components are tested while avoiding unnecessary testing of low-risk areas.

- **Efficient Resource Allocation:** Effective test planning involves the efficient allocation of resources, including time, personnel, and tools. It requires balancing the need for thorough testing with the constraints of the project timeline and budget. Prioritizing high-impact tests and leveraging automation can help in maximizing the use of available resources, ensuring that testing efforts are both practical and efficient.
- **Mitigating Risks:** A strategic test plan includes identifying potential risks and defining measures to mitigate them. This involves anticipating possible failure points and planning tests to validate those areas. By proactively addressing risks, we can minimize the likelihood of defects slipping through to production and ensure a higher quality product.
- **Documentation and Communication:** Effective test planning also involves thorough documentation and clear communication. Documenting the test strategy, objectives, scope, and resource allocation ensures that all stakeholders are aligned and that there is a clear reference for the testing process. Regular communication with the development team, project managers, and other stakeholders helps in addressing issues promptly and keeping the testing efforts on track.

By understanding and applying these test design principles and strategic planning practices, you will be well-equipped to create robust and effective test plans. In the following sections, we will delve deeper into the concepts of layered testing, explore the nuances of testing APIs and microservices, and introduce the tools and technologies that will be used throughout this book.

Introduction to Layered Testing

Layered testing is a strategic approach that goes beyond surface-level UI testing, diving into the multiple layers of an application. This section will introduce you to the concept of layered testing, emphasizing the importance of testing at every level—from individual components to integrated systems—to ensure a robust and reliable software product. We will start by understanding the Test Pyramid, a crucial framework that helps structure your testing strategy, and then explore how we can redesign this pyramid to implement layered testing effectively.

Understanding the Test Pyramid

As software systems have grown more complex, the need for a structured approach to testing has become increasingly important. Layered testing, an enhanced version of the test pyramid, is a strategic approach that distributes tests across different levels to ensure comprehensive coverage and efficient resource use.

The test pyramid is a model that represents the ideal distribution of tests across various levels of an application. Coined by Mike Cohn, the pyramid emphasizes the importance of having a large number of fast, automated unit tests at the base, followed by a smaller number of integration tests, and an even smaller number of End-to-End (E2E) tests at the top. This structure helps to achieve a balance between test coverage, execution speed, and maintenance effort.

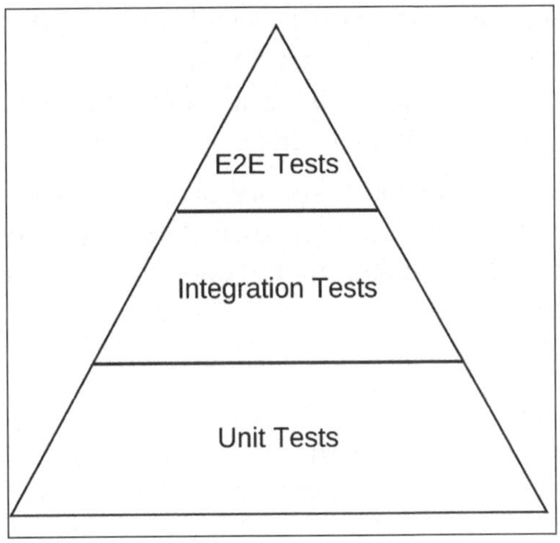

Figure 1.1: *Test Pyramid*

Unit Tests

- **Description:** Unit tests form the foundation of the test pyramid. They are designed to verify the functionality of individual components or units of code in isolation. Unit tests are typically written and maintained by developers, and they run quickly, providing immediate feedback on code changes.
- **Purpose:** The primary goal of unit tests is to ensure that each component functions correctly on its own. By testing components in isolation, unit tests help identify and fix defects early in the development process, reducing the cost and effort of debugging later.
- **Characteristics:** Unit tests are small, fast, and highly focused. They should be easy to write and maintain and should cover a wide range of scenarios for each component.

Unit Test Example:

```
def test_calculate_discount():
    # Test a pricing service's discount calculation
    price = 100
    discount_percentage = 20
    expected_price = 80
    assert calculate_discount(price, discount_percentage)
== expected_price
```

Integration Tests

- **Description:** Integration tests are the middle layer of the test pyramid. They verify the interactions between different application components or modules and ensure that the integrated parts of the system work together as expected.
- **Purpose:** Integration tests aim to catch defects that may arise from the interaction between components. These tests help identify issues related to data flow, API communication, and integration points, ensuring that the system functions correctly as a whole.
- **Characteristics:** Integration tests are broader in scope than unit tests and may require more setup and teardown. They typically run slower than unit tests but are crucial for validating the cooperation between different parts of the application.

Integration Test Example:

```
Integration Test example:
def test_order_creation_flow():
    # Test interaction between Order and Inventory services
    order = create_order({"product_id": "123", "quantity": 2})
    assert order.status == "created"
    assert check_inventory_level("123") == 98  # Reduced from 100
```

End-to-End Tests

- **Description:** End-to-end (E2E) tests are at the top of the test pyramid and focus on testing the application as a whole. These tests simulate real user scenarios, verifying that the entire system works together seamlessly from start to finish.
- **Purpose:** The primary goal of E2E tests is to validate the application's functionality from the user's perspective. They ensure that all components, including front-end and back-end systems, work together to deliver the expected results.
- **Characteristics:** E2E tests are the most comprehensive but also the most expensive in terms of time and resources. They are slower to execute and more challenging to maintain, making it essential to use them sparingly and focus on critical user journeys.

End-to-End Test Example

```
from playwright.sync_api import expect

def test_user_purchase_flow():
    """
    E2E test demonstrating a complete user purchase flow:
    - User logs in
```

```
    - Searches for a product
    - Adds to cart
    - Completes checkout
    - Verifies order confirmation
    """
    # Start browser and navigate to site
    page.goto("https://myecommerce.com")

    # Login
    page.fill("#email", "test@example.com")
    page.fill("#password", "testpass123")
    page.click("#login-button")
    expect(page.locator(".user-profile")).to_be_visible()

    # Search for product
    page.fill("#search", "laptop")
    page.click("#search-button")
    expect(page.locator(".product-results")).to_contain_
text("laptop")

    # Add to cart
    page.click(".add-to-cart-button")
    expect(page.locator("#cart-count")).to_have_text("1")

    # Checkout process
    page.click("#checkout-button")
    page.fill("#shipping-address", "123 Test St")
    page.fill("#card-number", "4111111111111111")
    page.click("#place-order")

    # Verify order confirmation
    expect(page.locator(".order-confirmation")).to_be_visible()
    expect(page.locator(".order-number")).to_be_visible()
```

The Importance of the Test Pyramid

The test pyramid offers several significant advantages:

- **Early Defect Detection:** By emphasizing unit tests at the base of the pyramid, defects can be identified and addressed early in the development process. This reduces the cost and effort associated with fixing bugs discovered later in the cycle.
- **Efficient Resource Utilization**: Layered testing ensures that resources are used efficiently. Fast-running unit tests provide immediate feedback to developers, while integration and E2E tests offer broader coverage without overwhelming the testing process.

- **Balanced Test Coverage:** The pyramid structure promotes a balanced approach to test coverage. While unit tests offer granular validation, integration, and E2E tests ensure that the system as a whole functions correctly, providing comprehensive coverage across different levels.
- **Reduced Maintenance Effort:** Focusing on a larger number of unit tests, which are easier to write and maintain, reduces the overall maintenance effort. Integration and E2E tests, being fewer in number, are easier to manage and update as the application evolves.

By understanding and implementing the principles of the test pyramid, you can create a robust testing strategy that ensures thorough coverage, early defect detection, and efficient resource use. This approach not only enhances the quality of your applications but also streamlines the testing process, making it more effective and manageable.

Layered Testing: Redesigning the Test Pyramid

While the test pyramid provides a solid foundation for understanding the distribution of test types, a more detailed look at layered testing offers insights into testing the different layers of an application, much like an iceberg, where the visible UI is just the tip and much of the complexity lies beneath. In this section, we will explore how to design tests across various layers, ensuring comprehensive coverage and effective test strategies.

The Iceberg Model of Layered Testing

Imagine the structure of your application as an iceberg. The visible part above the waterline represents the UI layer, which users interact with directly. Below the surface lie multiple layers of the system, including APIs, services, databases, and other backend components. Effective layered testing ensures that each of these layers is thoroughly tested, maintaining the integrity and performance of the entire system.

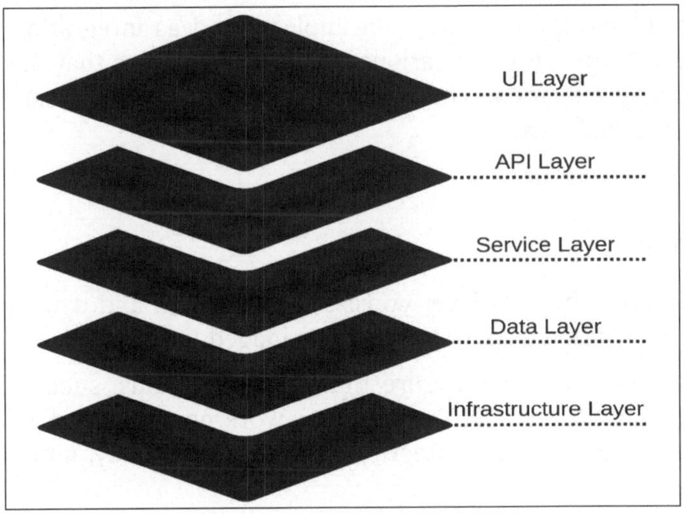

***Figure 1.2**: Layered Testing Architecture*

UI Layer

- **Description:** The UI layer is the most visible part of the application, where users interact with the system through graphical interfaces. Testing at this layer ensures that the user experience is smooth, functional, and free of bugs.
- **Focus:** End-to-end (E2E) tests are crucial at this layer to simulate real user interactions and validate the complete user journey. These tests should cover critical paths and ensure that the application behaves as expected from the user's perspective.
- **Tools:** Selenium, Cypress, Playwright

API Layer

- **Description:** APIs act as the intermediaries between the frontend and backend systems. They handle requests and responses, facilitating communication and data exchange between different parts of the application.
- **Focus:** API tests validate the functionality, performance, and security of the API endpoints. These tests ensure that the APIs return the correct responses, handle edge cases, and maintain data integrity.
- **Tools:** Postman, RestAssured, Requests

Service Layer

- **Description:** The service layer includes business logic and processing components that perform specific functions, such as calculations, data processing, and decision-making.

- **Focus:** Service layer tests, often implemented as integration tests, validate the interactions between various services and ensure that the business logic is correctly executed. These tests verify that different services can work together seamlessly.
- **Tools:** PyTest, JUnit, TestNG

Data Layer

- **Description:** The data layer consists of databases and data storage systems where application data is stored and managed.
- **Focus:** Data layer tests ensure that data operations, such as Create, Read, Update, and Delete (CRUD) functions, work correctly and efficiently. These tests also validate data integrity, schema consistency, and database query performance.
- **Tools:** SQLAlchemy (Python), Hibernate (Java), Entity Framework (C#)

Infrastructure Layer

- **Description:** This layer includes the underlying infrastructure that supports the application, such as servers, networks, and cloud services.
- **Focus:** Infrastructure tests validate the deployment and configuration of the infrastructure, ensuring that the environment is set up correctly and can support the application. These tests include deployment scripts, configuration files, and Infrastructure as Code (IaC) scripts.
- **Tools:** Terraform, Ansible, Docker

Implementing Layered Testing

Implementing layered testing requires a strategic approach to design, execute, and maintain tests across different layers. Here are some best practices to follow:

- **Automate Where Possible:** Automation is key to executing tests efficiently across different layers. Utilize appropriate tools and frameworks to automate tests at each layer.
- **Focus on Test Design:** Invest time in designing robust tests that cover a wide range of scenarios. Well-designed tests are crucial for achieving comprehensive coverage and reliable results.
- **Maintain a Clear Hierarchy:** Ensure a clear hierarchy and separation of tests at different layers. This helps manage and execute tests efficiently, avoiding overlap and redundancy.

- **Monitor and Optimize:** Continuously monitor the execution of tests and optimize them based on feedback. Identify and address any bottlenecks or flakiness in the test suite to maintain efficiency and reliability.

Shifting Left in Layered Testing

Shift-left testing is a critical concept that aligns perfectly with the principles of layered testing. Shifting left means incorporating testing early in the development lifecycle, often at the stage where developers are writing the application logic. This proactive approach helps catch defects early, reducing the cost and effort required to fix them later in the process.

Shift-Left Testing Strategies

- **Test-Driven Development (TDD):** Write tests before writing the code. This approach ensures that testing is an integral part of the development process, guiding the design and implementation of the application.
- **Continuous Integration (CI):** Integrate code changes frequently and run automated tests as part of the CI pipeline. This practice ensures that tests are executed regularly, providing immediate feedback on code changes.
- **Collaborative Testing:** Encourage collaboration between developers, testers, and other stakeholders to identify and address issues early in the development process. This collaborative approach fosters a shared responsibility for quality.

By adopting a layered testing approach and shifting left, you can create a robust testing strategy that ensures comprehensive coverage, early defect detection, and efficient use of resources. This approach not only enhances the quality of your applications but also streamlines the testing process, making it more effective and manageable.

Overview of APIs and Microservices

In the current software development landscape, APIs and microservices have become integral to building robust, scalable, and flexible applications. The shift from monolithic architectures to microservices, coupled with the pervasive use of APIs, has revolutionized how software systems are designed, developed, and maintained. This transformation is driven by the need for modularity, scalability, and rapid deployment cycles in response to ever-changing market demands. Organizations across various industries are increasingly adopting APIs and microservices to enhance their agility, improve resource utilization, and streamline communication between disparate systems. Understanding these concepts is crucial for designing effective tests and ensuring the robustness of your applications.

APIs: The Building Blocks of Communication

Application Programming Interfaces (APIs) are sets of rules and protocols that allow different software components to communicate with each other. They define the methods and data structures that developers can use to interact with the functionality provided by an application, service, or platform.

Types of APIs

- **REST APIs:** Representational State Transfer (REST) is a widely used architectural style for designing networked applications. REST APIs use standard HTTP methods (GET, POST, PUT, DELETE) and are designed to be stateless, meaning each request from a client to a server must contain all the information needed to understand and process the request.
- **SOAP APIs:** Simple Object Access Protocol (SOAP) is a protocol for exchanging structured information in the implementation of web services. SOAP APIs are known for their robustness and security features but are generally more complex and heavier compared to REST APIs.
- **GraphQL APIs:** GraphQL is a query language for APIs and a runtime for executing those queries. It allows clients to request exactly the data they need, making it more efficient and flexible than REST in some scenarios.

API Components

- **Endpoints:** These are specific URLs where the API's resources can be accessed. Each endpoint corresponds to a specific function or data set provided by the API.
- **Methods:** The actions that can be performed on the API's resources, such as creating, reading, updating, or deleting data.
- **Requests and Responses:** APIs handle requests from clients and return responses. A request includes the method, endpoint, headers, and body, while the response includes the status code, headers, and body.

Benefits of Using APIs

- **Modularity:** APIs enable modular design, allowing developers to build and integrate components independently.
- **Interoperability:** APIs facilitate communication between different systems, platforms, and programming languages.
- **Reusability:** APIs promote reusability by allowing the same functionality to be accessed and used by multiple applications or services.

Microservices: A Modular Approach to Application Design

Microservices architecture is an approach to designing applications as a collection of loosely coupled, independently deployable services. Each microservice is a small, self-contained unit that performs a specific business function and communicates with other services through APIs.

Characteristics of Microservices

- **Single Responsibility:** Each microservice is designed to handle a specific piece of functionality, adhering to the single responsibility principle.
- **Independence:** Microservices can be developed, deployed, and scaled independently of each other. This independence facilitates continuous delivery and deployment.
- **Decentralized Data Management:** Microservices often manage their own databases, allowing for more flexibility and scalability in data handling.

Communication Between Microservices

- **Synchronous Communication:** Involves direct communication between services, typically through HTTP requests. This method is straightforward but can lead to tight coupling and potential bottlenecks.
- **Asynchronous Communication:** Uses message brokers or event streams to facilitate communication. This method decouples services, making the system more resilient and scalable.

Benefits of Microservices

- **Scalability:** Individual services can be scaled independently, allowing for efficient resource utilization.
- **Resilience:** The failure of one microservice does not necessarily impact the entire system, enhancing overall resilience.
- **Flexibility:** Teams can choose different technologies and frameworks for different services, promoting flexibility and innovation.

Integrating APIs and Microservices

The combination of APIs and microservices forms a powerful paradigm for modern application development. APIs serve as the communication layer between microservices, enabling them to work together seamlessly. This integration offers several advantages:

- **Enhanced Modularity:** APIs and microservices together promote a modular architecture where each service can be developed and maintained independently.
- **Improved Scalability:** Both APIs and microservices support independent scaling, allowing specific parts of the application to handle increased load without affecting others.
- **Greater Flexibility:** The decoupled nature of microservices and the interoperability provided by APIs allow teams to adopt the best technologies for each service.

Testing APIs and Microservices

Testing APIs and microservices requires a comprehensive approach to ensure that each component functions correctly and that the system as a whole performs as expected. This includes:

1. **Unit Testing:** Testing individual units of code within each microservice to ensure they work as intended.
2. **Integration Testing:** Verifying that different microservices and their APIs interact correctly.
3. **Contract Testing:** Ensuring that the communication contracts between services are adhered to, preventing integration issues.
4. **Component Testing:** Testing individual components or services in isolation, focusing on their functionality, dependencies, and interactions within a controlled environment. This approach ensures that each microservice behaves as expected before integrating it into the broader system.
5. **End-to-End Testing:** Testing the entire workflow from the user's perspective to validate the interaction of all components.

In the subsequent chapters, we will delve deeper into the specific techniques and strategies for testing APIs and microservices, leveraging tools and frameworks to achieve comprehensive coverage and high-quality results. By mastering these concepts, you will be well-equipped to tackle the challenges of modern software testing and ensure the robustness of your applications.

Tools and Technologies

In this book, we will utilize a variety of tools and technologies to illustrate concepts and provide practical examples. These tools and technologies are essential for implementing effective layered-testing strategies for the Application. Understanding and mastering these will equip you with the necessary skills to design, execute, and maintain a robust test suite.

Programming Language: Python

Python is a versatile and widely used programming language that offers simplicity and readability. Due to its rich ecosystem of libraries and frameworks, it is a popular choice for test automation.

- **Advantages:**
  - Easy to learn and use, making it accessible for beginners.
  - Extensive library support for various testing needs.
  - Strong community support and documentation.

Libraries: Requests, PyTest, Selenium, and Playwright

To effectively demonstrate the concepts in this book, we will rely on powerful libraries such as Requests for handling HTTP requests, PyTest for test automation, and Selenium and Playwright for robust UI testing. These libraries offer the flexibility and functionality needed to build reliable and scalable test suites across different layers of your application.

Requests

- **Description:** A simple yet powerful library for making HTTP requests in Python.
- **Use Case:** Facilitates API testing by allowing you to send HTTP requests and handle responses with ease.
- **Key Features:**
  - Simplifies the process of making API calls.
  - Supports various HTTP methods (GET, POST, PUT, DELETE).
  - Handles authentication, cookies, and sessions.

PyTest

- **Description:** A robust and flexible testing framework for Python.
- **Use Case:** Provides a framework for writing and executing unit tests, integration tests, and more.
- **Key Features:**
  - Simple syntax and powerful features for test discovery and organization.

  - Supports fixtures for setup and teardown operations.
  - Extensive plugin support for additional functionalities (for example, pytest-html for HTML reports).

Selenium

- **Description:** A tool for automating web browsers.
- **Use Case:** Used to automate web application testing to ensure they work as expected.
- **Key Features:**
  - Supports multiple browsers (Chrome, Firefox, Safari, and so on).
  - Enables the simulation of user interactions with web pages.
  - Integrates with various programming languages.

Playwright

- **Description**: Microsoft's newer browser automation tool.
- **Use Case:** Enables end-to-end testing for web applications.
- **Key Features**:
  - Supports multiple browsers.
  - Provides features for testing modern web applications.
  - Allows for the recording of tests and automation scripts.

Tools: Postman, Docker, and Allure

In this book, we will utilize Postman for checking APIs, Docker for containerization, and Allure for comprehensive test reporting. These tools will help streamline your testing processes, ensure consistency across environments, and provide insightful reporting to enhance the quality of your automation efforts.

Postman

- **Description:** A popular tool for testing APIs with a user-friendly interface.
- **Use Case:** Allows you to create, share, test, and document APIs.
- Key Features:
  - Easy to create and manage API requests.
  - Supports automated testing through collections.
  - Provides detailed logs of API interactions.

Docker

- **Description:** A platform for developing, shipping, and running applications in containers.
- **Use Case:** Ensures consistency across different environments by containerizing applications and their dependencies.
- **Key Features:**
  - Simplifies the setup of testing environments.
  - Enables isolation of test environments to prevent conflicts.
  - Supports scalability and parallel test execution.

Allure

- **Description:** A flexible and lightweight reporting tool.
- **Use Case:** Used for generating test reports.
- **Key Features:**
  - Supports multiple testing frameworks.
  - Provides clear and concise test reports.
  - Helps in identifying and resolving issues.

Software/Platform: GitHub Actions, Kubernetes

To support continuous integration and delivery in modern software development, we will be leveraging powerful platforms such as GitHub Actions and Kubernetes. These tools will enable seamless automation and deployment, ensuring that your testing workflows are efficient, scalable, and adaptable to complex environments.

GitHub Actions

- **Description:** A CI/CD platform that allows you to automate your build, test, and deployment pipeline.
- **Use Case:** Integrates with GitHub repositories to automate workflows.
- **Key Features:**
  - Easy setup with GitHub repositories.
  - Supports a wide range of actions and workflows.
  - Provides detailed logs and status checks.

Kubernetes

- **Description:** An open-source platform for automating the deployment, scaling, and management of containerized applications.
- **Use Case:** Orchestrates containerized applications to ensure efficient resource utilization and high availability.
- **Key Features:**
  - Manages containerized applications across multiple hosts.
  - Automates the deployment and scaling of applications.
  - Supports rolling updates and rollbacks.

Technologies: APIs, Microservices, and Layered Testing

APIs, microservices, and layered testing are core technologies that drive modern software architecture. This book will guide you through understanding and applying these technologies to create effective and efficient testing strategies, ensuring comprehensive coverage and seamless integration across your application's various components.

APIs

- **Description:** Interfaces that allow different software components to communicate with each other.
- **Use Case:** Essential for integrating and testing various parts of an application.
- **Key Features:**
  - Facilitate communication between frontend and backend systems.
  - Enable modular design and reusability of components.

Microservices

- **Description:** Architectural style where applications are composed of small, independent services.
- **Use Case:** Enhances scalability, flexibility, and maintainability of applications.
- **Key Features:**
  - Each service performs a specific business function.
  - Services communicate via APIs, promoting loose coupling.

Layered Testing

- **Description:** Approach to testing different layers of an application, from the UI to the backend.
- **Use Case:** Ensures comprehensive coverage by testing each layer independently and in combination.
- **Key Features:**
  - Involves different types of tests (unit, integration, component, end-to-end).
  - Focuses on testing the interactions and dependencies between layers.

Knowledge Level Required

To effectively understand and apply the concepts and tools discussed in this book, a basic to intermediate level of knowledge in the following areas is recommended:

- **Programming with Python:**
  - Basic understanding of Python syntax and programming constructs.
  - Familiarity with writing simple scripts and functions.
  - Knowledge of Python libraries and how to install and use them.
- **HTTP and Web Services:**
  - Basic understanding of HTTP methods (GET, POST, PUT, DELETE).
  - Familiarity with RESTful APIs and how they work.
  - Ability to make API calls and handle responses.
- **Software Testing Fundamentals:**
  - Basic understanding of different types of tests (unit, integration, end-to-end).
  - Familiarity with the testing lifecycle and best practices.
  - Knowledge of common testing tools and frameworks.
- **Containerization with Docker:**
  - Basic understanding of Docker concepts and commands.
  - Familiarity with creating and managing Docker containers.
  - Knowledge of Dockerfile syntax and container orchestration.
- **Microservices Architecture:**
  - Basic understanding of microservices principles and benefits.
  - Familiarity with service-oriented architecture and its components.

- Knowledge of inter-service communication and data management.

Flexibility in Tool and Technology Choices

While this book primarily uses Python, Requests, PyTest, and Docker as examples, it is important to note that these are not the only tools and technologies suitable for testing APIs and microservices. The context of your team, existing infrastructure, and specific requirements may necessitate different choices. Similar tools and programming languages can also be used to implement the concepts discussed in this book.

Alternative Tools and Technologies

- **Programming Languages:**
  - **JavaScript:** Using frameworks such as Mocha or Jest for testing.
  - **Java:** Utilizing tools such as JUnit, TestNG, and RestAssured.
  - **Ruby:** Employing frameworks such as RSpec and Capybara.
- **API Testing Tools:**
  - **Postman:** A popular tool for testing APIs with a user-friendly interface.
  - **SoapUI**: A powerful tool for testing SOAP and REST APIs.
- **UI Testing Tools:**
  - **Cypress**: A popular tool for automating tests for Web UI in JavaScript/TypeScript
  - **Low Code/No Code Tools**: Multiple LC/NC tools are also present for browser automation.
- **Containerization Alternatives:**
  - **Kubernetes**: For container orchestration at scale.
  - **Podman:** An alternative to Docker for container management.

By understanding the core principles and techniques, you can apply them with the tools and technologies that best fit your context. Throughout this book, alternative tools and languages will also be highlighted to provide a broader perspective and adaptability. This approach ensures that you can implement effective testing strategies regardless of the specific tools and technologies at your disposal.

Best Practices for Test Distribution

Effective test distribution is a crucial aspect of strategic test design. It ensures that tests are organized, executed efficiently, and provide comprehensive coverage. By following best practices for test distribution, you can optimize your testing efforts and achieve higher-quality outcomes. Here, we outline some key best practices that will be elaborated on in subsequent chapters.

Understand the Test Pyramid

The test pyramid emphasizes the importance of different types of tests at various levels. Ensuring a balanced distribution of tests across the pyramid helps maintain a fast feedback loop and reduces the cost of maintaining the test suite.

- **Unit Tests:** Form the foundation of the pyramid. They are fast, isolated, and cover individual components or functions.
- **Integration Tests:** Focus on the interactions between components or systems, validating that they work together as expected.
- **End-to-End Tests:** These tests simulate real user scenarios, testing the entire system from start to finish. They provide high confidence but are slower and more expensive to maintain.

Prioritize High-Value Tests

Not all tests are created equal. Prioritizing high-value tests ensures that the most critical aspects of your application are covered.

- **Risk-Based Testing:** Identify the areas of your application that pose the highest risk and focus your testing efforts there.
- **Business-Critical Paths:** Ensure that the most important user journeys and business functions are thoroughly tested.

Implement Shift-Left Testing

Shifting left means integrating testing activities earlier in the development lifecycle. This approach helps catch defects early when they are cheaper and easier to fix.

- **Test-Driven Development (TDD):** Write tests before the code to ensure that requirements are clear and that the code is thoroughly tested from the outset.
- **Continuous Integration (CI):** Integrate code changes frequently and run tests automatically to detect issues early.

Use Automation Strategically

Automation is key to efficient test distribution. However, it is essential to use automation strategically to maximize its benefits.

- **Automate Repetitive Tasks:** Automate tests that need to be run frequently, such as regression tests, to save time and reduce human error.

- **Balance Automation and Functional Testing:** While automation is powerful, some tests are better suited for manual execution, such as exploratory testing or usability testing.

Maintain Test Isolation

Test isolation ensures that tests do not interfere with each other, leading to more reliable and consistent results.

- **Mocking and Stubbing:** Use mocks and stubs to isolate the component under test and simulate dependencies.
- **Independent Test Data:** Ensure that tests use independent data to avoid conflicts and maintain repeatability.

Optimize Test Execution

Efficient test execution helps reduce feedback time and improves the overall development process.

- **Parallel Testing:** Run tests in parallel to speed up execution times, especially for large test suites.
- **Continuous Delivery (CD):** Implement CD pipelines to automate the deployment process and run tests in different environments.

Monitor and Maintain Test Health

Regular monitoring and maintenance of the test suite ensure that it remains effective and up-to-date.

- **Flaky Tests:** Identify and fix flaky tests that produce inconsistent results, as they can undermine the reliability of the test suite.
- **Test Coverage Analysis:** Regularly review test coverage to identify gaps and areas for improvement.
- **Test Refactoring:** Periodically refactor tests to improve readability, maintainability, and performance.

Leverage Metrics and Reporting

Using metrics and reporting helps track the effectiveness of your testing efforts and make data-driven decisions.

- **Test Execution Metrics:** Monitor metrics such as test pass rate, execution time, and failure rate to assess the health of your test suite.
- **Code Coverage:** Use code coverage tools to identify untested areas of your codebase and improve coverage.

- **Quality Gates:** Implement quality gates in your CI/CD pipeline to ensure that code meets predefined quality standards before merging or deploying.

By following these best practices for test distribution, you can create a robust and efficient testing strategy that ensures comprehensive coverage and high-quality results. We will explore more about each practice, providing detailed guidance and examples to help you implement them effectively in your projects. Understanding and applying these principles will equip you with the tools and knowledge needed to excel in the field of test automation and deliver reliable, high-quality software.

Think About It

Let us apply what we have learned to some real-world scenarios. Consider these situations and think about how you would approach them:

Microservices Migration

You are working on a team that is migrating a monolithic e-commerce application to microservices.

- How would you distribute tests across different layers?
- What specific challenges could arise when testing service interactions?
- How would you ensure the same level of test coverage during and after the migration?

Test Automation Strategy

Your team has been manually testing APIs but wants to move to automation.

- Which testing layers would you prioritize first?
- How would you balance the test pyramid for API testing?
- What tools from this chapter would you choose and why?

Performance versus Coverage

You notice your test suite takes 45 minutes to run in CI/CD.

- How would you analyze which tests are causing the slowdown?
- What strategies could you use to improve execution time without sacrificing coverage?
- How would you apply the layered testing approach to solve this?

Testing in Production

Your team is considering implementing testing in production alongside your existing test strategy.

- What types of tests would be safe to run in production?
- How would you modify your test pyramid to accommodate this?
- What additional tools or safeguards would you need?

These scenarios reflect common challenges in modern testing. As you progress through this book, we will explore solutions to similar real-world situations, building on the foundational concepts covered in this chapter.

Conclusion

In this chapter, we laid the groundwork for understanding strategic test design and its crucial role in modern software development. A well-defined test strategy becomes indispensable as we navigate the complexities of testing with different layers of application.

Here is a cheat sheet summarizing the key points covered in this chapter:

- **Importance of Test Design:** Effective test design is the backbone of robust test automation. It ensures comprehensive coverage, high-quality results, and efficient testing processes.
- **Test Pyramid:** The test pyramid highlights the significance of different test types, emphasizing a balanced distribution of unit, integration, and end-to-end tests to maintain a fast feedback loop and reduce maintenance costs.
- **Layered Testing:** Building upon the test pyramid, layered testing involves designing tests across various layers of the application, such as unit, service, and end-to-end layers, to ensure thorough validation at each stage.
- **APIs and Microservices:** Understanding the fundamental concepts of APIs and microservices is crucial for effective testing. This chapter introduced the basics and the importance of testing these components.
- **Tools and Technologies:** We discussed the essential tools and technologies, such as Python, PyTest, Requests, and Docker, which will be used to demonstrate concepts throughout the book. These tools provide a practical framework for implementing the strategies discussed.
- **Best Practices for Test Distribution:** Key practices include understanding the test pyramid, prioritizing high-value tests, implementing shift-left testing, using automation strategically, maintaining test isolation, optimizing test execution, monitoring test health, and leveraging metrics and reporting.

By grasping these foundational concepts, you are now equipped to delve deeper into the world of strategic test design. In the subsequent chapters, we will explore each of these topics in greater detail, providing practical examples, case studies, and step-by-step guides to help you implement these strategies effectively.

As you continue your journey through this book, remember that the principles of strategic test design are adaptable and can be applied to various contexts and technologies. The goal is to empower you to create reliable, efficient, and maintainable test automation frameworks that enhance the quality and performance of your software.

In the next chapter, we will delve into the world of test design patterns, exploring how they can transform your approach to automation by ensuring your tests are both maintainable and scalable.

Key Takeaways

- **Strategic Test Design**: Central to effective test automation.
- **Test Pyramid:** Balance between unit, integration, and end-to-end tests.
- **Layered Testing:** Comprehensive validation across all layers.
- **APIs and Microservices:** Critical components for modern applications.
- **Tools and Technologies:** Practical framework for implementation.
- **Best Practices:** Guide to optimizing test distribution and execution.

CHAPTER 2
Understanding Test Design Patterns

Introduction

Building on our understanding of automation and layered testing from the previous chapter, we now focus on the strategic patterns that make test automation more effective and maintainable. While *Chapter 1, Introduction to Strategic Test Design*, established why we need automation and what to test, this chapter explores how to design these tests for maximum impact and longevity.

Test design patterns provide proven solutions to common challenges in test automation. Just as software design patterns help developers write better code, test design patterns help testers create more robust and maintainable test suites. These patterns have emerged from years of industry experience and represent best practices in structuring automated tests.

By the end of this chapter, you will master various test design patterns and learn when to apply each one. You will understand how to select the right patterns for different testing scenarios, avoid common automation pitfalls, and combine patterns effectively. This knowledge will enable you to create test suites that not only find bugs effectively but also remain maintainable as your application evolves.

Structure

In this chapter, we delve into the world of test design patterns, which are crucial for building scalable and maintainable automation frameworks. Here is what we will cover:

- Introduction to Test Design Patterns
- Key Test Design Patterns
- Implementing Test Design Patterns
- Real-World Examples and Case Studies
- Best Practices for Implementing Test Design Patterns

Introduction to Test Design Patterns

Test design patterns are standardized approaches to creating automated tests that ensure they are not only functional but also maintainable, scalable, and adaptable. Just as design patterns in software development provide solutions to common coding challenges, test design patterns offer strategies for addressing the complexities and intricacies of test automation. They guide the structure and organization of tests, helping testers avoid common pitfalls such as redundancy, fragility, and inefficiency.

At their core, test design patterns are about creating tests that are modular, reusable, and easy to understand. This is especially important in automated testing, where poorly structured tests can quickly become a burden—difficult to maintain, prone to breaking, and challenging to extend as the application under test evolves. By following these patterns, testers can develop automation frameworks that are not only effective in detecting issues but also sustainable over the long term.

In this chapter, we will dive into the key test design patterns that form the foundation of effective test automation. From the simple yet powerful Arrange-Act-Assert pattern to more sophisticated approaches such as Data-Driven and Keyword-Driven Testing, we will explore how these patterns can be implemented to create robust and flexible test suites. By mastering these patterns, you will be well-equipped to design automation tests that stand the test of time, adapting smoothly to changes in your application's codebase.

Differences Between Manual and Automation Test Designs

Manual test designs typically focus on what testers can see and interact with directly—the User Interface (UI). In manual testing, the tester's primary tools are the application's screens, forms, and buttons, where they verify functionality based on user interactions. Since functional testers often have limited access to the underlying code or system architecture, they concentrate on testing the application's behavior from the user's perspective.

However, when transitioning from manual to automated testing, the scope of what can be tested expands significantly. Automation opens the door to deeper layers of the application, allowing tests to interact not just with the UI but with the underlying components such as APIs, databases, and even individual functions within the code. This shift requires a different approach to test design, where the focus is on identifying the most efficient and effective layer to execute each test.

Rather than testing everything through the UI, which can be slow and fragile, automation allows you to distribute tests across different layers. For instance, business logic that resides within a specific component can be validated more efficiently at the component level rather than through a UI test. By understanding the application's architecture, you can determine where a particular test case should be executed—whether it is at the unit, integration, or UI level—ensuring that the tests are both more efficient and less brittle.

In summary, while manual testing is often constrained to the UI layer, automated testing empowers you to access and test individual components, APIs, and even internal functions. This approach not only enhances the speed and reliability of your test suite but also ensures that each part of the application is tested in the most appropriate and effective way.

Common Flaws in Automating Functional Tests

Automating functional tests is a critical component of modern software development, but it comes with its own set of challenges and pitfalls. Recognizing and addressing these flaws early can significantly improve the effectiveness of your test automation strategy. Here are some common flaws often encountered in automating functional tests:

- **Heavy Dependence on UI Test Automation**: One of the most prevalent mistakes is an over-reliance on UI test automation. While UI tests are essential, they are often the slowest and most brittle type of tests due to frequent changes in the user interface. This over-dependence can lead to increased maintenance efforts and slower feedback cycles. The test pyramid suggests a more balanced approach, emphasizing unit and integration tests over UI tests. Automating at the API or component level can provide faster and more reliable feedback while reducing the fragility of the test suite.
- **Not Considering Scalability While Building the Framework**: Scalability is crucial in test automation, especially as the application grows in complexity. A common flaw is designing a test automation framework that cannot scale with the application's needs. This includes not considering parallel test execution, inadequate handling of large datasets, and lack of support for distributed testing environments. A scalable test automation framework should be designed with future growth in mind, allowing for the addition of new tests and the expansion of test coverage without a significant increase in execution time or maintenance efforts.
- **Inadequate Research on Frameworks and Tools**: Selecting the right tools and frameworks is foundational to the success of any test automation project. A common mistake is jumping into automation without thoroughly researching the available options. This can lead to the adoption of tools that are not well-suited for the specific needs of the project, resulting in inefficiencies and limited capabilities. Proper research should include evaluating the compatibility of the tools with the existing technology stack, the ease of integration, community

support, and the long-term viability of the tools. Additionally, the selected framework should align with the team's skill set to ensure effective utilization.

- **Neglecting the Importance of Test Maintenance**: Automation is not a one-time effort. Over time, applications evolve, and so should the automated test suite. A common flaw is failing to regularly review and update test scripts to ensure they remain relevant and effective. This can lead to false positives, missed defects, and a general decline in the value of the test suite. Regular evaluation and refactoring of test scripts are essential to maintain their effectiveness. This includes removing obsolete tests, updating existing ones to reflect changes in the application, and continuously improving the test design to enhance coverage and reliability.
- **Lack of Clear Test Objectives**: Without clear objectives, test automation efforts can become unfocused and ineffective. A common issue is automating tests without a clear understanding of what they are intended to achieve. This can result in redundant or low-value tests that do not contribute to the overall quality of the software. Setting clear, measurable objectives for each automated test ensures that the test suite is aligned with the overall goals of the project, whether that is to increase test coverage, reduce manual testing effort, or improve the speed of feedback.
- **Overlooking Non-Functional Requirements**: Functional tests are essential, but neglecting non-functional requirements such as performance, security, and usability can lead to gaps in the overall testing strategy. Often, automation efforts focus solely on validating functional aspects of the application, ignoring the critical non-functional elements. This flaw can result in a system that works as expected under normal conditions but fails under stress or is vulnerable to security threats. Incorporating non-functional testing into the automation strategy ensures a more comprehensive evaluation of the software's quality.
- **Inconsistent Test Data Management**: Reliable test data is the backbone of effective test automation. A common flaw is the inconsistent or ad-hoc management of test data, leading to flaky tests and unreliable results. Without a structured approach to managing test data, tests may fail intermittently due to data issues rather than actual defects in the application. Implementing a robust test data management strategy that ensures consistent, reusable, and relevant data for all automated tests is crucial for maintaining test reliability.

To overcome the flaws in automating functional tests, we will explore various advanced test design patterns tailored specifically for layered testing. These patterns provide a strategic blueprint for creating maintainable, scalable, and efficient automation frameworks, focusing on optimizing the distribution of tests across different layers. The patterns we will delve into include:

- **Foundation-First Testing**: Starts building test coverage from the lowest layer, progressively covering higher layers, ensuring a solid base of test coverage where most logic resides.

- **Layer-Specific Logic Testing**: Focuses on automating tests at the same layer as the logic they are testing, aligning tests with the layer of their respective logic for relevancy and effectiveness.
- **Balanced Layer Distribution**: Emphasizes an equal distribution of tests across various layers to ensure comprehensive coverage without overemphasizing any single layer.
- **Simplicity-Driven Testing**: Prioritizes automating simpler tests first, typically at layers where implementation is less complex, leading to quicker development and earlier bug detection.
- **Risk-Based Layer Coverage**: Prioritizes test automation based on the risk assessment of different application layers, focusing more on areas that are critical to the application's stability and performance.
- **Feedback-Focused Testing**: Aims to create automated tests in layers that provide the quickest feedback for developers, which is helpful, especially in agile environments.

These patterns help reduce reliance on UI tests, ensuring scalability and fostering a more organized approach to test maintenance and execution. In the upcoming sections, we will explore these patterns in more detail with practical examples, demonstrating how they can be effectively implemented to enhance your automation strategy.

Key Test Design Patterns

As we delve deeper into the realm of test automation, understanding and applying key test design patterns becomes essential for crafting effective and resilient testing strategies. These patterns not only optimize the testing process but also ensure that the automation efforts deliver lasting value. In this section, we will explore several pivotal test design patterns that have proven their effectiveness across various applications and industries. These patterns will be dissected to illustrate their core principles, practical applications, and the specific challenges they address within automated testing frameworks. By integrating these patterns into your test design, you can achieve more targeted, efficient, and scalable testing outcomes.

Foundation-First Testing

The Foundation-First Testing pattern builds upon the test pyramid principles discussed in the previous chapter, providing a strategic approach to implementing layered testing. This pattern guides teams on how to sequence their test automation efforts, starting with the foundational layers of the application.

Concept and Application

The core idea behind Foundation-First Testing is to ensure that each component of the application is thoroughly vetted in isolation before integrating with other components. By starting at the lowest layer, testers can catch and address fundamental issues early in the development cycle, which reduces the complexity and cost of fixing bugs found in later stages.

For instance, consider an e-commerce application where the shopping cart functionality is critical. Using Foundation-First Testing, you would first write unit tests for individual functions within the shopping cart module–such as adding items to the cart, calculating totals, and applying discounts. These unit tests ensure that each function performs as expected in isolation.

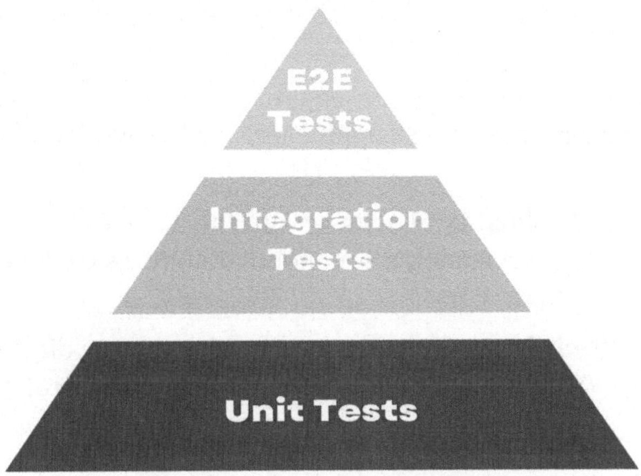

***Figure 2.1**: Foundation First Testing*

Technical Details

In a typical setup, you might use a testing framework such as PyTest for Python to write and execute these unit tests. Each test would be designed to run independently, without relying on external services or the integration of other modules. This isolation is achieved using mocking and stubbing techniques, where dependencies (such as database calls or external APIs) are replaced with mock objects that simulate the behavior of real components.

Here is a simple example of a unit test for a shopping cart:

example_2_1.py

```
import pytest
from shopping_cart import ShoppingCart
```

```
@pytest.fixture
def cart():
    return ShoppingCart()

def test_add_item_to_cart(cart):
    cart.add_item("apple", 3)
    assert cart.total_items() == 3
    assert cart.total_cost() == 9  # Assuming the cost of an
apple is $3
```

In this example, the **ShoppingCart** class is tested to ensure items are added correctly. Tests for other functionalities, such as removing items or applying discounts, would follow similar patterns, focusing on the individual responsibilities of the shopping cart module.

Benefits

- **Early Bug Detection**: Bugs are caught at the earliest possible stage in the development process, which significantly reduces the cost and complexity of fixes.
- **Improved Code Quality**: Focusing on the lowest layers first encourages developers to write cleaner, more modular code, as each component must be testable in isolation.
- **Faster Feedback Loop**: Unit tests run quickly, providing rapid feedback to developers, which is crucial for agile development environments.

Summary

Foundation-First Testing is a foundational pattern in the arsenal of test design strategies. It ensures that the building blocks of the application are solid before moving on to more complex testing scenarios, thereby enhancing the overall stability and reliability of the software.

Layer-Specific Logic Testing

Layer-Specific Logic Testing is a test design pattern that focuses on ensuring that tests are conducted at the appropriate layer in the software architecture, corresponding directly to where the application logic resides. This approach enables more precise and effective testing by targeting the layer that most directly impacts the functionality being tested.

Concept and Application

Layer-Specific Logic Testing is based on the understanding that different components of an application can be more effectively tested at the layer where their core logic is implemented. This not only improves the accuracy of the tests but also enhances test efficiency by avoiding unnecessary complications that come with higher-level testing, such as through the UI.

For example, if the business logic for processing payments in an e-commerce application is contained within a service layer, it would be more effective to write integration tests that directly interact with this service layer rather than conducting these tests through the UI. This direct approach allows for more detailed testing of the business rules and logic, ensuring that all scenarios are thoroughly validated.

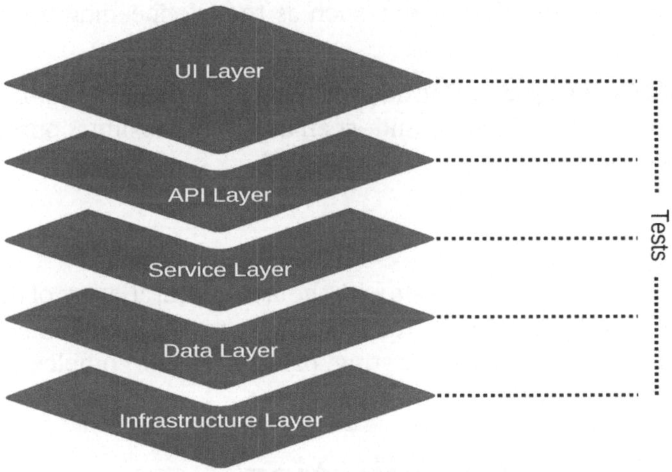

***Figure* 2.2**: *Layer-Specific Logic Testing*

Technical Details

In practice, using a framework such as PyTest along with a tool such as Postman for API testing can facilitate Layer-Specific Logic Testing. Test cases can be designed to interact directly with the API endpoints that encapsulate the business logic, allowing testers to validate responses, error handling, and performance under various conditions.

Here is an example of how you might test the payment processing logic via API tests:

example_2_2.py

```
import requests

def test_payment_processing():
    response = requests.post("http://api.example.com/payments/
process", json={"amount": 100, "currency": "USD"})
    assert response.status_code == 200
    assert response.json()['status'] == 'success'
    assert 'transaction_id' in response.json()
```

In this example, the API endpoint for processing payments is tested directly to ensure that it handles payment transactions correctly under normal conditions.

Benefits

- **Enhanced Test Precision**: By focusing tests on the layer where the logic is implemented, you can achieve greater control and accuracy in your testing efforts.
- **Reduced Overhead**: Testing closer to the logic reduces the overhead of navigating through other layers, such as the UI, speeding up test execution and simplifying test scenarios.
- **Increased Coverage and Confidence**: This pattern allows for comprehensive testing of all logic paths and scenarios, increasing confidence in the robustness of the application.

Summary

Layer-Specific Logic Testing aligns tests with the architectural layers of the application, ensuring that each component is tested in its most relevant context. This approach leads to more efficient and accurate testing, particularly for complex systems with a clear separation of concerns across different layers.

Balanced Layer Distribution

Balanced Layer Distribution is a test design pattern that emphasizes equitable distribution of tests across all layers of an application to ensure comprehensive coverage and maintain the resilience of the testing strategy. This pattern helps in achieving a balanced test suite that neither overemphasizes nor neglects any particular layer.

Concept and Application

The Balanced Layer Distribution pattern advocates for a proportional approach to testing, where the allocation of tests is based on the complexity and criticality of each layer. This approach ensures that while lower layers, such as unit tests, receive a substantial number of tests due to their lower cost and higher speed, higher layers, such as integration and UI tests, are also adequately covered to ensure the application functions correctly as a whole.

For example, in a typical web application, instead of heavily loading either the unit tests or the UI tests, this pattern would guide the test strategy to distribute tests across the unit, service, and UI layers. Each layer would receive attention proportional to its importance and role in the application's functionality, ensuring that tests are well-rounded and effective across the board.

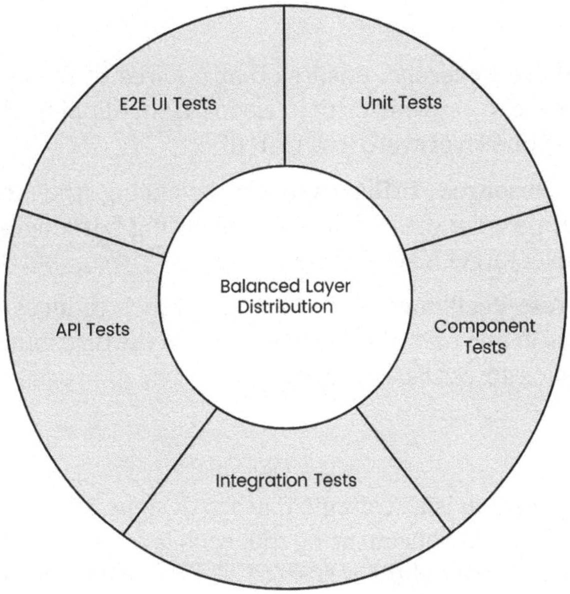

Figure 2.3: *Balanced Layer Distribution*

Technical Details

Implementing this pattern might involve setting specific targets for coverage metrics at each layer. Tools such as PyTest for unit testing, Selenium for UI testing, and intermediate service testing tools can be orchestrated to achieve the desired balance.

Consider an online bookstore application:

- **Unit Tests**: Focusing on models and data manipulation functions.
- **Service Tests**: Testing the APIs that handle user requests, such as adding a book to a cart or processing a payment.
- **UI Tests**: Ensuring that the user interface provides the correct inputs to the user and correctly displays results from the back-end services.

Here is a simple example of how tests might be structured across different layers:

- **Unit Layer**: Tests individual functions and classes.
- **Service Layer**: Tests API endpoints and their interactions with the database.
- **UI Layer**: Tests the end-to-end flow from a user perspective, such as completing a purchase.

Benefits

- **Comprehensive Coverage**: Ensures that no area of the application is under-tested, which can prevent critical issues from slipping through cracks that might exist if one layer were less tested.
- **Optimized Resource Utilization**: By balancing the tests across layers, resources are used more efficiently, preventing bottlenecks that occur when too many tests target a single layer.
- **Enhanced Test Resilience**: A balanced approach reduces the risk associated with changes in one part of the application, as the distributed tests can quickly pinpoint issues across various areas.

Summary

Balanced Layer Distribution is a strategic pattern designed to optimize test coverage across all layers of an application, ensuring that each layer is adequately tested without overwhelming any single part of the test suite. This balance helps maintain the agility and responsiveness of the development process while ensuring a high-quality final product. In the next section, we will continue to explore other vital test design patterns that further enhance the robustness of our testing strategies.

Simplicity-Driven Testing

Simplicity-Driven Testing is a test design pattern that focuses on prioritizing tests based on their complexity and ease of implementation. This approach advocates for automating simpler tests first, typically targeting the less complex layers of an application, which often leads to quicker development and earlier identification of defects.

Concept and Application

Simplicity-Driven Testing operates on the principle that starting with less complex tests can provide quick wins and build momentum in the test automation process. This strategy is particularly effective in the early stages of development or in projects where rapid deployment is critical. By focusing on simpler tests, teams can establish a baseline of stability and functionality, upon which more intricate tests can later be built.

For example, in an application with a complex business logic layer but a relatively straightforward user interface, it would be more practical to first automate UI tests that verify basic functionalities such as navigation, form submissions, and data displays before moving on to more intricate API or unit tests involving business logic.

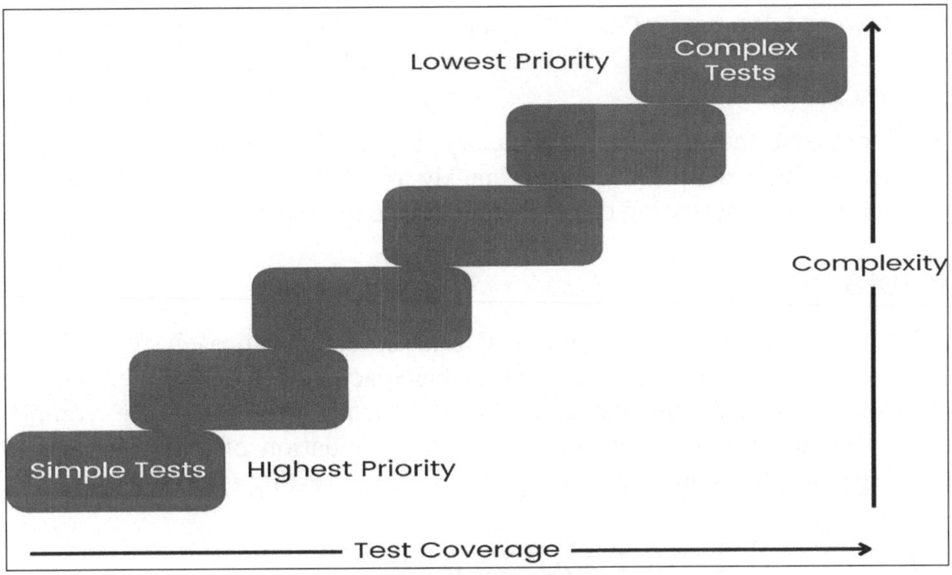

***Figure 2.4**: Simplicity-Driven Testing*

Technical Details

Implementing Simplicity-Driven Testing typically involves:

- **Identifying Test Complexity**: Breaking down each test scenario by its technical and logical complexity.
- **Prioritizing Based on Simplicity**: Arranging test cases in order to increase complexity and start automation with the simplest ones.
- **Iterative Expansion**: Gradually expanding the test suite by adding more complex tests as the foundation of simpler tests solidifies.

Here is an example scenario for an e-commerce site:

- **Simple UI Tests**: Verifying that product pages load correctly and display the expected information.
- **Intermediate Service Tests**: Checking that the shopping cart correctly updates when items are added or removed.
- **Complex Business Logic Tests**: Ensuring that promotions and discounts apply correctly under various conditions.

Benefits

- **Quick Feedback**: Automating simpler tests first can provide quick feedback on the fundamental aspects of the application, allowing for early detection of critical issues.

- **Lower Maintenance Costs**: Simpler tests are typically easier to maintain and less prone to breakage, which can reduce the overall maintenance cost of the test suite.
- **Increased Test Coverage Efficiency**: By focusing initially on less complex areas, the test coverage can quickly reach a significant portion of the application, increasing the efficiency of the testing effort.

Summary

Simplicity-Driven Testing is a practical and efficient approach to building an automation suite, especially beneficial in fast-paced development environments or projects with tight deadlines. By systematically increasing the complexity of automated tests, teams can ensure a solid foundation of test coverage while minimizing disruptions and maximizing the impact of testing efforts.

Risk-Based Layer Coverage

Risk-Based Layer Coverage is a test design pattern that focuses on allocating testing resources according to the risk associated with different layers of an application. This method prioritizes testing efforts based on the potential impact of defects in each layer, ensuring that higher-risk areas receive the most thorough testing.

Concept and Application

Risk-Based Layer Coverage leverages a strategic approach to testing by identifying and assessing the risk level of each component or layer within the system. Risks can be evaluated based on various factors such as business impact, user interaction frequency, complexity of the code, and historical defect trends. By prioritizing layers that are deemed higher risk, this pattern ensures that testing efforts are concentrated where they are most needed, enhancing the effectiveness of the test suite.

For instance, in a financial application, components handling transactions and data privacy may be identified as high-risk areas. Therefore, these components would be prioritized for more intensive testing compared to less critical features such as user profile updates or notification settings.

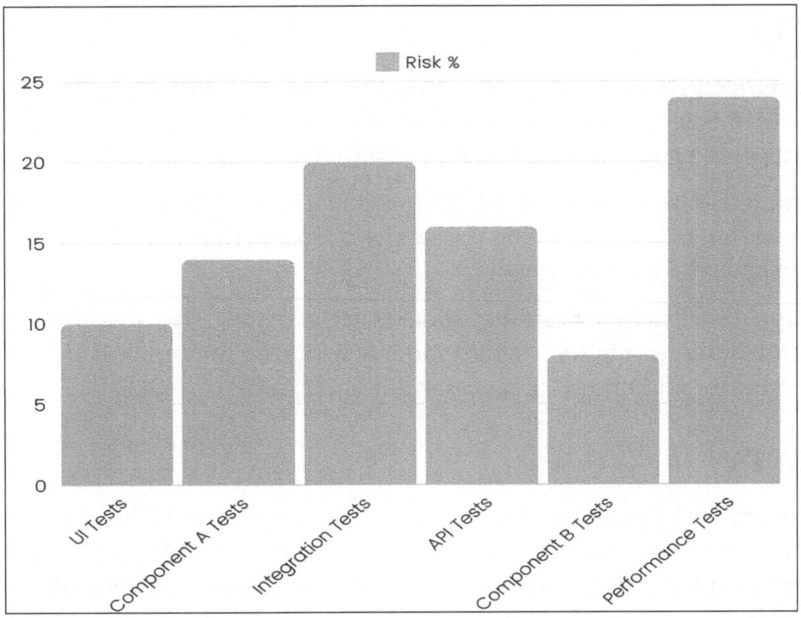

***Figure 2.5**: Risk-Based Layer Coverage*

Technical Details

Implementing Risk-Based Layer Coverage involves several key steps:

- **Risk Assessment**: Conducting a thorough analysis of each layer to determine the risk associated with potential defects. This might involve stakeholder interviews, analysis of usage data, and reviews of past incident reports.
- **Test Prioritization**: Assigning a priority level to each test based on the risk assessment. Higher-risk areas might require more comprehensive testing strategies, including a mix of unit, integration, and end-to-end tests.
- **Resource Allocation**: Distributing resources such as time, testing tools, and team efforts according to the prioritization, ensuring that high-risk areas are adequately covered.

An example might be a web-based CRM system:

- **High-Risk Layer (Data Integrity)**: Ensuring all database operations related to customer data are rigorously tested for accuracy and security.
- **Medium-Risk Layer (API Functionality)**: Focusing on API endpoints that handle customer data transactions, requiring robust testing but less so than direct data handling.
- **Lower-Risk Layer (User Interface)**: Conducting basic functionality tests on UI elements that have a lower impact on the core business operations.

Benefits

- **Enhanced Focus on Critical Areas**: By concentrating on high-risk areas, this pattern ensures that the most critical parts of the application are thoroughly tested, reducing the likelihood of severe defects.
- **Efficient Use of Resources**: Risk-based prioritization helps in the optimal allocation of limited testing resources, ensuring that they are used where they can have the greatest impact.
- **Improved Product Stability and Security**: Prioritizing testing based on risk contributes to higher stability and security of the application, as the most vulnerable and crucial areas are robustly tested.

Summary

Risk-Based Layer Coverage is a strategic and targeted approach to test design that aligns testing efforts with the risk profile of the application. This pattern is particularly valuable in complex systems where resources are limited and not all components can be tested with equal intensity. Up next, we will explore additional patterns that complement Risk-Based Layer Coverage, further enhancing the security and reliability of the testing strategy.

Feedback-Focused Testing

Feedback-Focused Testing is a test design pattern that prioritizes the speed and efficiency of receiving feedback from test executions. This approach is particularly beneficial in agile development environments where quick iterations and fast feedback loops are essential for the continuous improvement of the product.

Concept and Application

Feedback-Focused Testing emphasizes the importance of designing tests that provide immediate and actionable feedback to developers. By strategically placing tests at layers of the application where they can quickly and accurately detect issues, this pattern helps to streamline the development process and enhance the quality of the software.

For example, in a continuous integration environment, implementing automated unit tests that run on every code check-in provides developers with immediate feedback on their changes. Similarly, integrating automated smoke tests that quickly assess the critical functionalities of an application after each deployment ensures that any major issues can be addressed promptly.

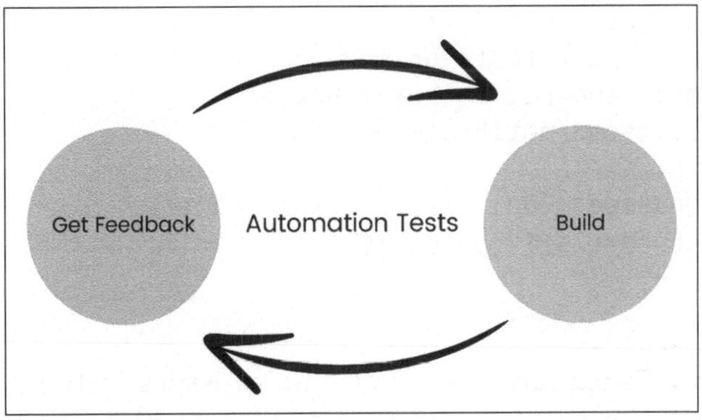

Figure 2.6: *Feedback Focused Testing*

Technical Details

Implementing Feedback-Focused Testing involves several key strategies:

- **Integration with Development Workflow**: Embedding automated tests within the development and deployment pipelines to ensure they are run at key points where feedback is most useful.
- **Selection of Fast-Running Tests**: Prioritizing the creation of tests that execute quickly, such as unit tests or targeted integration tests, to minimize the feedback loop duration.
- **Use of Real-Time Monitoring Tools**: Implementing tools that provide real-time test results to developers as soon as they are available. Tools such as Jenkins or GitHub Actions can be configured to send notifications or create reports immediately after test executions.

Here is an example of setting up a Feedback-Focused Test in a CI pipeline using GitHub Actions:

example_2_3.yaml

```
name: CI
on: [push]
jobs:
  build:
    runs-on: ubuntu-latest
    steps:
    - uses: actions/checkout@v2
    - name: Set up Python
      uses: actions/setup-python@v2
      with:
        python-version: '3.8'
    - name: Install dependencies
      run: pip install -r requirements.txt
```

```
    - name: Run Unit Tests
      run: pytest tests/unit
    - name: Send Feedback Notification
      uses: some/notification-action@v1
      with:
        message: "Unit Tests Completed"
        status: ${{ job.status }}
```

Benefits

- **Rapid Issue Detection**: Early detection of issues in the development cycle helps in reducing the time and cost associated with fixing bugs.
- **Improved Developer Productivity**: Quick feedback allows developers to address issues immediately before they move on to other tasks, which can enhance overall productivity.
- **Higher Quality Software**: Regular and immediate testing ensures that the quality of the software is consistently monitored and maintained throughout its development.

Summary

Feedback-Focused Testing is crucial for projects that value quick iterations and rely on continuous feedback to drive development. By ensuring that testing is integrated into the development process and that feedback is promptly delivered, this pattern supports a more agile, responsive, and effective development workflow. Up next, we will explore how these testing strategies can be integrated into broader test automation frameworks to maximize efficiency and effectiveness.

Implementing Test Design Patterns

Implementing test design patterns effectively requires a strategic approach that considers the specific needs and nuances of your project. Selecting the right patterns and adapting them to fit within your development environment can significantly enhance the effectiveness of your test automation efforts. This section will guide you through the process of implementing these patterns, choosing the appropriate ones for your project, and understanding why these choices may differ from one project to another.

How to Implement Test Design Patterns

1. **Assess Your Testing Needs**: Begin by understanding the specific requirements and challenges of your project. Consider factors such as the complexity of the application, the criticality of different features, the development methodology (Agile, Waterfall, and so on), and the existing testing practices. This assessment

will help identify gaps in your current strategy and pinpoint areas where specific test design patterns could be beneficial.

2. **Choose Appropriate Patterns**: Based on your needs assessment, select patterns that best address the identified challenges. For instance, if your project suffers from slow feedback loops, consider implementing the Feedback-Focused Testing pattern. If your application has a high-risk business logic layer, the Risk-Based Layer Coverage pattern might be more appropriate.
3. **Plan the Implementation**: Develop a detailed plan for how the selected patterns will be implemented. This plan should include the tools and technologies needed, the scope of changes to the existing test suite, and a timeline for the rollout. It is important to involve all stakeholders in this planning phase to ensure alignment and address any concerns.
4. **Educate Your Team**: Ensure that your team understands the selected patterns and the rationale behind them. Providing training or resources can help team members adapt to new approaches and technologies, facilitating a smoother implementation process.
5. **Iteratively Integrate Patterns**: Gradually integrate the new test design patterns into your existing testing processes. Start with pilot projects or smaller test cases to evaluate the effectiveness of the patterns before fully scaling them across the project.
6. **Monitor and Optimize**: Continuously monitor the outcomes of the implemented patterns. Use metrics such as defect detection rates, test coverage, and execution times to evaluate their impact. Be prepared to make adjustments based on feedback and changing project requirements.

Selecting Between Test Design Patterns

Choosing the right test design patterns involves considering several key factors:

- **Project Size and Complexity**: Larger and more complex projects might benefit from more sophisticated patterns, such as Risk-Based Layer Coverage or Balanced Layer Distribution, to manage the scale and diversity of testing needs.
- **Team Skillset**: The existing skills and expertise of your team can influence which patterns are feasible to implement. Patterns requiring advanced tooling or programming skills may require additional training.
- **Development Methodology**: Agile projects might prioritize patterns such as Feedback-Focused Testing that support rapid iterations, whereas Waterfall projects might lean towards comprehensive patterns such as Foundation-First Testing.

Project-to-Project Variability

The effectiveness of test design patterns can vary significantly from one project to another due to differences in application architecture, team dynamics, project goals, and external constraints. It is crucial to conduct thorough research and possibly even preliminary testing to determine which patterns are most likely to succeed in your specific context.

- **Research and Pilot Testing**: Before fully committing to a pattern, conduct research and pilot tests to gauge its effectiveness within your project environment. This preliminary phase can prevent costly missteps and guide better decision-making.
- **Customization of Patterns**: Adapt patterns to fit the unique challenges and requirements of your project. Customization might involve tweaking the implementation details or combining several patterns to address complex needs.

Implementing test design patterns is a strategic process that requires careful planning, thoughtful selection, and continuous optimization. By understanding your project's specific needs, selecting appropriate patterns, and customizing them to your environment, you can build a more effective and efficient testing strategy. This approach not only improves the quality of your software but also enhances the agility and responsiveness of your development process.

Real-World Examples and Case Studies

Implementing test design patterns effectively can transform the quality and efficiency of your software testing processes. Here, we present several real-world examples and case studies that illustrate the successful application of various test design patterns in diverse environments. These examples highlight the practical benefits and strategic importance of adopting specific patterns based on project needs.

Case Study 1: Implementing Risk-Based Layer Coverage in Financial Software

Background: A large financial institution faced challenges with its legacy systems, which often led to high-severity bugs slipping through to production. The complexity and critical nature of the financial transactions required a more robust testing approach.

Implementation:

- **Risk Assessment**: The team conducted a thorough risk assessment to identify high-risk areas, particularly focusing on modules handling transactions and customer data.

- **Pattern Implementation**: The Risk-Based Layer Coverage pattern was chosen to prioritize testing efforts. High-risk areas received more intensive testing, including both integration and end-to-end tests.
- **Tools Used**: Advanced tools such as Selenium for UI testing and Postman for API testing were integrated to ensure comprehensive coverage.

Outcome: The implementation of the Risk-Based Layer Coverage pattern led to a significant reduction in critical bugs reaching production. The focused approach allowed the team to allocate resources more effectively, improving overall software reliability and customer trust.

Case Study 2: Adopting Feedback-Focused Testing in a Continuous Delivery Environment

Background: A tech startup developing a real-time data analytics platform needed to accelerate its development cycle without compromising the quality of its application, which was crucial for its real-time decision-making features.

Implementation:

- **Integration with CI/CD**: Feedback-Focused Testing was integrated directly into their continuous integration and deployment pipeline.
- **Rapid Testing Tools**: The team used GitLab CI for continuous testing, integrating lightweight unit tests and smoke tests that could run quickly and frequently.
- **Feedback Mechanisms**: Real-time feedback mechanisms were established to alert developers immediately if tests failed, using tools such as Slack for notifications.

Outcome: The adoption of Feedback-Focused Testing significantly speeds up the development process by providing developers with instant feedback on their commits. This enabled faster iterations and helped maintain high code quality, which was crucial for the platform's success.

Case Study 3: Enhancing Test Efficiency with Simplicity-Driven Testing in an E-Commerce Application

Background: An e-commerce company was experiencing delays in its release cycles due to lengthy and complex testing processes, especially as their product offerings expanded.

Implementation:

- **Simplifying Test Cases**: The company implemented the Simplicity-Driven Testing pattern, starting with automating simple, high-impact tests across the user journey.
- **Phased Approach**: They began with critical paths, such as cart addition and checkout processes, using Playwright for UI and API Automation.
- **Iterative Expansion**: Over time, more complex scenarios were automated, building on the stable foundation of simpler tests.

Outcome: This approach not only streamlined the testing process but also helped identify key issues faster, reducing the overall testing time and speeding up the release cycle. The simpler tests proved easier to maintain and adapt, supporting the rapid scaling of their testing efforts as new features were developed.

These case studies demonstrate the transformative potential of implementing test design patterns in a strategic manner. By understanding the specific challenges and needs of each project, teams can select and apply the most effective patterns to enhance testing efficiency, reduce risks, and ultimately deliver higher quality software. As we continue to explore more patterns and their applications, it becomes evident that a thoughtful approach to test design is crucial for achieving excellence in software development.

Best Practices for Implementing Test Design Patterns

Implementing test design patterns effectively is a critical component of a successful automation strategy. This section discusses the best practices that can help ensure that these patterns are applied effectively, efficiently, and in a way that brings tangible improvements to your testing processes. These practices are derived from industry standards and refined through real-world application in numerous projects.

Understand Your Application and Requirements

- **Comprehensive Requirement Analysis**: Before selecting and implementing test design patterns, thoroughly understand your application's architecture, dependencies, and business requirements. This deep understanding will guide which patterns are applicable and how they can be customized to fit your specific needs.
- **Identify Testable Components**: Break down the application into testable components and layers. This helps in applying layer-specific patterns such as Risk-Based Layer Coverage or Simplicity-Driven Testing more effectively.

Select the Right Test Design Patterns

- **Align Patterns with Project Goals**: Choose test design patterns that align with your project's goals and challenges. For example, if rapid development cycles are crucial, consider Feedback-Focused Testing to enhance the speed of feedback.
- **Balance Between Pattern Types**: Ensure a balance between structural, behavioral, and creational patterns to cover various aspects of testing effectively. For instance, combine Foundation-First Testing (structural) with Data-Driven Testing (behavioral) to enhance both the foundation and flexibility of your tests.

Implement Patterns Systematically

- **Iterative Implementation**: Implement test design patterns iteratively. Start small with a pilot area before rolling out the pattern across the entire project. This approach allows you to gauge the pattern's effectiveness and make necessary adjustments before widespread implementation.
- **Integrate into Existing Processes**: Seamlessly integrate these patterns into existing development and testing workflows. Avoid disruption in current processes by introducing changes incrementally.

Training and Documentation

- **Educate Your Team**: Provide training and resources for your team on the selected test design patterns. Understanding the purpose, benefits, and implementation details of these patterns is crucial for their successful adoption.
- **Maintain Comprehensive Documentation**: Document how each pattern is implemented, including the rationale behind choosing each pattern, the specific cases it addresses, and any modifications made to fit your context. This documentation will be invaluable for onboarding new team members and scaling your testing efforts.

Monitor and Adapt

- **Continuous Monitoring**: Regularly monitor the effectiveness of implemented test design patterns. Use metrics such as defect escape rates, test coverage, and testing time to evaluate their impact.
- **Be Adaptive**: Be prepared to adapt or change strategies based on monitoring outcomes and evolving project needs. Flexibility is key to maintaining an effective testing strategy as the project and its environment evolve.

Leverage Tools and Automation

- **Use Appropriate Tools**: Utilize tools that complement the selected test design patterns. For example, a tool such as Jenkins for Feedback-Focused Testing can automate feedback loops, or PyTest can implement Foundation-First Testing to leverage its powerful unit-testing capabilities.
- **Automate Wisely**: Automate the application of test design patterns where possible, such as automatic code analysis tools to enforce certain patterns or automated test case generation based on templates aligned with selected patterns.

Adopting these best practices for implementing test design patterns can dramatically improve the structure, effectiveness, and efficiency of your testing processes. By carefully selecting, implementing, and monitoring the impact of these patterns, you can ensure that your testing strategy not only meets but also exceeds the demands of modern software development environments. This approach not only enhances the quality of the software but also optimizes the testing efforts to support continuous improvement and innovation.

Conclusion

In this chapter, we thoroughly explored the role of test design patterns in enhancing the effectiveness of automation frameworks. By adopting and implementing various strategic patterns, such as Foundation-First Testing, Layer-Specific Logic Testing, Balanced Layer Distribution, Simplicity-Driven Testing, Risk-Based Layer Coverage, and Feedback-Focused Testing, you can address a wide range of testing challenges. These patterns are not just theoretical concepts but practical tools that, when applied correctly, can significantly improve the quality and efficiency of your testing processes.

Here is a summary of the key points covered in this chapter: **Foundation-First Testing** involves building a strong base of unit tests before progressing to higher test layers. **Layer-Specific Logic Testing** places tests at the layer where the logic resides, improving precision and efficiency. **Balanced Layer Distribution** ensures that tests are proportionally distributed across all layers for comprehensive coverage. **Simplicity-Driven Testing** focuses on starting with the simplest tests to quickly build coverage and detect major issues early. **Risk-Based Layer Coverage** prioritizes testing efforts based on the risk associated with different application layers. Lastly, **Feedback-Focused Testing** integrates tests that provide quick and actionable feedback, supporting agile development practices.

These design patterns provide a framework for crafting tests that are not only effective at catching defects but are also manageable and adaptable to changes in the application and its environment.

As we move forward, the next chapter will delve into the intricacies of unit testing, a fundamental aspect of any robust testing strategy. We will begin by discussing the **Importance of Unit Testing in the Test Pyramid**, highlighting its role in ensuring the stability and functionality of individual components. We will also compare unit tests with other types of tests to clarify their unique benefits and applications.

Key Takeaways

- **Strategic Application of Test Design Patterns**: Understanding and applying the right test design patterns can dramatically improve the effectiveness of your testing strategy by addressing specific challenges unique to your project.
- **Customization and Flexibility**: Test design patterns should be customized to fit the specific context and requirements of your project. Flexibility in their implementation is key to adapting to project changes and achieving optimal results.
- **Thorough Understanding and Selection Process**: Carefully selecting which test design patterns to implement based on a thorough understanding of your application's architecture and risk profile is crucial for maximizing the impact of your testing efforts.
- **Integrative Approach for Implementation**: Successfully integrating test design patterns into your existing development and testing workflows ensures minimal disruption and enhances overall testing efficacy.
- **Continuous Evaluation and Adaptation**: Continuously monitoring the effectiveness of implemented patterns and being willing to adapt them as necessary can help maintain the relevance and efficiency of your testing processes over time.

These takeaways encapsulate the core lessons from this chapter, providing a strategic framework for employing test design patterns effectively within your software testing and development practices. This foundation sets the stage for diving deeper into specific testing strategies, starting with unit testing in the next chapter.

CHAPTER 3
Unit Testing Strategies

Introduction

In the previous chapter, we delved into the world of test design patterns, exploring how these strategic frameworks can significantly enhance the effectiveness and maintainability of your test automation efforts. We examined key patterns such as Foundation-First Testing, Layer-Specific Logic Testing, and Risk-Based Layer Coverage, each offering unique solutions to common testing challenges. By understanding and implementing these patterns, you have laid the groundwork for a more structured and efficient testing approach that spans across different layers of your application.

Building on this foundation, this chapter focuses on unit testing, the cornerstone of any robust test automation strategy. Unit testing is where the smallest pieces of your code—individual functions or methods—are put under the microscope. This chapter will explore why unit testing is so crucial within the test pyramid, how it differs from other types of tests, and the best practices for writing effective unit tests. We will also dive into advanced topics such as mocking and stubbing, which are essential for isolating units and ensuring that your tests are focused and reliable.

As we progress through this chapter, you will gain a comprehensive understanding of how to implement unit testing strategies that improve code quality and integrate seamlessly into your development workflow. From practical examples to real-world case studies, this chapter is designed to equip you with the tools and knowledge needed to write and maintain unit tests that provide reliable, actionable feedback, ultimately enhancing the overall quality and stability of your software.

Structure

In this chapter, we will explore the critical role of unit testing in maintaining high-quality software. Here is what we will cover:

- Introduction to Unit Testing
- Importance of Unit Testing in the Test Pyramid
- Writing Effective Unit Tests: Principles and Practices
- Integrating Unit Tests in CI/CD Pipelines
- Best Practices and Common Pitfalls in Unit Testing

Introduction to Unit Testing

Unit testing is a fundamental practice in software development, playing a critical role in ensuring the quality and reliability of code. At its core, unit testing involves the verification of the smallest testable parts of an application, known as units. These units are typically individual functions, methods, or classes that can be isolated from the rest of the application to be tested independently. By focusing on these small components, unit testing allows developers to ensure that each piece of code performs as expected, even before it is integrated into the larger system.

The concept of unit testing is rooted in the idea of breaking down an application into its most basic elements and verifying that each element behaves correctly. This granular approach to testing is crucial because it allows for the early detection of defects within the codebase. When issues are identified at the unit level, they are often easier and less costly to fix compared to problems discovered later in the development process. This early detection is particularly valuable in agile environments, where continuous integration and frequent code changes are the norm. By catching bugs early, unit testing helps maintain the stability and integrity of the application as it evolves.

In addition to ensuring code correctness, unit testing serves several other vital functions within the development lifecycle, such as:

- **Documentation**: Unit tests serve as a form of documentation, providing clear examples of how individual units are intended to function. This is particularly helpful when onboarding new developers to a project, as they can quickly understand the expected behavior of specific parts of the codebase through the unit tests.
- **Facilitates Refactoring and Maintenance**: Unit testing makes refactoring and code maintenance safer and more manageable. Since unit tests validate the behavior of code, they provide a safety net that allows developers to refactor or optimize code with confidence, knowing that any unintended changes will be caught by the tests.

- **Enhances Test Coverage**: Unit testing contributes to the overall test coverage of an application, ensuring that even the smallest parts of the code are tested. This comprehensive coverage increases the robustness and reliability of the software, as potential defects are more likely to be identified and resolved early in the development process.

Another key aspect of unit testing is its role in Test-Driven Development (TDD), a development methodology where tests are written before the code itself. In TDD, the development process is guided by the creation of unit tests that define the desired behavior of the code. Developers first write a unit test that fails (since the code to pass it does not yet exist), then write the minimal amount of code necessary to pass the test, and finally refactor the code while ensuring that it still passes the test. This cycle of testing, coding, and refactoring ensures that the code is not only functional but also clean and maintainable. TDD has gained popularity in modern software development because it encourages good coding practices and results in code that is inherently testable.

Despite the clear benefits of unit testing, it is important to recognize that it is not a silver bullet. Unit tests are just one part of a comprehensive testing strategy that also includes integration tests, end-to-end tests, and more. While unit tests are excellent for verifying the correctness of individual components, they do not test how these components interact with each other in the context of the full application. This is why unit testing is typically positioned at the base of the test pyramid, forming a strong foundation upon which other types of testing are built. The test pyramid emphasizes that while the majority of tests should be unit tests due to their speed and low cost, they should be complemented by higher-level tests that validate the interactions between components.

In conclusion, unit testing is an essential practice for any software development team committed to delivering high-quality code. It provides early defect detection, acts as documentation, facilitates refactoring, and supports methodologies such as TDD. However, it should be understood as part of a broader testing strategy that includes other forms of testing to ensure comprehensive coverage and reliability. As we move forward in this chapter, we will explore the importance of unit testing within the test pyramid, the differences between unit tests and other types of tests, and the best practices for writing effective unit tests that contribute to a robust and maintainable codebase.

Linking Unit Testing to Test-Driven Development (TDD)

Unit testing is not only a critical component of the test pyramid but also the backbone of Test-Driven Development (TDD), a development methodology that has gained significant traction in modern software engineering. TDD fundamentally changes the way code is written by placing unit tests at the very start of the development process. In TDD, developers write unit tests before they write the actual code that will be tested. This approach flips the traditional development cycle, ensuring that the code is driven by the need to pass tests rather than the other way around.

The TDD Process

The TDD cycle typically follows a simple but powerful workflow:

1. **Write a Failing Unit Test**: The developer begins by writing a unit test for a new function or feature that does not yet exist. This test is expected to fail since there is no corresponding code to pass it. This step ensures that the test is indeed valid and that it will only pass when the correct functionality is implemented.
2. **Write the Minimum Code to Pass the Test**: Once the failing test is in place, the developer writes the minimal code necessary to make the test pass. This approach encourages simplicity and ensures the codebase remains lean, as only the necessary code is written to meet the test requirements.
3. **Refactor the Code**: After making the test pass, the developer refactors the code to improve its structure, readability, or performance, all while ensuring that the test continues to pass. The refactoring step is crucial in TDD as it allows the code to evolve without sacrificing quality.

This cycle—often referred to as "Red-Green-Refactor"—promotes the development of code that is inherently testable, clean, and aligned with the application's requirements. By writing tests first, developers are forced to think about their code's desired behavior and outcomes before diving into the implementation, leading to better-designed software.

Benefits of TDD

- **Increased Test Coverage**: Since tests are written before any code, TDD naturally leads to high test coverage. This ensures that every part of the code is tested, reducing the likelihood of bugs slipping through.
- **Improved Code Quality**: TDD encourages writing only the necessary code to meet the test requirements, which results in a cleaner, more maintainable codebase. The constant refactoring in TDD also ensures that the code structure remains optimal over time.
- **Faster Debugging**: When a test fails in TDD, it fails close to where the bug is introduced, making debugging and fixing issues easier and faster.
- **Better Design and Requirements Understanding**: Writing tests first forces developers to clarify their understanding of the requirements, leading to better-designed features that closely align with user needs.

Incorporating unit testing through TDD enhances code quality and reliability and fosters a deeper understanding of the requirements, ultimately leading to better-designed software. By integrating unit tests early and often, teams can ensure that their development process is efficient and aligned with the end goals, creating a robust foundation for future iterations.

Importance of Unit Testing in the Test Pyramid

Unit testing is not just a foundational practice in software development; it is the cornerstone upon which a robust and effective testing strategy is built. The test pyramid, which we have discussed earlier, also emphasizes the need to focus on different types of tests at varying levels, with unit tests forming the base. This section explores the critical role that unit testing plays within the test pyramid and how it contributes to the overall quality and reliability of software.

- **The Foundation of the Testing Strategy**: Unit tests ensure that the building blocks of an application are reliable. They catch bugs at the earliest stage, preventing them from cascading into more complex levels. For example, if a function handling data processing is flawed, no amount of higher-level tests can fix the issue. Unit tests guarantee that such core functionalities are stable before integrating them into larger systems.
- **Speed and Cost-Effectiveness**: Unit tests are quick to run and inexpensive to maintain, making them ideal for Continuous Integration (CI) pipelines. By catching bugs early in development, they reduce the cost of fixing defects and provide fast feedback to developers, enabling quicker iterations and higher development velocity.
- **Early Defect Detection and Isolation**: Unit tests help isolate defects at the source, allowing developers to identify and fix issues quickly. This aligns well with agile development, where frequent code changes require immediate validation. Testing components in isolation simplifies debugging and allows for targeted fixes, improving overall software quality.
- **Supporting Agile and Continuous Integration**: Unit tests support agile methodologies and continuous integration practices by providing rapid feedback during code changes. They also make refactoring safer, ensuring that code improvements do not introduce new bugs. Developers can confidently make changes knowing that unit tests validate the core functionality.
- **Complementing Higher-Level Tests**: While unit tests are foundational, they work best in conjunction with integration and E2E tests. Integration tests ensure components work well together, while E2E tests validate complete workflows. For example, in an e-commerce application, unit tests might verify

price calculations, while integration tests ensure they work with payment systems, and E2E tests simulate a full user checkout process.

- **Facilitating Code Maintenance and Refactoring**: As software evolves, unit tests provide a safety net, allowing developers to refactor or optimize code without fear of breaking functionality. By testing specific components in isolation, developers can ensure that changes do not compromise the integrity of the codebase.

Differences Between Unit Tests and Other Types of Tests

Understanding the distinctions between unit tests, integration tests, and End-to-End (E2E) tests is crucial for building an effective testing strategy.

- **Unit Tests**: Focus on individual pieces of code, such as functions or methods. They are fast, isolated, and granular, targeting specific behaviors in the smallest units of code. Their primary benefits include early defect detection and support for code refactoring.
- **Integration Tests**: Validate how different components work together. These tests focus on the interactions between units, catching issues that arise from data passing between modules or services. While slower than unit tests, they are essential for ensuring system cohesion and verifying correct data flow between components.
- **End-to-End Tests (E2E)**: Simulate real user interactions with the application. These tests verify that the entire system functions correctly from start to finish. E2E tests are comprehensive but slow, making them ideal for validating full workflows rather than individual components.

The Need for a Balanced Testing Strategy

While unit tests are essential for ensuring the correctness of individual components, they are not sufficient on their own. Integration and E2E tests are necessary to validate the interactions between components and to ensure that the system as a whole behaves correctly. A balanced testing strategy, therefore, requires a mix of unit, integration, and E2E tests.

For instance, a team might start by writing comprehensive unit tests to ensure that the basic building blocks of the application work correctly. They would then add integration tests to verify that these blocks work together as intended. Finally, they would implement E2E tests to simulate real user interactions and ensure the system functions as expected. This layered approach ensures that defects are caught at the earliest possible stage while providing confidence that the application will perform correctly in production.

Writing Effective Unit Tests: Principles and Practices

Unit testing is a fundamental practice in software development that ensures the smallest components of your application function as expected. Writing effective unit tests is crucial not only for catching bugs early but also for maintaining a clean, reliable, and scalable codebase. Effective unit tests are more than just code that checks if a function works—they are carefully crafted pieces of your development process that help safeguard the integrity of your software over time.

In this section, we will explore the principles and best practices that guide the writing of effective unit tests. From structuring tests in a way that makes them easy to understand and maintain to ensuring they cover all possible scenarios without redundancy, this section will provide you with the tools and knowledge to write unit tests that are not just functional but invaluable to your development process.

By focusing on key principles such as isolation, determinism, and readability, you will learn how to create unit tests that provide consistent, reliable feedback on your code's behavior. We will also discuss how to approach testing different types of code, including pure functions, stateful components, and error-handling routines. Whether you are dealing with new code or integrating tests into a legacy system, the practices covered here will help you develop a robust suite of unit tests that support continuous development and high software quality.

Introduction to Writing Effective Unit Tests

Unit tests serve as the bedrock of a solid testing strategy, offering the first line of defense against defects in your codebase. When written effectively, unit tests can dramatically reduce the number of bugs that make it into production, saving time and resources by catching issues early in the development cycle. However, the effectiveness of unit tests depends heavily on how they are written. Poorly written tests can lead to false positives, missed bugs, and a test suite that is difficult to maintain, ultimately defeating the purpose of testing.

Effective unit tests are those that are reliable, maintainable, and provide clear, actionable feedback. They isolate the code being tested from external dependencies, ensuring that the test results are not influenced by factors outside the unit's control. They are also deterministic, meaning they produce the same result every time they are run, regardless of the environment or the order in which they are executed. Additionally, effective unit tests are easy to read and understand, which is crucial for maintaining them over time, especially as teams change and projects evolve.

Moreover, writing effective unit tests requires a strategic approach that considers the type of code being tested, the potential edge cases, and the overall testing strategy of the project. Whether you are testing simple functions, complex classes, or error-handling mechanisms, the principles outlined in this section will guide you in creating tests that truly add value to your codebase.

Principles of Writing Effective Unit Tests

Writing effective unit tests is not just about ensuring that your code works; it is about crafting tests that are robust, maintainable, and meaningful. These tests should provide consistent and reliable feedback, helping to prevent bugs from reaching production and ensuring that the code remains clean and functional over time. The following are the key principles that should guide the writing of effective unit tests:

Isolation

Isolation is a fundamental principle of unit testing. A unit test should focus solely on the behavior of the unit being tested–typically a function, method, or class–without being affected by external dependencies. This means that any interactions with databases, external APIs, file systems, or other components outside the unit should be removed or simulated using mocks, stubs, or other techniques.

Why Isolation Matters:

- **Consistency**: By isolating the unit from external factors, you ensure that the test results are consistent and reliable. A unit test that depends on an external service might fail due to issues with that service, not because of a problem in the code being tested.
- **Simplicity**: Isolated tests are simpler and easier to understand because they focus on a single unit of code. This simplicity makes it easier to identify the cause of a test failure, which speeds up debugging and maintenance.

Example: If you are testing a function that processes user input and saves it to a database, the unit test should not interact with the actual database. Instead, you might mock the database interaction so that the test only verifies that the function behaves correctly when saving data.

Deterministic Outcomes

Effective unit tests must be deterministic, meaning they should produce the same results every time they are run, regardless of the environment or the order in which they are executed. Determinism is crucial for trust in your test suite; if a test passes sometimes and fails at other times, it can lead to confusion and a lack of confidence in the results.

Why Determinism Matters:

- **Reliability**: Tests that produce consistent results are more reliable and help to ensure that changes in the codebase do not introduce unexpected behavior.

- **Debugging**: When a test fails, a deterministic test makes it easier to reproduce the issue, which is essential for effective debugging.

Example: A test that depends on the current system time might produce different results depending on when it is run. To ensure determinism, you could mock the system time or pass it as an argument to the function, allowing you to control the time during the test.

Readability and Maintainability

Unit tests should be written in a way that is easy to read and understand. This principle is vital because tests are not just for the original author–they are for anyone who works on the code in the future. Readable tests help ensure that the intent of the test is clear, making it easier to maintain and extend the test suite as the codebase evolves.

Why Readability and Maintainability Matter:

- **Collaboration**: Clear, well-structured tests make it easier for team members to understand what is being tested and why. This facilitates collaboration, especially in larger teams or open-source projects.
- **Long-Term Maintenance**: As the codebase evolves, tests will need to be updated. Readable tests make it easier to understand how they should be modified, reducing the likelihood of introducing errors during maintenance.

Best Practices for Readability:

- **Use Descriptive Names**: Test names should clearly describe what is being tested and the expected outcome. For example, instead of naming a test **`test1`**, use a descriptive name such as **`test_user_can_login_with_valid_credentials`**.
- **Keep Tests Focused**: Each test should focus on a single behavior or aspect of the code. Avoid combining multiple tests into one, as this can make the test harder to understand and maintain.
- **Comment Sparingly**: Comments can help clarify complex parts of a test, but over-commenting can clutter the code. Aim for clarity in the test code itself, using comments only when necessary.

Testing Edge Cases and Boundaries

Effective unit tests go beyond testing the "*happy path*" and include scenarios that cover edge cases and boundary conditions. Edge cases are the extreme conditions under which the code might behave differently, such as very large or very small input values, null values, or unexpected input formats. Boundary testing involves checking the behavior at the limits of allowable input, ensuring that the code handles these cases correctly.

Why Testing Edge Cases and Boundaries Matters:

- **Comprehensive Coverage**: Edge cases and boundary conditions are often where bugs occur, so testing these scenarios helps ensure that the code is robust and can handle a wide range of inputs.
- **Preventing Regression**: By covering edge cases, you can catch potential regressions or issues that might arise when the code is modified in the future.

Example: If you have a function that calculates the sum of two integers, you should test not only typical values but also cases such as the maximum and minimum integer values, negative numbers, and zero. These tests ensure that the function behaves correctly under all possible input conditions.

Adhering to these principles–Isolation, Determinism, Readability, and Edge Case Testing–will help you write unit tests that are not only effective in catching bugs but also maintainable over the long term. By focusing on these key aspects, you can build a test suite that provides reliable feedback, supports continuous development, and ensures the overall quality of your software. As we continue through this section, we will explore how to apply these principles in practice, ensuring that your unit tests are both valuable and robust.

Test Structure and Naming Conventions

Writing effective unit tests is not just about what you test but also about how you structure your tests and name them. A well-structured test not only ensures clarity and consistency but also makes it easier for developers to understand the purpose of the test, troubleshoot failures, and maintain the test suite over time. Naming conventions further enhance readability by clearly communicating what each test is intended to verify.

The AAA Structure: Arrange, Act, Assert

One of the most widely used patterns in unit testing is the AAA structure: Arrange, Act, Assert. This pattern provides a clear, logical flow that makes it easier to write and understand tests. It divides the test into three distinct sections, each serving a specific purpose:

1. **Arrange**: In this first step, you set up the test environment. This involves initializing objects, setting up mock data, and configuring any dependencies or conditions that are required for the test. The goal is to prepare everything necessary before executing the code under test.

   Example:

   ```
   # Arrange
   user = User("john_doe", "password123")
   ```

```
database = MockDatabase()
database.add_user(user)
```

2. **Act**: The second step involves executing the code or function that you are testing. This is the action part of the test, where the behavior you want to validate takes place.

   Example:

```
# Act
result = database.authenticate_user("john_doe", "password123")
```

3. **Assert**: In the final step, you verify that the outcome of the action matches your expectations. This is done by comparing the actual result with the expected result using assertions. If the test passes, it confirms that the code behaves as expected for the given scenario.

   Example:

```
# Assert
assert result == True
```

The AAA structure provides a clear and organized way to write tests, ensuring that each test is easy to follow and understand. It separates setup logic from execution and verification, which helps to isolate potential issues when tests fail.

Naming Conventions: Clarity and Descriptive Power

The names you give to your tests are crucial because they serve as the first line of communication about what the test is supposed to accomplish. A good test name should be descriptive enough that someone reading it can immediately understand the purpose of the test without needing to read through the test code itself.

Best Practices for Naming Tests:

- **Be Descriptive**: Test names should clearly describe what is being tested and the expected behavior. Instead of generic names such as **`testFunction`**, use descriptive names such as **`test_user_login_with_valid_credentials`**.
- **Follow a Consistent Pattern**: Adopting a consistent pattern for naming tests helps maintain readability across the test suite. One common pattern is to describe the scenario being tested followed by the expected result, such as **`test_calculate_discount_with_no_items_returns_zero`**.
- **Include Edge Cases**: When testing edge cases, it is helpful to indicate this in the test name. For example, **`test_calculate_discount_with_negative_quantity_throws_exception`**.
- **Keep Names Short but Informative**: While it is important to be descriptive, avoid overly long test names. Aim for a balance between clarity and brevity.

Examples of Good Test Names:

- `test_add_item_to_cart_increases_item_count`
- `test_remove_item_from_cart_decreases_item_count`
- `test_calculate_total_with_discount_applies_correctly`
- `test_login_with_invalid_password_returns_false`

These names provide clear information about what each test is doing, making it easier to understand the purpose of each test at a glance.

Structuring Tests for Maintainability

Maintaining a large test suite can be challenging, especially as a project evolves over time. By organizing tests in a consistent and logical structure, you can make it easier to manage and maintain your tests.

- **Organize Tests by Functionality**: Group related tests together based on the functionality they are testing. For instance, if you are testing an e-commerce application, you might have separate test files or classes for **`Cart`**, **`Checkout`**, and **`Payment`** functionalities.
- **Use Test Classes to Group Related Tests**: In languages such as Python, using test classes to group related tests can improve organization. For example, you might have a **`TestCart`** class that contains all tests related to the shopping cart functionality.

  Example:

  ```
  class TestCart:
      def test_add_item_to_cart_increases_item_count(self):
          # test implementation

      def test_remove_item_from_cart_decreases_item_count(self):
          # test implementation
  ```
- **Keep Tests Focused and Independent**: Each test should focus on a single aspect of the functionality. Avoid combining multiple assertions that test different behaviors within a single test. If a test fails, it should be immediately clear which behavior is broken.
- **Commenting and Documentation**: While tests should generally be self-explanatory, comments can be helpful for explaining the intent behind complex tests or unusual scenarios. However, avoid over-commenting; the code itself should be clear enough that comments are only needed for additional context.

Example of a Well-Structured Test:

```
class TestUserAuthentication:

    def test_login_with_valid_credentials_returns_true(self):
        # Arrange
        user = User("john_doe", "password123")
        database = MockDatabase()
        database.add_user(user)

        # Act
        result = database.authenticate_user("john_doe",
"password123")

        # Assert
        assert result == True

    def test_login_with_invalid_credentials_returns_false(self):
        # Arrange
        user = User("john_doe", "password123")
        database = MockDatabase()
        database.add_user(user)

        # Act
        result = database.authenticate_user("john_doe", "wrong_
password")

        # Assert
        assert result == False
```

In this example, the tests are clearly named, follow the AAA structure, and are grouped logically within a test class. This structure makes the test suite easy to navigate and maintain, ensuring that each test is clear, focused, and effective.

By adhering to the principles of the AAA structure and following clear, consistent naming conventions, you can create unit tests that are not only effective but also easy to maintain and understand. A well-structured test suite is an invaluable asset in any development project, providing reliable feedback, supporting refactoring efforts, and ensuring the long-term health of your codebase.

Writing Tests for Different Types of Code

Not all code is created equal, and different types of code require different testing approaches. Writing effective unit tests involves understanding the nature of the code you are testing and applying the right strategies to ensure comprehensive coverage. In this section, we will explore how to write unit tests for various types of code, including pure functions, stateful components, and error-handling mechanisms.

Testing Pure Functions

Pure functions are those that always produce the same output given the same input and do not cause any side effects. Because of their deterministic nature, pure functions are the easiest to test and are often the first candidates for unit testing.

Characteristics of Pure Functions:

- **Deterministic**: A pure function will always return the same result for the same input, making it highly predictable and straightforward to test.
- **No Side Effects**: Pure functions do not alter any external state, such as modifying global variables or interacting with external systems.

Testing Strategy:

- **Input-Output Matching**: The primary goal when testing pure functions is to verify that for a given input, the function returns the expected output.
- **Edge Cases**: In addition to standard cases, it is important to test edge cases, such as empty inputs, large numbers, or special characters, depending on the function's purpose.

Example: Let us consider a simple pure function that calculates the square of a number:

```
def square(x):
    return x * x
```

A unit test for this function might appear as follows:

```
def test_square():
    assert square(2) == 4
    assert square(-3) == 9
    assert square(0) == 0
    assert square(100) == 10000
```

In this example, the tests are straightforward and cover a range of inputs, including negative numbers and zero.

Testing Stateful Components

Stateful components are those that maintain an internal state between function calls. Unlike pure functions, stateful components can produce different outputs depending on their internal state, making them more complex to test.

Characteristics of Stateful Components:

- **Internal State**: The output of stateful components can vary depending on the current state of the object.
- **Side Effects**: Stateful components often interact with other parts of the system, potentially modifying shared resources or triggering additional actions.

Testing Strategy:

- **State Initialization**: Ensure that the state is correctly initialized before each test. This might involve resetting the state or setting up the component in a known state before testing.
- **State Transitions**: Test how the component behaves as its state changes. This includes verifying that the state transitions occur as expected and that the component produces the correct output for each state.
- **Multiple Scenarios**: Because stateful components can behave differently depending on their state, it is important to test multiple scenarios to ensure comprehensive coverage.

Example: Consider a simple counter class that maintains a count and provides methods to increment and reset the count:

```
class Counter:
    def __init__(self):
        self.count = 0

    def increment(self):
        self.count += 1

    def reset(self):
        self.count = 0

    def get_count(self):
        return self.count
```

Unit tests for this class might appear as follows:

```
def test_counter_initial_state():
    counter = Counter()
    assert counter.get_count() == 0

def test_counter_increment():
    counter = Counter()
    counter.increment()
    assert counter.get_count() == 1
    counter.increment()
    assert counter.get_count() == 2

def test_counter_reset():
    counter = Counter()
    counter.increment()
    counter.reset()
    assert counter.get_count() == 0
```

These tests check the initial state of the counter, ensure that increments work correctly, and verify that the reset method functions as expected.

Testing Error Handling and Exceptions

Error handling is a critical part of any application, and testing how your code responds to various error conditions is essential for building robust software. Unlike regular functionality, error handling requires tests that deliberately trigger failures and verify that the code responds appropriately.

Characteristics of Error Handling:

- **Exceptional Scenarios**: These are scenarios that fall outside the normal operation of the code, such as invalid inputs, network failures, or resource limitations.
- **Error Propagation**: Error handling often involves catching exceptions and either recovering from them or propagating them up the call stack.

Testing Strategy:

- **Triggering Exceptions**: Write tests that intentionally trigger errors by passing invalid inputs or simulating failure conditions. Ensure that the code throws the correct exceptions and handles them as expected.
- **Verifying Error Messages**: In some cases, it is important to verify that the correct error messages or codes are returned. This can be crucial for debugging and for providing meaningful feedback to users.
- **Edge Case Testing**: Similar to testing pure functions, ensure that edge cases, such as the lowest and highest possible inputs, are tested for error handling.

Example: Consider a function that calculates the square root of a number but should raise an exception if a negative number is provided:

```
import math

def calculate_square_root(x):
    if x < 0:
        raise ValueError("Cannot calculate square root of a nega-
tive number")
    return math.sqrt(x)
```

Unit tests for this function might appear as follows:

```
import pytest

def test_calculate_square_root_valid_input():
    assert calculate_square_root(4) == 2.0
    assert calculate_square_root(0) == 0.0

def test_calculate_square_root_invalid_input():
    with pytest.raises(ValueError) as excinfo:
        calculate_square_root(-1)
```

```
        assert str(excinfo.value) == "Cannot calculate square root of
    a negative number"
```

In this example, the first test verifies that the function returns the correct result for valid inputs. The second test deliberately passes an invalid input to check that the function raises the appropriate exception and provides a meaningful error message.

Testing different types of code requires tailored strategies that address the unique challenges posed by each type. Pure functions are straightforward to test due to their deterministic nature, while stateful components and error-handling mechanisms require more complex approaches to ensure that all possible scenarios are covered. By understanding these differences and applying the right testing strategies, you can write unit tests that are both effective and comprehensive, providing a solid foundation for reliable software.

Testing Strategies for Legacy Code

Legacy code is code that is inherited from previous projects or versions and often lacks sufficient documentation or tests–it presents unique challenges in software development. Unlike new code, legacy code was typically written without modern testing practices in mind, making it difficult to introduce unit tests and ensure reliability. However, testing legacy code is crucial for maintaining and enhancing the software without introducing new bugs. In this section, we will explore strategies for effectively testing legacy code, enabling you to improve its quality and maintainability.

Understanding the Challenges of Legacy Code

Before diving into specific strategies, it is important to understand why testing legacy code is particularly challenging:

- **Lack of Documentation**: Legacy code often lacks comprehensive documentation, making it difficult to understand the code's intent and behavior. This absence of documentation can complicate the process of writing meaningful tests.
- **Tightly Coupled Components**: Legacy systems are frequently characterized by tightly coupled components, where different parts of the system are highly interdependent. This tight coupling can make it challenging to isolate individual units for testing, a crucial step in writing effective unit tests.
- **Fear of Breaking the System**: Introducing tests or making changes to legacy code can be intimidating, especially in systems that are critical to business operations. Developers might fear that even minor modifications could break the system in unexpected ways.
- **Technical Debt**: Over time, legacy codebases accumulate technical debt–shortcuts or outdated practices that were acceptable at the time of writing

but now hinder the software's performance, scalability, or maintainability. Addressing this technical debt often requires significant refactoring, which is difficult without a solid test suite.

Start with Characterization Tests

One of the most effective strategies for testing legacy code is to begin with characterization tests. These tests do not necessarily verify the correctness of the code according to its original intent (which may be unclear) but instead capture the current behavior of the system. Characterization tests serve as a safety net, ensuring that any changes made to the code do not alter its existing behavior.

Implementation of Characterization Tests:

- **Identify Key Behaviors**: Begin by identifying the key behaviors of the legacy code that must remain consistent. These might include outputs for specific inputs, interactions with other components, or performance characteristics.
- **Write Tests Based on Existing Behavior**: Write tests that reflect how the system currently behaves, regardless of whether that behavior is correct or ideal. The goal is to document what the code does now, providing a baseline for future refactoring or enhancements.
- **Incrementally Improve**: Once you have a suite of characterization tests, you can begin refactoring or improving the code with confidence, knowing that the tests will alert you if any existing behavior changes unexpectedly.

Example: Consider a legacy function that calculates a customer's discount based on various factors. If the logic is unclear, start by writing tests that capture the current discounts for a range of customer profiles. These tests document the function's behavior, allowing you to refactor or update the code later without changing its output.

Refactor to Facilitate Testing

Refactoring is the process of restructuring existing code without changing its external behavior. In legacy systems, refactoring is often necessary to make the code more testable. The goal is to decouple tightly bound components, reduce dependencies, and simplify the code so that it can be easily unit-tested.

Refactoring Strategies:

- **Break Down Large Functions**: Legacy code often contains large, monolithic functions that perform multiple tasks. Break these down into smaller, more focused functions that are easier to test individually.
- **Introduce Dependency Injection**: Legacy code might directly instantiate dependencies within the code, making it difficult to replace these dependencies with mocks or stubs during testing. Introducing dependency injection allows

you to pass dependencies into a function or class, making it easier to control and isolate them in tests.

- **Encapsulate Complex Logic**: If certain parts of the legacy code contain complex logic, consider encapsulating this logic in a new class or module. This allows you to isolate and test the logic separately from the rest of the code.

Example: Suppose you are dealing with a legacy method that interacts with a database and performs multiple calculations. Start by refactoring the method to separate the database interaction from the calculations. You can then write unit tests for the calculation logic independently of the database, ensuring that each part of the code is tested in isolation.

Prioritize High-Risk Areas

When dealing with a large legacy codebase, it is often impractical to test everything at once. Instead, focus on the areas of the code that are most critical to the system's operation or that have the highest risk of causing issues if they fail. Prioritizing these high-risk areas ensures that your testing efforts provide the greatest possible value.

Identifying High-Risk Areas:

- **Business-Critical Functions**: Focus on testing functions that are essential to the core business operations. These might include payment processing, data validation, or user authentication.
- **Frequently Changed Code**: Code that is frequently modified is more likely to contain bugs, especially if it has not been tested previously. Prioritize adding tests to these areas to catch potential issues early.
- **Complex or Bug-Prone Code**: Complex code is inherently more difficult to understand and maintain, making it more likely to contain hidden bugs. Similarly, code that has a history of bugs should be prioritized for testing.

Example: If your legacy system processes financial transactions, prioritize writing tests for the functions that calculate totals, apply taxes, or handle payments. Ensuring these critical functions are well-tested can prevent costly errors and enhance the system's reliability.

Gradual Integration of Tests

Testing legacy code is often a gradual process that cannot be completed overnight. Instead of attempting to test the entire codebase at once, integrate tests gradually as you work on different parts of the system. This incremental approach allows you to build up a suite of tests over time without overwhelming your development efforts.

Strategies for Gradual Integration:

- **Test-Driven Bug Fixes**: Whenever you encounter a bug in the legacy code, write a unit test that reproduces the issue before fixing it. This approach ensures that the bug is not reintroduced in the future.
- **Adopt a "Boy Scout Rule"**: Follow the principle of leaving the codebase better than you found it. Whenever you work on a piece of legacy code, add or improve tests for that part of the system.
- **Celebrate Small Wins**: Testing legacy code can be daunting, so it is important to celebrate small victories. Each new test you add increases the overall reliability of the system.

Example: If you are tasked with adding a new feature to a legacy system, start by writing tests for the existing functionality in the area where the new feature will be implemented. This ensures that the current behavior is documented and protected, allowing you to confidently introduce the new feature.

Testing legacy code is a challenging but essential part of maintaining and improving existing systems. By employing strategies such as characterization tests, refactoring for testability, prioritizing high-risk areas, and gradually integrating tests, you can make legacy code more reliable and easier to maintain. While the process may be slow and require careful planning, the long-term benefits–reduced technical debt, fewer bugs, and a more maintainable codebase–are well worth the effort.

Ensuring Test Coverage and Avoiding Over-Testing

Test coverage is a critical metric in software development that indicates the extent to which your codebase is tested. High test coverage is generally desirable because it suggests that more of your code is verified against potential bugs. However, achieving optimal test coverage requires a balanced approach to avoid the pitfalls of over-testing, where the test suite becomes bloated and difficult to maintain. This section explores strategies for ensuring adequate test coverage while avoiding unnecessary tests that do not add significant value.

Understanding Test Coverage

Test coverage refers to the percentage of your codebase that is exercised by your tests. It is commonly measured using tools that track which lines of code are executed when the test suite is run. The goal is to ensure that all critical parts of your code are tested, particularly those that are complex, prone to errors, or essential to the application's functionality.

Types of Test Coverage:

- **Line Coverage**: The percentage of executed lines of code during testing. It is the most basic form of coverage, indicating how much of the codebase is being tested.
- **Branch Coverage**: Measures the percentage of code branches (for example, if-else statements) that have been tested. This type of coverage is important for ensuring that all possible paths through the code are verified.
- **Function Coverage**: Tracks the percentage of functions or methods that have been tested, ensuring that every function in your codebase is executed at least once during testing.
- **Condition Coverage**: Goes a step further by verifying that each boolean condition within the code has been tested for both true and false outcomes.

Example: Consider a simple function that calculates a discount based on customer type:

```
def calculate_discount(customer_type):
    if customer_type == "VIP":
        return 20
    elif customer_type == "Regular":
        return 10
    else:
        return 0
```

To achieve comprehensive coverage for this function, you would write tests that cover all possible inputs: VIP, Regular, and other customer types.

Achieving Adequate Test Coverage

To ensure that your code is well-covered, follow these guidelines:

- **Identify Critical Code Paths**: Focus your testing efforts on the parts of the codebase that are most critical to the application's functionality. This includes business logic, data processing, and areas where errors could have serious consequences, such as financial calculations or user authentication.
- **Use Coverage Tools**: Leverage code coverage tools to identify untested parts of your code. These tools can provide valuable insights into areas that might need additional testing. However, coverage tools should be used as a guide, not as the sole measure of test quality.
- **Balance Coverage with Test Value**: Not all code needs to be covered by tests. For instance, trivial code such as getters and setters or boilerplate code generated by frameworks may not need extensive testing. Focus on covering code that involves logic and decision-making or has a higher likelihood of containing bugs.

- **Test Edge Cases and Boundaries**: Ensure that your tests cover edge cases and boundary conditions. These are often where bugs are most likely to occur, and thorough testing of these scenarios is crucial for robust software.

Example: In the discount calculation function mentioned earlier, you should test edge cases, such as an unrecognized customer type or a null input, to ensure that the function handles unexpected inputs gracefully.

Avoiding Over-Testing

While high test coverage is important, over-testing can lead to a bloated and fragile test suite. Over-testing occurs when tests are written for code that is unlikely to fail, such as trivial functions, or when redundant tests are added, leading to unnecessary maintenance work.

Signs of Over-Testing:

- **Redundant Tests**: Multiple tests that check the same functionality in slightly different ways without adding new value. These tests increase the test suite size without improving its effectiveness.
- **Testing Trivial Code**: Writing tests for simple or boilerplate code that is unlikely to contain bugs, such as getters, setters, or automatically generated code.
- **Excessive Mocking**: When too many mocks and stubs are used, the tests may become disconnected from the real code, leading to a false sense of security. Over-mocking can also make tests harder to maintain and understand.

Strategies to Avoid Over-Testing:

- **Prioritize High-Value Tests**: Focus on writing tests that cover complex logic, high-risk areas, and business-critical functions. Ensure that each test adds value by addressing a specific, meaningful scenario.
- **Eliminate Redundancy**: Review your test suite regularly to identify and remove redundant tests. Consolidating similar tests into a single, comprehensive test can reduce maintenance overhead and improve clarity.
- **Use Test Metrics Wisely**: While test coverage metrics are useful, they should not be the sole determinant of your testing strategy. Aiming for 100% coverage is often unnecessary and can lead to over-testing. Instead, strive for meaningful coverage that ensures critical paths are well-tested.

Example: If you have a test that verifies the setter and getter methods for a class, consider whether these methods are critical enough to warrant testing. In many cases, these tests add little value and can be safely omitted, allowing you to focus on more complex and impactful parts of the code.

Maintaining a Balanced Test Suite

Achieving and maintaining the right balance between adequate coverage and avoiding over-testing is an ongoing process. As your codebase evolves, your test suite should adapt to ensure it continues to provide value without becoming a burden.

Best Practices for Maintaining Balance:

- **Regular Test Suite Reviews**: Periodically review your test suite to identify areas that are over-tested or under-tested. Adjust your tests as necessary to maintain optimal coverage.
- **Refactor Tests Alongside Code**: Just as you refactor code to improve its structure and performance, your test suite should also be refactored to remove redundancies, improve readability, and enhance maintainability.
- **Involve the Whole Team**: Encourage collaboration between developers, testers, and other stakeholders to ensure that the test suite remains focused on delivering value. Different perspectives can help identify areas where testing can be improved or streamlined.

Example: As part of your sprint retrospectives, include a review of the test suite to discuss any issues related to test coverage, redundancy, or maintenance. This regular check-in helps keep the test suite lean and effective, ensuring it continues to serve its purpose without becoming a burden.

Ensuring adequate test coverage is essential for building reliable software, but it is equally important to avoid the pitfalls of over-testing. By focusing on high-value tests, eliminating redundancy, and maintaining a balanced approach, you can create a test suite that provides meaningful coverage without unnecessary complexity. This balanced strategy will help you maintain a healthy, efficient testing process that supports the ongoing quality and stability of your software.

Mocking and Stubbing in Unit Tests

In unit testing, the goal is to isolate the unit of code being tested from external dependencies. However, many functions and classes interact with external systems or other parts of the application, such as databases, file systems, APIs, or services. To effectively test these units in isolation, developers use techniques such as mocking and stubbing to simulate these external dependencies. These techniques allow you to control the behavior of dependencies, ensuring that your unit tests remain focused on the code under test and not on the behavior of external systems.

Understanding Mocks and Stubs

Mocks and **stubs** are both test doubles–objects that stand in for real components during testing–but they serve slightly different purposes:

- **Stubs**: Stubs are simplified, controlled versions of dependencies that return predefined responses to method calls. They are primarily used to provide the necessary data or behavior to the unit under test. Stubs do not track how they are used; they merely provide canned responses to the inputs they receive.
- **Mocks**: Mocks, on the other hand, are more sophisticated. They not only provide controlled responses like stubs but also allow you to verify that certain interactions with the mock occurred. Mocks can track method calls, arguments passed to those methods, and how many times methods were called, enabling you to verify the correctness of interactions within the test.

Example of a Stub: Suppose you have a function that retrieves data from a database and processes it. To unit test this function, you can create a stub of the database that returns a predefined dataset, allowing you to test the processing logic without relying on an actual database.

```
class DatabaseStub:
    def get_data(self):
        return {"id": 1, "name": "Test Item"}

def process_data():
    db = DatabaseStub()
    data = db.get_data()
    return f"Processed {data['name']}"

def test_process_data():
    result = process_data()
    assert result == "Processed Test Item"
```

Example of a Mock: Imagine you have a service that sends notifications via an email system. To test whether the service correctly sends an email, you can create a mock of the email system that tracks whether the **`send_email`** method was called.

```
from unittest.mock import Mock

def notify_user(email_system, user_email):
    message = "You have a new notification"
    email_system.send_email(user_email, message)

def test_notify_user():
    email_system_mock = Mock()

    notify_user(email_system_mock, "user@example.com")
```

```
    email_system_mock.send_email.assert_called_once_with("user@
example.com", "You have a new notification")
```

In this example, the mock object verifies that the **send_email** method was called exactly once with the correct arguments, ensuring that the **notify_user** function behaves as expected.

Appropriate Use of Mocks and Stubs

The decision to use mocks or stubs depends on the nature of the dependency and what you need to verify in your test:

- **Use Stubs**: When you need to provide a controlled input or response to the unit under test without worrying about verifying interactions with the dependency. Stubs are ideal when the interaction with the dependency is simple, and you only care about the output.
- **Use Mocks**: When you need to verify that specific interactions with a dependency occurred, such as method calls, argument values, or the number of times a method was invoked. Mocks are useful for testing complex interactions and ensuring that your code correctly communicates with other components.

Example: If you are testing a function that calculates a report based on data from an API, you might use a stub to return a fixed dataset for the test. However, if you also want to verify that the function correctly logs an error when the API is unavailable, you would use a mock to simulate the API's behavior and check that the logging method was called appropriately.

Best Practices for Using Mocks and Stubs

While mocking and stubbing are powerful tools, they should be used carefully to ensure that your tests remain reliable and maintainable:

- **Keep Tests Focused**: Mocks and stubs should be used to isolate the unit under test, not to simulate the entire system. Avoid creating overly complex mocks or stubs that replicate large parts of the application. The goal is to focus on the specific behavior you want to test.
- **Avoid Over-Mocking**: Over-mocking occurs when too many interactions are mocked, leading to tests that are brittle and difficult to maintain. If your test relies on many mocks, it might be a sign that the code is too tightly coupled or that the unit under test is doing too much.
- **Use Mocks and Stubs Judiciously**: Only mock or stub the parts of the code that are necessary for the test. If a real object or component can be used without compromising the test's isolation, it might be better to use the actual component instead of a mock.

- **Keep It Simple**: The simpler the mock or stub, the better. Avoid adding unnecessary complexity to your test doubles. They should be as straightforward as possible while still fulfilling the needs of the test.
- **Verify Critical Interactions**: When using mocks, ensure that you verify only the most critical interactions. Avoid verifying every method call, as this can lead to fragile tests that break whenever the implementation changes slightly.

Example: In a test for a payment processing system, you might mock the payment gateway to ensure that the `process_payment` method is called correctly. However, you would not mock every part of the system–just the interactions that are critical to the behavior you are testing.

Challenges and Limitations

While mocks and stubs are invaluable for isolating units during testing, they come with their own set of challenges:

- **Mocking Complex Dependencies**: Some dependencies are difficult to mock effectively, especially if they involve complex interactions or states. In such cases, it may be necessary to refactor the code to make it more testable.
- **False Sense of Security**: Mocks can give a false sense of security if the tests pass, but the real dependency behaves differently than the mock. To mitigate this, consider writing integration tests that use the actual dependencies in a controlled environment.
- **Test Maintenance**: Tests that rely heavily on mocks can become difficult to maintain as the codebase evolves. This is especially true if the tests are tightly coupled to the implementation details rather than the behavior of the code.

Example: Suppose you mock an external API's response in your tests. If the API changes its response format, your tests might still pass, but the actual application could fail. This highlights the importance of complementing unit tests with integration tests that use the real API.

Mocking and stubbing are essential techniques in unit testing, enabling developers to isolate the unit of code under test from its external dependencies. By using these tools effectively, you can write tests that are both reliable and focused, ensuring that your code behaves as expected even in complex scenarios. However, like any tool, mocks and stubs should be used judiciously, with an awareness of their limitations and potential pitfalls. By following best practices and maintaining a balance between simplicity and functionality, you can leverage mocks and stubs to build a robust and maintainable test suite.

Integrating Unit Tests in CI/CD Pipelines

Continuous Integration and Continuous Deployment (CI/CD) pipelines have become a cornerstone of modern software development, enabling teams to deliver high-quality software quickly and reliably. Integrating unit tests into CI/CD pipelines is essential for maintaining the integrity of the codebase as it evolves. By automatically running unit tests whenever code changes are made, teams can catch and address issues early, ensuring that new code does not introduce bugs or regressions. This section explores the benefits, best practices, and key considerations for integrating unit tests into CI/CD pipelines.

The Role of Unit Tests in CI/CD

Unit tests play a crucial role in the CI/CD pipeline by providing fast and reliable feedback on the quality of the code. Because unit tests are focused on individual components of the codebase, they can quickly identify defects in newly written or modified code. When integrated into a CI/CD pipeline, unit tests serve as the first line of defense against potential issues, ensuring that only code that passes all tests is merged into the main branch or deployed to production.

Benefits of Integrating Unit Tests in CI/CD:

- **Early Defect Detection**: Unit tests help catch defects immediately after code changes are made, reducing the likelihood of issues propagating through the development process.
- **Faster Development Cycles**: By automating the testing process, developers can receive immediate feedback on their code, enabling them to fix issues quickly and move forward with their work.
- **Increased Confidence in Code Changes**: With unit tests integrated into the CI/CD pipeline, developers can confidently make changes to the codebase, knowing that any unintended consequences will be caught early.

Example: Imagine a scenario where a developer adds a new feature to an application. As soon as the code is committed, the CI/CD pipeline automatically runs the unit tests. If any tests fail, the pipeline alerts the developer, who can then address the issue before the code is merged or deployed. This process helps maintain the stability and reliability of the application.

Setting Up Unit Tests in a CI/CD Pipeline

Integrating unit tests into a CI/CD pipeline involves configuring the pipeline to run the tests automatically whenever certain events occur, such as code commits or pull requests. Here is how to set up unit tests in a typical CI/CD pipeline:

1. **Choose a CI/CD Tool**:
    - **Popular CI/CD Tools**: Jenkins, GitHub Actions, GitLab CI, Travis CI, CircleCI, and Azure Pipelines are some of the popular CI/CD tools

available. Each of these tools provides features for automating the build, test, and deployment processes.

- **Tool Configuration**: Depending on the chosen tool, you will need to configure the pipeline using a configuration file (for example, **`.jenkinsfile`** for Jenkins, **`.github/workflows`** for GitHub Actions). This file defines the steps in the pipeline, including running the unit tests.

2. **Define the Pipeline Stages**:

   - **Source Code Checkout**: The first stage in the pipeline typically involves checking out the latest code from the repository.
   - **Build Stage**: If the project requires compilation (for example, Java, C#), the build stage compiles the code.
   - **Test Stage**: This is where unit tests are executed. The pipeline should be configured to run all relevant unit tests and report the results.

Example Configuration: Here is an example of a GitHub Actions workflow that runs unit tests for a Python project:

```
name: CI Pipeline

on:
  push:
    branches:
      - main
  pull_request:
    branches:
      - main

jobs:
  test:
    runs-on: ubuntu-latest

    steps:
      - name: Checkout code
        uses: actions/checkout@v2

      - name: Set up Python
        uses: actions/setup-python@v2
        with:
          python-version: 3.8

      - name: Install dependencies
        run: |
          python -m pip install --upgrade pip
          pip install -r requirements.txt
```

```
      - name: Run unit tests
        run: |
          pytest
```

In this example, the workflow triggers whenever code is pushed to the **`main`** branch or when a pull request is made. The pipeline checks out the code, sets up Python, installs dependencies, and then runs the unit tests using **`pytest`**.

3. **Handle Test Results:**

   - **Reporting**: CI/CD pipelines should provide clear and actionable feedback on the results of the unit tests. Most CI/CD tools generate test reports that highlight which tests passed, which failed, and any errors encountered during execution.
   - **Failing the Pipeline**: If any unit tests fail, the pipeline should be configured to halt further stages, preventing broken code from being merged or deployed. This ensures that only code that meets the quality standards is allowed to progress.

Example: In the aforementioned GitHub Actions example, if any of the **`pytest`** tests fail, the pipeline will be marked as failed, and the developer will be notified. This allows the issue to be addressed before the code is merged.

Best Practices for Integrating Unit Tests in CI/CD

Integrating unit tests into CI/CD pipelines is not just about running tests; it is about ensuring that the testing process is effective, efficient, and reliable. Here are some best practices to consider:

1. **Keep Tests Fast**:

   - **Efficiency**: Unit tests should be fast to execute, allowing the CI/CD pipeline to provide rapid feedback. Slow tests can delay the entire pipeline, reducing the effectiveness of the CI/CD process.
   - **Test Selection**: If the test suite is large, consider running only the most relevant tests for each code change. Some CI/CD tools allow for selective test execution based on the modified files.

2. **Maintain Test Reliability**:

   - **Avoid Flaky Tests**: Flaky tests, which pass or fail unpredictably, can undermine confidence in the test suite. Regularly review and fix flaky tests to ensure that the pipeline results are reliable.
   - **Stable Environments**: Ensure that the test environment is consistent and stable across pipeline runs. Use containerization tools such as Docker to create isolated environments for testing, reducing the risk of environment-related issues.

3. **Automate Test Coverage Reports**:
   - **Coverage Metrics**: Integrate tools that generate test coverage reports as part of the CI/CD pipeline. These reports help identify untested parts of the codebase and guide developers in writing additional tests.
   - **Code Quality Gates**: Implement quality gates that enforce minimum coverage thresholds. If the coverage drops below a certain level, the pipeline can fail, prompting developers to add more tests before merging the code.

Example: Incorporating tools such as `coverage.py` for Python or `JaCoCo` for Java into the CI/CD pipeline can provide detailed coverage reports, helping the team maintain high test coverage over time.

4. **Parallelize Tests for Speed**:
   - **Parallel Execution**: If your test suite is large, consider parallelizing the tests to speed up the pipeline. Many CI/CD tools support running tests in parallel across multiple agents or containers.
   - **Divide and Conquer**: Break down the test suite into smaller chunks that can be executed simultaneously. This approach can significantly reduce the total execution time, allowing the pipeline to complete faster.

Handling Failures and Feedback

Failures are an inevitable part of the CI/CD process, but they provide valuable insights into the quality of the code. Properly handling test failures and providing timely feedback is crucial for maintaining an effective CI/CD pipeline.

1. **Immediate Feedback**:
   - **Notifications**: Configure the CI/CD pipeline to notify the relevant developers immediately when a test fails. This can be done through email, messaging platforms such as Slack, or the CI/CD tool's own notification system.
   - **Detailed Logs**: Ensure that the pipeline provides detailed logs and error messages when tests fail. This helps developers quickly identify and address the root cause of the issue.
2. **Addressing Failures Promptly**:
   - **Fixing Issues**: Encourage developers to address test failures as soon as they are identified. Delaying fixes can lead to more significant issues down the line, as broken code accumulates and complicates further development.
   - **Re-Run Failed Tests**: Some CI/CD tools allow for automatically re-running failed tests to rule out transient issues. This can be useful for distinguishing between true failures and temporary glitches.

Example: If a unit test fails due to a transient network issue, the pipeline can be configured to re-run the test up to a certain number of times before marking it as a failure. This prevents the pipeline from failing due to intermittent problems.

Integrating unit tests into CI/CD pipelines is essential for maintaining code quality and ensuring that new changes do not introduce regressions. By automating the testing process, providing immediate feedback, and adhering to best practices, development teams can create a robust and efficient CI/CD pipeline that supports rapid, reliable software delivery. As your codebase grows and your testing needs evolve, continually refining the integration of unit tests into your CI/CD pipeline will help you maintain high standards of quality and accelerate your development cycles.

Best Practices and Common Pitfalls in Unit Testing

Unit testing is a critical component of software development, ensuring that individual units of code function correctly and reliably. However, writing effective unit tests requires more than just technical knowledge–it requires an understanding of best practices and an awareness of common pitfalls that can undermine the effectiveness of your tests. This section provides guidance on how to maximize the benefits of unit testing while avoiding common mistakes that can lead to unreliable, difficult-to-maintain tests.

Best Practices in Unit Testing

- **Write Tests Before Code (Test-Driven Development - TDD)**

  One of the most effective ways to ensure that your code is thoroughly tested is to adopt a Test-Driven Development (TDD) approach. TDD involves writing unit tests before the actual code. This practice forces you to think about the requirements and design of your code before implementation, leading to cleaner, more testable code.

  - **Benefits**:
    - Encourages better code design by focusing on testability.
    - Ensures comprehensive test coverage from the outset.
    - Provides immediate feedback on the correctness of new code.

- **Keep Tests Small and Focused**

  Unit tests should be small and focused on testing a single aspect of the code. Each test should verify one behavior or a specific piece of functionality, making it clear what the test is intended to validate.

- **Best Practices**:
  - Write tests that are easy to understand and describe in one sentence.
  - Avoid testing multiple behaviors in a single test. If a test covers too much ground, it can be challenging to diagnose failures.
  - Use clear and descriptive names for your tests to indicate their purpose.

- **Ensure Tests Are Independent and Isolated**

  Each unit test should be independent of others, meaning that it should not rely on the outcome of another test or share state with other tests. This isolation ensures that tests can be run in any order without affecting the results, making your test suite more reliable.

  - **Best Practices**:
    - Avoid global state or shared resources between tests.
    - Use setup and teardown methods (for example, `@Before` and `@After` in JUnit) to prepare the test environment and clean up afterward.
    - Mock external dependencies to isolate the unit of code being tested.

- **Use Meaningful Assertions**

  Assertions are the heart of unit tests—they verify that the code behaves as expected. Using meaningful assertions that clearly express the intent of the test is crucial for understanding test failures.

  - **Best Practices**:
    - Use specific assertions (for example, **`assertEqual`**, **`assertTrue`**) rather than generic ones.
    - Include error messages in assertions to provide context when a test fails.
    - Assert all relevant conditions, not just the primary outcome.

- **Regularly Review and Refactor Tests**

  Just as production code requires regular refactoring to improve its structure and maintainability, unit tests should also be reviewed and refactored. This process helps ensure that tests remain relevant and easy to maintain as the codebase evolves.

  - **Best Practices**:
    - Periodically review tests to remove redundancy and improve clarity.
    - Refactor tests alongside production code to keep them aligned with code changes.
    - Consolidate similar tests to reduce duplication.

- **Prioritize Test Readability and Maintainability**

  Unit tests are often read more frequently than they are written, especially during debugging and maintenance. Ensuring that your tests are easy to read and maintain is crucial for their long-term effectiveness.

  - **Best Practices**:
    - Use clear and consistent naming conventions for tests and variables.
    - Keep tests concise and avoid unnecessary complexity.
    - Comment tests only when necessary to explain non-obvious behaviors.

- **Achieve Balance in Test Coverage**

  While high test coverage is desirable, it is important to focus on covering the most critical and complex parts of the code. Aiming for 100% coverage is often impractical and can lead to over-testing, where trivial code is unnecessarily tested.

  - **Best Practices**:
    - Focus on testing critical business logic and areas with a high likelihood of defects.
    - Use code coverage tools to identify untested areas, but do not rely solely on coverage metrics.
    - Test edge cases and error conditions to ensure robustness.

- **Automate Unit Tests in CI/CD Pipelines**

  Integrating unit tests into your Continuous Integration/Continuous Deployment (CI/CD) pipeline ensures that tests are run automatically whenever code is committed. This practice helps catch issues early and prevents regressions.

  - **Best Practices**:
    - Ensure that all unit tests are run as part of the CI/CD pipeline.
    - Use CI/CD tools to generate test reports and provide feedback to developers.
    - Maintain fast-running unit tests to keep the CI/CD pipeline efficient.

Common Pitfalls in Unit Testing

- **Testing Implementation Details Instead of Behavior**

  A common mistake in unit testing is focusing too much on the implementation details of the code rather than its behavior. Tests that are tightly coupled to the implementation can become brittle and require frequent changes, even for minor refactoring.

- **Pitfall Example**:
  - Writing a test that checks the internal state of an object instead of its output. If the implementation changes but the behavior remains the same, the test may fail unnecessarily.
- **Avoidance Strategy**:
  - Focus on testing the observable behavior and outcomes of the code, not how it is implemented.

- **Over-Reliance on Mocks**

  While mocking is a powerful tool for isolating units during testing, over-reliance on mocks can lead to tests that are disconnected from the real behavior of the application. Over-mocked tests can give a false sense of security, as they may pass even when the actual dependencies are broken.

  - **Pitfall Example:**
    - Mocking every dependency in a test to the point where the test no longer resembles real-world usage.
  - **Avoidance Strategy**:
    - Use mocks judiciously and only when necessary to isolate the unit under test. Complement unit tests with integration tests that use real components.

- **Neglecting Edge Cases and Error Handling**

  It is easy to focus on the "happy path" when writing unit tests, but neglecting edge cases and error conditions can leave your code vulnerable to unexpected failures.

  - **Pitfall Example**:
    - Writing tests that only validate correct inputs and expected outcomes while ignoring invalid inputs, boundary conditions, or exceptions.
  - **Avoidance Strategy**:
    - Ensure that your test suite includes tests for edge cases, invalid inputs, and potential error conditions.

- **Ignoring Test Performance**

  As your test suite grows, slow-running tests can become a bottleneck in your development and CI/CD processes. Ignoring test performance can lead to longer feedback cycles, reducing the effectiveness of your tests.

  - **Pitfall Example**:
    - Including expensive operations such as database access or network calls in unit tests, leading to slow execution times.

- **Avoidance Strategy**:
    - Keep unit tests fast by avoiding external dependencies and focusing on small, isolated units of code. Use integration tests for scenarios that require real interactions.

- **Letting the Test Suite Decay**

  Over time, a test suite can become outdated, with tests that no longer reflect the current state of the codebase. Decayed test suites can lead to false positives (tests passing when they should not) or false negatives (tests failing for invalid reasons), reducing trust in the tests.

  - **Pitfall Example**:
    - Keeping old tests that no longer match the code's functionality, leading to confusion and wasted time during debugging.
  - **Avoidance Strategy**:
    - Regularly review and update tests to ensure they remain relevant and accurate. Remove or refactor tests that no longer serve a purpose.

- **Writing Tests That Are Too Complex**

  Unit tests should be simple and straightforward. Writing overly complex tests can make them difficult to understand, maintain, and debug, defeating the purpose of unit testing.

  - **Pitfall Example**:
    - Writing tests that involve multiple steps, complex logic, or extensive setup, making it hard to pinpoint the cause of a failure.
  - **Avoidance Strategy**:
    - Keep tests focused on a single behavior or outcome. Simplify test setup and use helper methods or test data builders to streamline complex scenarios.

Unit testing is an essential practice for ensuring the reliability and quality of your code, but it is important to approach it with a clear understanding of best practices and common pitfalls. By following best practices such as writing small, focused tests, maintaining test independence, and integrating tests into CI/CD pipelines, you can create a robust and maintainable test suite. At the same time, being aware of common pitfalls—such as over-reliance on mocks, neglecting edge cases, and letting the test suite decay—will help you avoid issues that can undermine the effectiveness of your tests. By adhering to these guidelines, you can ensure that your unit tests provide real value, supporting the ongoing development and maintenance of high-quality software.

Conclusion

In this chapter, we delved into the fundamental aspects of unit testing, exploring its critical role in ensuring code quality and stability. We began by understanding the importance of unit testing within the broader context of the test pyramid, highlighting how it serves as the foundation for reliable software development. We discussed the principles of writing effective unit tests, emphasizing the need for isolation, determinism, and maintainability. By adhering to best practices such as writing small, focused tests and integrating them into CI/CD pipelines, we can ensure that our unit tests provide consistent and meaningful feedback throughout the development process.

We also covered essential topics such as testing different types of code—whether pure functions, stateful components, or error-handling routines—each requiring a tailored approach to ensure comprehensive coverage. The chapter further explored strategies for dealing with legacy code, demonstrating how to introduce tests incrementally to improve its reliability. Finally, we examined common pitfalls in unit testing, providing guidance on how to avoid issues such as over-reliance on mocks, neglecting edge cases, and letting the test suite decay.

As we move forward, the next chapter will build on this foundation by focusing on **Integration Testing Approaches**. While unit tests verify individual components in isolation, integration tests are crucial for ensuring that these components work together as expected. In the upcoming chapter, we will explore various strategies for conducting integration tests, including the challenges and best practices associated with testing the interactions between different modules and services. By understanding and applying these integration testing approaches, you will be equipped to ensure that your application functions correctly as a whole, beyond just its individual parts.

Key Takeaways

- **Foundational Role of Unit Testing**: Unit tests are the backbone of a robust testing strategy, providing the first line of defense against bugs by ensuring the correctness of individual components in isolation.
- **Effective Test Principles**: Writing effective unit tests involves following key principles such as isolation, determinism, and readability, which help create reliable, maintainable, and meaningful tests.
- **Tailored Testing Strategies**: Different types of code—such as pure functions, stateful components, and error-handling routines—require specific testing approaches to ensure comprehensive coverage.

- **Managing Legacy Code**: Introducing unit tests to legacy code requires careful strategies such as characterization tests and refactoring to improve testability and maintainability over time.
- **Best Practices and Pitfalls**: Adhering to best practices such as integrating unit tests into CI/CD pipelines, and avoiding common pitfalls such as over-reliance on mocks and neglecting edge cases, is essential for maintaining an effective test suite.

These takeaways distill the key insights from this chapter, providing a strong basis for applying unit testing principles effectively in your development workflow. With these concepts in mind, you are ready to build on this knowledge as we delve into integration testing approaches in the next chapter, where the focus will shift to validating the interactions between various components of your application.

CHAPTER 4
Integration Testing Approaches

Introduction

In the previous chapter, we explored unit testing in depth, discussing its role as the foundational layer in the test pyramid and its importance in ensuring the quality of individual components within your application. We covered strategies for writing effective unit tests, highlighting the principles of isolation and rapid feedback. Additionally, we delved into advanced topics such as mocking and stubbing, which are essential for maintaining test focus and ensuring code behavior is thoroughly validated. By the end of the chapter, you gained a strong understanding of how unit tests help safeguard the integrity of your codebase.

In this chapter, we shift our focus to integration testing, the next essential layer in the test pyramid. Integration testing examines how different components or services interact within your application. While unit tests verify the functionality of individual units, integration tests ensure that these units work together seamlessly. This chapter will cover the differences between unit and integration testing, the role of integration testing in your testing strategy, and various approaches to conducting these tests. We will also introduce tools and technologies such as PyTest, Requests, SQLAlchemy, and Docker, as well as best practices for setting up effective integration test environments.

By the end of this chapter, you will have a comprehensive understanding of how to implement integration testing in your development workflow. You will be able to identify and address issues that arise when components or services interact, ensuring that your application functions smoothly as a whole. With real-world examples and case studies, this chapter will equip you with the knowledge and skills needed to create robust integration tests that catch complex bugs early, ultimately improving the reliability and performance of your software.

Structure

In this chapter, we will explore the vital role of integration testing in ensuring that the various components of your application work harmoniously together. Here is what we will cover:

- Introduction to Integration Testing
- Integration Testing in the Test Pyramid
- Strategies for Effective Integration Testing
- Setting Up Integration Test Environments
- Mocking External Dependencies
- Best Practices and Common Pitfalls in Integration Testing

Introduction to Integration Testing

Integration testing is a fundamental step in the software testing lifecycle that ensures different modules or services of an application work together harmoniously. While unit testing focuses on individual components, integration testing takes a broader perspective, testing how these individual pieces interact and function when combined. This phase of testing is particularly critical in complex systems where various software modules, APIs, and external services need to communicate and exchange data seamlessly. Integration testing verifies that these interactions are correct and that the application functions as intended when its parts work together.

Integration testing can be viewed as the next layer in the testing pyramid, sitting just above unit testing and just below system testing. It is a bridge between testing individual units and testing the complete system. The primary goal of integration testing is to ensure that the interfaces between different components are working as expected and to validate that data flows between these components without errors. In modern software development, where microservices architecture and API-driven development are prevalent, integration testing has gained even more significance.

Purpose of Integration Testing

One of the key purposes of integration testing is to identify defects that occur due to the interaction between modules, which might not be detectable during unit testing. For example, while a function may work perfectly in isolation, problems could arise when it interacts with other functions or external systems. This could be due to mismatched data formats, improper handling of error conditions, or performance bottlenecks. Integration testing helps uncover these issues before they can propagate further down the development pipeline, ensuring a smoother transition to system and acceptance testing.

Types of Integration Testing

There are various approaches to conducting integration testing, depending on the system architecture and project requirements. Common types include:

- **Top-Down Integration Testing**: This approach involves testing the higher-level modules first and then progressively integrating lower-level modules. Stubs (temporary replacements for lower-level modules) are often used during this phase to simulate the behavior of components that are not yet integrated. This method helps in the early validation of high-level interactions, but lower-level module defects might not be detected until later in the process.
- **Bottom-Up Integration Testing**: As the opposite of top-down testing, this approach starts with testing the lower-level modules and works its way up. Here, drivers (which act as placeholders for higher-level modules) are used to facilitate testing of the lower layers. This approach is particularly useful when the lower modules are complex and need to be validated early.
- **Big Bang Integration Testing**: This strategy involves integrating all modules at once after they have been developed and tested individually. While simple in theory, this method can be risky because it delays the identification of issues related to module interactions until late in the development process, which can make debugging and troubleshooting more difficult.
- **Incremental Integration Testing**: Incremental integration testing is a more systematic approach, where modules are integrated and tested in small, manageable increments. By testing smaller parts of the system progressively, it is easier to identify and fix issues before moving on to the next phase. This is the preferred method in most Agile and continuous integration environments, as it allows for earlier detection of defects and smoother integration overall.

Challenges in Integration Testing

While integration testing is essential, it comes with its own set of challenges. One of the biggest difficulties is dealing with dependencies. Since integration testing involves multiple components, ensuring that all dependencies are available and functioning correctly during testing can be complex. External services, databases, APIs, and third-party systems may not always be reliable or available during the testing phase, leading to false positives or negatives in test results.

To overcome this, testers often rely on techniques such as **mocking** and **stubbing**. Mocking refers to simulating the behavior of external components or services during testing, allowing the integration test to proceed even if the real external system is not available. Stubbing involves creating temporary replacements for modules that are not yet integrated, providing predefined responses that simulate how the real module would behave. Both techniques allow for greater flexibility and control during integration testing, ensuring that dependencies do not hinder the testing process. We will learn more about mocking and stubbing later in the chapter.

Integration Testing in the Test Pyramid

As we have already discussed the concept of the Test Pyramid and the critical role of unit tests in previous chapters, we now shift focus to where integration testing fits within this structure. In the Test Pyramid, integration tests lie between unit tests and End-to-End (E2E) tests. While unit tests target individual components in isolation, integration tests focus on validating the interaction between multiple components or services. Their role is crucial in ensuring that different parts of the application function correctly together.

While unit tests offer rapid feedback by verifying the behavior of isolated functions or methods, they cannot expose issues that arise when components are integrated. This is where integration testing becomes invaluable. By testing how well the components or modules collaborate, integration tests catch defects related to miscommunication between services, database connection issues, API response inconsistencies, and other integration-related problems that unit tests might miss.

The Importance of Integration Testing in the Test Pyramid

Integration testing plays a pivotal role in ensuring the system's integrity because it checks whether the interactions between different parts of the application are functioning as intended. While unit tests ensure that each piece of code works in isolation, integration tests verify that components work together in a realistic environment. The following are some of the primary reasons why integration testing is essential within the context of the test pyramid:

- **Identifying Interface Issues**: Many defects in complex systems stem from issues at the boundaries between components, such as APIs, databases, or third-party services. Integration tests ensure that these boundaries are tested and that the communication between modules is functioning as expected.
- **Validating Data Flow**: Different modules in an application often rely on each other for data. Integration tests verify that data is passed correctly from one component to another, whether it is between internal services or external systems. For example, integration tests will ensure that data retrieved from a database is correctly used by another component in the application.
- **Catching Early Defects**: By identifying and addressing issues during the integration phase, defects can be detected early in the development lifecycle. This early detection helps reduce the cost of fixing bugs and prevents larger

issues during end-to-end or system testing. Moreover, resolving issues at this stage leads to a smoother and more reliable end-to-end test process.

- **Ensuring System Stability**: Integration tests ensure that changes made in one module do not break the functionality of another module, promoting system stability as the application evolves. With Continuous Integration and Continuous Delivery (CI/CD) pipelines, integration tests provide quick feedback on the health of the system, making sure that each module remains compatible with the others as new features are added or existing ones are modified.

Integration Testing versus Unit Testing in the Pyramid

While both unit and integration testing are essential, they serve distinct purposes. Unit tests are more granular, verifying the correctness of individual functions or classes, but they do not account for how these elements interact with one another. Integration tests, on the other hand, take a more holistic approach by focusing on how components function together. They are less numerous than unit tests but provide a deeper level of validation regarding system-wide interactions.

A key takeaway is that integration testing is not a replacement for unit testing but rather a complementary practice. By having a solid foundation of unit tests, integration tests can focus on verifying module interactions without needing to retest the individual logic of those modules. This separation of concerns allows for efficient and scalable testing strategies.

Strategies for Effective Integration Testing

In this section, we will explore a range of integration testing strategies that enable effective testing of how different components of an application interact with each other. A well-planned strategy is crucial for identifying issues that arise when individual modules are combined, ensuring that the system functions as a cohesive unit. We will dive into various integration testing approaches, each with its unique strengths and challenges, and understand how to choose the right method based on your application architecture and testing requirements.

We will begin by examining different types of integration testing, including the **Top-Down**, **Bottom-Up**, **Big Bang**, **Incremental**, and **Sandwich (Hybrid)** approaches. Each of these methodologies offers distinct advantages and limitations depending on the complexity of the system and the priority of the modules being tested. For example, Top-Down and Bottom-Up focus on testing different levels of the application hierarchy, while Big Bang involves testing all components together at once. Incremental and

Hybrid methods offer more flexibility and are often favored in modern, distributed architectures.

After understanding the pros and cons of these strategies, we will focus on **Contract Testing**, which plays a critical role in ensuring smooth integration in microservices-based architectures. Contract testing allows different components or services to communicate based on predefined contracts, reducing the risk of integration failures. This section will highlight how contract testing can streamline testing efforts, especially in systems with multiple dependencies, and provide practical tools for its implementation.

Types of Integration Testing

When it comes to integration testing, different strategies can be employed to test how various components of an application interact. Each type of integration testing serves a different purpose depending on the structure of the application, the dependencies between components, and the priority of the testing effort. In this section, we will explore the most common types: **Top-Down**, **Bottom-Up**, **Big Bang**, **Incremental**, and the **Sandwich (Hybrid)** approach. Each of these methods has its own advantages and limitations, and choosing the right one is crucial to the success of your testing strategy.

Top-Down Integration Testing

Top-down integration testing is a method where testing starts from the top of the module hierarchy and progresses downward. This strategy is particularly effective for applications built with a hierarchical structure, where the higher-level modules call the lower-level ones. The testing begins with the topmost modules (often referred to as "*high-level modules*"), and progressively lower-level modules are integrated and tested.

Advantages:

- **Early Discovery of Design Flaws**: Since testing begins with high-level modules, issues related to the overall architecture and design can be identified early.
- **Test-Driven Development Compatibility**: This approach works well with test-driven development, as testing at higher levels can guide the creation of stubs for untested lower-level components.
- **Focus on Critical Functionality**: Because the top modules are often where the core business logic resides, Top-Down testing ensures that critical functionality is tested first.

Limitations:

- **Stub Dependency**: Since lower-level modules may not be ready for integration when high-level modules are tested, stubs (temporary substitutes) must be used. These stubs may not fully replicate the behavior of actual modules, potentially leading to incomplete testing.

- **Late Identification of Low-Level Issues**: Errors in lower-level modules may not be discovered until later in the testing process, which could delay the overall testing cycle.

Bottom-Up Integration Testing

In **Bottom-Up Integration Testing**, testing starts from the bottom of the module hierarchy and works its way upward. This method is the opposite of Top-Down testing, focusing on integrating and testing the lowest-level modules (those that do not depend on any other modules) first.

Advantages:

- **Testing of Low-Level Components First**: This approach ensures that the foundational or supporting modules are tested thoroughly before moving to higher-level modules.
- **Simplifies Testing of Utility Functions**: Since utility functions often reside in lower-level modules, Bottom-Up testing ensures they are tested early and thoroughly.
- **Easier Debugging**: Testing from the bottom-up allows for easier identification of bugs in lower-level modules before they propagate to higher levels.

Limitations:

- **Late Discovery of System-Level Issues**: Since testing starts at the lowest levels, any issues with high-level business logic or overall architecture may not be discovered until later in the process.
- **Initial Absence of High-Level Business Logic**: Testers must often wait to test key functionalities until the lower-level components are integrated, which may slow down the testing progress.

Big Bang Integration Testing

Big Bang Integration Testing involves integrating all components or modules of an application at once and then performing the testing. This approach does not follow a step-by-step integration process but instead tests the entire system in one go after all modules have been developed.

Advantages:

- **No Need for Stubs or Drivers**: Since all components are integrated at once, there is no need to use stubs or drivers, simplifying the test environment.
- **Complete System Testing**: This method tests the application as a whole,

providing a clear picture of how all modules interact once the entire system is assembled.

Limitations:

- **High-Risk Strategy**: Since testing happens only after all modules are integrated, the chances of encountering a large number of issues at once are high. This can lead to significant delays in the project timeline.
- **Difficult to Isolate Bugs**: Because all components are tested together, it becomes challenging to isolate the root cause of bugs. Debugging and fixing issues can be time-consuming.
- **Late Discovery of Integration Issues**: Since no incremental testing occurs, integration issues are discovered only at the end, increasing the likelihood of a major rework.

Incremental Integration Testing

Incremental Integration Testing is a middle-ground approach where modules are integrated and tested incrementally rather than all at once. This can be done using either a Top-Down or Bottom-Up approach or a combination of both. In incremental testing, two or more modules that are logically related are tested together, and gradually, more modules are integrated and tested until the entire system is covered.

Advantages:

- **Early Detection of Integration Issues**: Since modules are integrated in small steps, any issues with interaction between components are discovered early in the process, making debugging and fixing easier.
- **Continuous Feedback**: Testers and developers receive continuous feedback as the system is tested incrementally, allowing them to make adjustments as needed.
- **Reduced Risk**: By testing in increments, the risk of major issues arising late in the testing process is significantly reduced.

Limitations:

- **Requires Planning and Organization**: Incremental testing requires careful planning to ensure that the right modules are integrated and tested in a logical order.
- **Need for Stubs and Drivers**: Depending on the approach (Top-Down or Bottom-Up), stubs or drivers may still be required to simulate the behavior of untested modules.

Sandwich (Hybrid) Integration Testing

The **Sandwich (Hybrid) Integration Testing** approach is a combination of Top-Down and Bottom-Up testing. It involves testing both high-level and low-level modules simultaneously, while middle-level modules are integrated later. This strategy is often used when both sets of modules—those at the top and those at the bottom—are critical to the system's functioning.

Advantages:

- **Best of Both Worlds**: By combining Top-Down and Bottom-Up testing, the Sandwich approach allows early testing of both high-level business logic and low-level utility functions.
- **Parallel Testing**: High- and low-level modules can be tested in parallel, saving time and speeding up the overall testing process.
- **Balanced Approach**: This method balances the focus between different layers of the system, ensuring that neither high-level nor low-level modules are neglected.

Limitations:

- **Complex Test Management**: Managing the parallel testing of high- and low-level modules can be complex and requires careful coordination between teams.
- **Incomplete Coverage of Middle Modules**: Since the focus is on testing the top and bottom modules first, issues in middle-level modules may not be identified until later in the process.

Each type of integration testing offers its own advantages and limitations, and choosing the right strategy depends on the specific needs of your application and testing goals. Whether you prioritize early detection of system-level issues or are more focused on thoroughly testing low-level utility functions, there is a strategy that fits your requirements. In most cases, a combination of these methods is often employed, especially when dealing with complex systems, to achieve optimal testing coverage.

As we move forward, we will explore other aspects of integration testing, including how to set up test environments and mock external dependencies to ensure robust and reliable testing across your entire application stack.

Setting Up Integration Test Environments

Setting up a robust and reliable integration test environment is a critical aspect of successful integration testing. Unlike unit tests, which focus on isolated components, integration tests require a more comprehensive setup that mimics the interactions between different modules, services, and external dependencies. A well-configured integration test environment ensures that all the necessary components are available, behaves similarly to the production environment, and allows for the accurate detection of bugs related to inter-service communication.

In this section, we will explore the key steps and considerations involved in setting up effective integration test environments. We will cover important topics such as managing dependencies, replicating production-like environments, using tools such as Docker for containerization, and handling database and API services. Additionally, we will discuss best practices for maintaining a stable and consistent test environment throughout the development lifecycle.

Key Considerations for Integration Test Environments

When setting up an integration test environment, there are several critical factors to consider:

- **Isolation and Consistency**: Integration test environments need to be isolated from other environments (such as development or production) to prevent interference. Each test run should start with a consistent and known state to ensure repeatable results.
- **Replicating Production-Like Conditions**: The integration test environment should closely mimic the production environment to catch bugs that could surface due to environment-specific factors, such as different configuration settings, hardware, or network conditions.
- **Managing External Dependencies**: Many modern applications depend on external services, such as third-party APIs, databases, or microservices. The integration test environment should simulate these external dependencies to ensure that the system behaves as expected in a realistic context.
- **Automation and Scalability**: Automation is essential for integration testing in Continuous Integration (CI) and Continuous Delivery (CD) pipelines. The test environment should support automated test executions and be scalable to handle multiple test runs in parallel.

Step 1: Use of Containerization for Test Environments (Docker)

One of the most effective ways to set up an integration test environment is through **containerization**. Tools such as **Docker** allow you to create isolated, reproducible environments that are easy to configure and manage. Docker is particularly useful in integration testing because it can mimic production-like environments while offering flexibility and scalability.

Benefits of Using Docker for Integration Testing:

- **Isolation**: Docker containers run in isolated environments, which means that each integration test can run independently without affecting other tests or the underlying system.
- **Reproducibility**: With Docker, you can create a test environment once and share it with different team members, ensuring that the same environment is used for all tests.
- **Scalability**: Docker makes it easy to scale integration testing by running multiple containers in parallel, simulating various parts of your application, such as databases, services, or APIs.
- **Consistency**: Since Docker containers are built from predefined configurations (Dockerfiles), the same environment can be spun up on any system, eliminating the "*it works on my machine*" problem.

Setting Up a Dockerized Integration Environment

1. **Create Dockerfiles for Services**: For each service or component involved in your integration testing, create a **`Dockerfile`** that defines the environment and dependencies required to run the service. For example, if you are testing a database-backed microservice, your Dockerfile might include the application code, a database setup, and any required middleware or libraries.

2. **Use Docker Compose for Multi-Service Integration**: Docker Compose is a tool that simplifies the management of multi-container environments. It allows you to define all the services your test environment needs (such as APIs, databases, and message brokers) in a single YAML file and then start all of them with one command.

   Example: Use **`docker-compose.yml`** file for setting up an integration test environment.

```
version: '3'
services:
  app:
    build: .
    ports:
      - "5000:5000"
  db:
    image: postgres:12
    environment:
      POSTGRES_USER: user
      POSTGRES_PASSWORD: password
      POSTGRES_DB: testdb
    ports:
      - "5432:5432"
```

```
api:
  image: my-api-service
  environment:
    API_KEY: "test-api-key"
```

3. **Network Configuration**: Docker Compose allows services to communicate with each other via a network. This is important in integration testing because you need services such as your application, database, and external APIs to interact seamlessly.

4. **Automating Environment Setup**: Automate the creation and teardown of your Dockerized environment within your CI pipeline. For example, use **`docker-compose up`** to start the services, run your integration tests, and then tear down the environment using **`docker-compose down`** once the tests are complete.

Step 2: Handling Databases in Integration Testing

Databases are a crucial component of many integration tests, and managing them properly within the test environment is essential. Since integration tests often involve creating, reading, updating, and deleting data in a database, you need to ensure that your database behaves predictably during testing.

Strategies for Database Management in Integration Testing:

1. **Use an In-Memory Database for Faster Tests**: One strategy is to use an in-memory database (such as SQLite in-memory mode) during integration tests. In-memory databases are faster than their on-disk counterparts because they do not require file system access. However, this may not be suitable if your production system uses a different database (for example, PostgreSQL or MySQL).

2. **Database Snapshots and Resetting State**: If you are using an actual database in your integration tests, it is important to ensure that each test starts with a clean database state. You can achieve this by taking database snapshots or using database migration tools to reset the database schema and data before each test run.

   Example: Use **`pytest fixtures`** to set up a database schema before running the tests and tear it down afterward to ensure consistent testing conditions.

   ```
   @pytest.fixture(scope="function")
   def setup_database():
       # Setup code here: create tables, populate with test data
       yield
       # Teardown code: drop tables, clean up data
   ```

3. **Mocking External Databases**: In some cases, it may be preferable to mock the database during integration testing, especially when the test does not rely heavily on the actual database behavior. Tools such as **SQLAlchemy** in Python make it easy to mock database queries and simulate interactions with the database without needing an actual connection.

Step 3: Managing External APIs and Dependencies

Most modern applications rely on external APIs or third-party services. In integration testing, it is important to account for these dependencies while maintaining control over the test environment. Here are some common approaches for handling external services during integration testing:

- **Mocking External APIs**: Mocking external APIs is a common strategy in integration testing when real services may not be available or you want to avoid the cost or side effects of hitting actual APIs. Mocking allows you to simulate the behavior of the external service and focus on the interactions between your application and the mocked service.
  - **Use Mock Servers**: Tools such as **WireMock** or **MockServer** can act as stand-ins for external services during integration tests. They allow you to define expected requests and responses so that your application behaves as if it is interacting with the real service.
  - **Postman Mock Servers**: If you are using Postman for API testing, you can also use its built-in mock server functionality to simulate API responses. This ensures that your tests do not depend on the availability or behavior of actual third-party services.
- **Service Virtualization**: Service virtualization goes beyond simple API mocking by creating realistic simulations of complex services, such as message brokers, payment gateways, or databases. This technique allows you to test integrations with services that may not be available during the testing process, such as staging environments or third-party systems with high usage costs.
  - **Tools for Service Virtualization**: Use tools such as **Mountebank** or **WireMock** to create virtual services that behave like the real services your application interacts with. These virtual services allow for more accurate integration tests by simulating real-world conditions, such as response delays or error states.
  - **Dynamic Responses**: With service virtualization, you can simulate various response scenarios (for example, success, failure, timeout) to ensure that your application handles all cases properly.

Step 4: Automation and Integration with CI/CD Pipelines

A key part of setting up an integration test environment is ensuring that it integrates smoothly with your CI/CD pipeline. Automating the environment setup and teardown is crucial for running integration tests efficiently in a continuous development workflow.

- **CI Tools**: Use CI tools such as Jenkins, CircleCI, GitHub Actions, or Travis CI to automate the deployment of your integration test environment. These tools allow you to spin up Docker containers, run your tests, and destroy the containers afterward.
- **Automated Database Resetting**: Use database migration tools or custom scripts to ensure that your database resets between test runs. This will help prevent flaky tests that pass or fail based on the data left over from previous test runs.
- **Parallel Test Execution**: As your integration test suite grows, running tests in parallel can save time. Tools such as **pytest-xdist** allow you to parallelize test execution across multiple containers, improving the efficiency of your testing pipeline.

Setting up a reliable and efficient integration test environment is a multi-step process that involves careful planning and the use of modern tools such as Docker, database management strategies, and service virtualization. By mimicking production-like conditions, isolating environments, and automating the setup process, you can ensure that your integration tests provide accurate and meaningful results. With a properly configured integration test environment, your development team will be well-equipped to identify and fix issues early in the development lifecycle, ensuring smoother deployments and higher software quality.

Mocking External Dependencies

In modern software development, applications often depend on external services, such as databases, third-party APIs, message queues, or other microservices. While integration testing aims to ensure that these components work together seamlessly, there are times when interacting with real external services during testing can be challenging or even impractical. For example, the external service may be unreliable, unavailable, or costly to use during the testing phase. Additionally, integration testing with real services can lead to unpredictable behavior, making it difficult to achieve consistent and repeatable test results.

This is where **mocking external dependencies** becomes an essential strategy in integration testing. By creating mock versions of external services, you can simulate their behavior and control their responses, allowing your tests to focus on the interactions between components without relying on real external systems. Mocking helps you isolate the part of the system under test, ensuring that external dependencies do not interfere with the test execution.

Now we will explore the concept of mocking in-depth, the scenarios in which it is useful, the advantages and limitations of mocking, and the tools and best practices for implementing it effectively in integration testing environments.

Understanding Mocking

Mocking is a technique used to simulate the behavior of external dependencies in software testing. When you mock a dependency, you replace the real implementation of that service or component with a mock version that behaves in a controlled way. These mocks can return predefined responses or simulate specific behaviors that are required for your tests.

For example, if your application relies on an external payment gateway to process transactions, you might not want to make real payment requests during your tests. Instead, you can mock the payment gateway by simulating different responses (for example, success, failure, network timeout), allowing you to test how your application handles these scenarios without making actual requests.

Mocks are particularly useful when testing:

- **APIs**: Mocking external APIs allows you to simulate responses from services that may not be available or reliable during testing.
- **Databases**: Mocking database interactions can help you avoid the overhead of setting up and tearing down database connections in each test.
- **Microservices**: In distributed architectures, mocking microservices ensures that each service can be tested in isolation, regardless of whether other services are available.
- **Third-Party Services**: Services such as authentication providers, cloud storage, or payment processors can be expensive or impractical to interact with in test environments, making mocking a valuable alternative.

Appropriate Scenarios for Mocking in Integration Testing

Mocking is not always necessary in every test scenario, but there are several situations where it becomes a crucial tool for integration testing, including:

- **Unreliable or Unavailable External Services**: If the external service is unreliable, frequently down for maintenance, or unavailable during testing, mocking allows you to simulate its behavior without relying on its availability.

- **Costly API Usage**: Some APIs, especially third-party services such as payment gateways or cloud platforms, may charge for each request. Mocking these APIs ensures that your tests are cost-effective by avoiding real requests that may incur charges.
- **Performance Considerations**: External services may introduce delays due to network latency or other factors. Mocking can help you avoid these delays and keep your tests fast and responsive, which is especially important in Continuous Integration (CI) pipelines where speed is critical.
- **Error Simulation**: Sometimes, you need to test how your application behaves in failure scenarios, such as when an external API returns an error or times out. Mocking allows you to simulate these edge cases and ensure that your application handles them correctly.
- **Consistency and Repeatability**: By mocking external dependencies, you can control the responses and ensure that your tests produce the same results each time they run. This is particularly useful when writing automated tests, as inconsistent behavior from external services can lead to false positives or negatives in the test results.

Types of Mocks

There are several types of mocks, each serving different purposes depending on the testing scenario, starting with:

1. **Stub**: A stub is a simple type of mock that provides predefined responses for specific inputs. It does not track or verify how it is used; it simply returns the data needed for the test. Stubs are useful when you need to simulate external services that provide fixed outputs based on known inputs, such as a database query returning a static dataset.

   Example:

   ```
   def get_user_data(user_id):
       # Stub that returns a static dataset
       return {"user_id": user_id, "name": "John Doe"}
   ```

2. **Spy**: A spy is similar to a stub, but it also records information about how it was used, such as how many times a method was called or with what parameters. This can be helpful when you need to verify that certain actions were taken during the test.

   Example:

   ```
   def payment_gateway_mock(amount, currency):
       # Spy that records the number of times it was called
       payment_gateway_mock.call_count += 1
       return {"status": "success"}
   payment_gateway_mock.call_count = 0
   ```

3. **Fake**: A fake is a lightweight implementation of an external service that has actual functionality but is simplified for testing purposes. For example, a fake database might store data in memory rather than on disk, allowing tests to interact with it as if it were a real database.

4. **Full Mock**: A full mock simulates both the behavior and the interface of the external dependency. It is used when you need complete control over how the dependency behaves during the test, including what data it returns, how it handles different inputs, and whether it throws errors.

   Example:

```
class PaymentGatewayMock:
    def process_payment(self, amount, currency):
        # Simulate success or failure based on input
        if amount > 1000:
            return {"status": "failure", "message": "Payment
declined"}
        return {"status": "success", "message": "Payment
approved"}
```

Mocking Tools and Libraries

Several tools and libraries are available to help implement mocks in integration testing. These tools allow you to easily create mock versions of external dependencies and define their behavior. The following are some popular options:

- **WireMock**: WireMock is a versatile tool used to mock HTTP-based APIs. It allows you to simulate API responses based on specific request patterns, making it ideal for testing applications that rely on external APIs. WireMock can also simulate latency, timeouts, and other network conditions to test how your application behaves in different scenarios.

  Key Features:

  - Supports JSON request/response stubbing.
  - It can simulate various HTTP error codes (404, 500, and so on).
  - Allows for response delays and network simulation.

  Example:

```
# WireMock configuration to mock a payment API response
request:
  method: POST
  url: /payment
response:
  status: 200
  jsonBody:
    { "status": "success", "transaction_id": "12345" }
```

- **MockServer**: MockServer is another popular tool that allows you to mock external services, such as RESTful APIs or databases, by simulating responses to specific requests. It can be used in both unit and integration testing environments and supports HTTP, HTTPS, and WebSocket protocols.
- **Mountebank**: Mountebank is a multi-protocol service virtualization tool that allows you to create mock servers for various types of services, including HTTP APIs, TCP services, and more. It is particularly useful when testing complex microservices architectures.
- **Mockito (Java)**: In Java-based applications, Mockito is a widely used library for creating mocks and verifying the interactions between components. It allows developers to replace real dependencies with mock objects during tests and assert that the correct interactions occurred.
- **PyTest-Mock (Python)**: For Python applications, **PyTest-Mock** is a popular library that integrates with PyTest, allowing developers to create and manage mock objects easily. It simplifies the process of replacing real dependencies with mock versions and provides tools for asserting that the correct behaviors occurred during testing.

Best Practices for Mocking in Integration Testing

While mocking can be a powerful tool in integration testing, it is important to use it effectively and avoid common pitfalls. The following are some of the best practices to consider when implementing mocks:

1. **Avoid Over-Mocking**: Over-relying on mocks can lead to a false sense of security in your tests. If too many components are mocked, you may miss issues that arise from real-world interactions between services. Strive to mock only the parts of the system that are external and outside of your control (for example, third-party APIs) while keeping internal components real whenever possible.
2. **Test Real Services Whenever Feasible**: Whenever practical, test with real services in a staging or test environment to ensure that your application can handle real-world conditions. Mocks should be used to simulate exceptional scenarios or to replace dependencies that are not under your control.
3. **Simulate Realistic Scenarios**: When mocking external services, try to simulate real-world conditions as closely as possible. For example, simulate network latency, timeouts, or error codes to test how your application handles various failure scenarios. This will help you catch edge cases and ensure that your application behaves as expected in production environments.

4. **Keep Mocks Updated**: External services evolve over time, and so should your mocks. Regularly review and update your mock implementations to ensure they reflect any changes in the API contracts, data formats, or behavior of the real services.
5. **Use Mocking for Edge Cases**: Mocks are particularly useful for testing how your application handles edge cases, such as when an external service returns an error or times out. Make sure your tests cover these scenarios by mocking different response types, such as HTTP 500 errors or failed database connections.
6. **Automate Mocking with CI Pipelines**: Ensure that your mock setup and teardown processes are automated in your CI/CD pipeline. This allows your tests to run consistently in any environment and ensures that mocks behave the same way during every test execution.

Mocking external dependencies is a valuable strategy for creating effective and reliable integration tests, especially in environments where real services are unavailable, unreliable, or costly. By simulating the behavior of external APIs, databases, or microservices, mocks allow you to isolate the components under test and focus on the interactions between them. With the right tools and practices, mocking can significantly enhance your integration testing strategy, providing faster feedback and more consistent test results. However, it is important to balance the use of mocks with real-world testing, ensuring that your application can handle actual production conditions.

Real-World Examples and Case Studies

To better understand how integration testing works in practice, it is essential to explore real-world examples and case studies. These examples highlight the challenges faced by development teams and how integration testing strategies, including the use of mocks, contract testing, and well-configured environments, were leveraged to solve complex integration issues. In this section, we will examine real-world scenarios that illustrate the practical benefits and common pitfalls of integration testing in various industries and applications.

Case Study 1: Microservices Architecture in an E-Commerce Platform

Scenario:

An e-commerce company operates a large microservices-based platform where services such as order processing, payment, inventory management, and shipping are decoupled. Each service is owned by a separate team, and the services communicate with one another through APIs. As the platform grew, the company faced several integration challenges due to the independent nature of these services.

Challenges:

- **Independent Deployments**: Each team deployed its services independently, leading to frequent integration issues. For instance, the payment service would introduce a change that broke the order processing service, causing checkout failures on the platform.
- **Third-Party Service Dependencies**: The platform depended on external payment gateways and shipping providers, which made testing in a production-like environment difficult. Testing against these third-party services was slow and unreliable.
- **Distributed Testing**: Teams found it difficult to ensure comprehensive integration tests across all microservices. This led to undetected bugs slipping into production, affecting the platform's functionality and user experience.

Solution:

The development teams implemented several integration testing strategies to address these issues:

- **Contract Testing**: They introduced consumer-driven contract testing using **Pact**. Each service defined a contract specifying how it would communicate with other services (such as what APIs to call and expected response formats). This ensured that even if one team deployed changes, the contracts were validated before deployment, ensuring backward compatibility between services. We will discuss contract testing more later.
- **Mocking External Services**: For third-party services such as payment gateways, the teams implemented **mock servers** using **WireMock**. These mocked versions of the payment and shipping services allowed the platform to simulate various real-world scenarios without relying on the availability or reliability of third-party services. This dramatically improved test coverage and helped identify edge cases, such as failed payments or delayed shipping responses.
- **CI/CD Pipeline Integration**: The company integrated automated integration testing into its Continuous Integration/Continuous Deployment (CI/CD) pipeline. Each microservice's deployment was gated by a suite of integration tests that ran against the mocked and real services in a staging environment. This allowed for quick feedback when any service introduced a breaking change.

Outcome:

By implementing contract testing and mocking third-party services, the e-commerce platform saw a reduction in production incidents caused by service incompatibility. Teams could develop and deploy independently while ensuring that their services adhered to agreed-upon contracts. Additionally, testing third-party dependencies with mocks sped up test execution and improved the reliability of test results, ultimately enhancing the overall platform's stability.

Case Study 2: Banking Application with a Monolithic to Microservices Transition

Scenario:

A traditional bank decided to modernize its core banking application by transitioning from a monolithic architecture to a microservices-based architecture. The bank's services, such as customer onboarding, account management, loan processing, and fraud detection, were broken down into individual microservices. During this transition, the bank faced significant integration testing challenges due to the complexity of the system and the need to maintain security and compliance.

Challenges:

- **Complex Inter-Service Dependencies**: The banking application had numerous inter-service dependencies, where microservices needed to exchange sensitive financial data. Ensuring that these interactions were secure, reliable, and compliant with industry regulations was a major concern.
- **Third-Party APIs**: The platform depended on several third-party services for credit checks, identity verification, and loan approval. Testing with these services in real time was expensive and impractical.
- **Data Sensitivity**: Due to the sensitive nature of the data (for example, customer financial details), testing against real customer data was prohibited. This created a challenge in validating the integration of services without using actual production data.

Solution:

To ensure robust integration between the newly created microservices, the bank implemented the following solutions:

- **Service Virtualization**: The development team used **Mountebank** for service virtualization. This allowed them to simulate the behavior of third-party services (such as credit bureaus and identity verification services) without interacting with real data. By virtualizing external dependencies, the team could test integration scenarios, such as failed identity verifications or credit check denials, while keeping costs low and maintaining data privacy.
- **Contract Testing for Secure Data Exchange**: Using **Spring Cloud Contract**, the teams implemented contract testing between microservices. Contracts

were written to specify how sensitive financial data should be exchanged between services, ensuring compliance with security protocols. Any changes to data formats or security policies were validated through these contracts before deployment, preventing breaches or data leaks.

- **Mock Databases**: The bank used **SQLAlchemy** for database interactions and set up mock databases for testing. These mock databases contained synthetic data, allowing the teams to simulate customer data without using real information. Tests were designed to verify database transactions, account balance updates, and loan approval processes, ensuring that the microservices interacted correctly with the database without violating compliance standards.

Outcome:

The bank successfully transitioned to a microservices architecture with minimal disruptions to its core banking operations. By leveraging service virtualization, contract testing, and mock databases, the teams ensured that sensitive financial data was securely transmitted between services. Moreover, the use of contract testing helped enforce strict validation rules, ensuring that no unauthorized data exchanges occurred between microservices, thus maintaining compliance with regulatory standards.

Case Study 3: Healthcare Application with External APIs and Data Synchronization

Scenario:

A healthcare application provider developed a platform that allowed hospitals and clinics to synchronize patient health records across multiple systems. The platform interacted with several external APIs, including insurance verification services, patient health record systems, and electronic prescription services. The primary challenge was ensuring that all these external systems could reliably exchange data with the healthcare platform without introducing errors or delays.

Challenges:

- **Data Synchronization**: The healthcare platform needed to sync patient health records in real-time with multiple systems. Any delays or errors in this synchronization could lead to incorrect medical treatments or diagnoses.
- **Regulatory Compliance**: The healthcare application had to comply with stringent data privacy regulations, including the Health Insurance Portability and Accountability Act (HIPAA). Testing with real patient data was prohibited, and maintaining the security of health records during integration testing was critical.

- **External API Dependencies**: The platform depended on several third-party APIs (for example, insurance companies and pharmacies). These APIs had limited availability during testing and often had strict usage limits, making real-time testing difficult.

Solution:

The development team adopted a combination of **contract testing**, **mocking** external APIs, and **data synchronization validation** to ensure the reliability and security of their integration tests.

- **Contract Testing for API Integration**: The team implemented contract testing to ensure that the healthcare platform's APIs conformed to the expectations of each external system. Contracts were written and validated using **Pact**, ensuring that the platform's requests to insurance providers, pharmacies, and health record systems met the expected formats and behaviors.
- **Mocking External APIs**: External APIs for insurance verification and electronic prescriptions were mocked using **Postman Mock Servers**. This allowed the team to simulate responses from these APIs (for example, insurance approvals and prescription authorizations) without hitting actual external systems, reducing the testing costs and avoiding rate limits imposed by third-party services.
- **Data Synchronization Testing with Synthetic Data**: To ensure patient records were accurately synchronized, the team used synthetic test data in a mocked database. Each service that accessed the patient data was tested to verify that it correctly processed the information. Mocks allowed the team to simulate real-world data synchronization issues, such as conflicting records or failed updates, without using real patient data.

Outcome:

By employing contract testing, API mocking, and data synchronization validation, the healthcare platform was able to achieve reliable integration between various external systems. The platform successfully maintained real-time synchronization of patient health records while complying with regulatory requirements. Mocking external APIs not only helped reduce testing costs but also ensured that the platform was prepared to handle real-world usage and edge cases in a production environment.

These case studies illustrate how integration testing strategies, including mocking, contract testing, and service virtualization, can solve complex challenges in real-world applications. Whether in e-commerce, banking, or healthcare, these techniques help teams ensure that components and external services interact reliably and securely. By implementing these strategies, development teams can reduce production incidents, maintain compliance with regulations, and improve the overall quality and performance of their systems.

Best Practices and Common Pitfalls in Integration Testing

Integration testing plays a critical role in ensuring that various components of an application work seamlessly together. It sits between unit testing and end-to-end testing, validating how modules interact within the system. When executed well, integration testing uncovers defects related to inter-service communication, data flow, and external dependencies. However, when poorly managed, integration testing can become time-consuming, fragile, and difficult to maintain.

In this section, we will explore some best practices to ensure successful integration testing and highlight common pitfalls to avoid.

Best Practices for Integration Testing

Integration testing plays a vital role in ensuring that different components of an application work together smoothly. To make the most of your integration testing efforts, it is essential to follow certain best practices that guide the testing process effectively. The following are the key strategies to consider:

Step 1. Plan and Prioritize Integration Tests

Planning and prioritizing what to test is crucial for an efficient integration testing strategy. Not every integration needs to be tested immediately or at the same depth. Start by identifying the most critical interactions—those with the highest risk of failure or the greatest business impact—and focus your testing efforts there.

- **Risk-Based Testing**: Prioritize testing interactions that involve high-risk components, such as payment gateways, user authentication, or data processing modules. Ensuring the reliability of these components early can prevent major failures in production.
- **Start Small, Then Expand**: Begin by testing simple interactions between two components and gradually expanding the scope to cover more complex interactions involving multiple services.

By focusing on the most critical areas first, you ensure that key functionality is working correctly before testing less critical interactions.

Step 2. Automate Integration Testing

Automation is a cornerstone of modern integration testing, particularly in Continuous Integration and Continuous Deployment (CI/CD) environments. Automating integration tests ensures that they are run consistently and can quickly provide feedback whenever new code is pushed to the repository.

- **CI/CD Integration**: Use CI/CD tools such as Jenkins, GitHub Actions, or CircleCI to automatically trigger integration tests after every commit or pull request. This ensures that code changes do not inadvertently break the integration between components.
- **Maintain a Fast Feedback Loop**: Automated integration tests should be designed to run quickly and efficiently. Optimize the test environment using tools such as Docker or cloud-based solutions to keep tests lightweight and fast.
- **Parallel Execution**: When integration tests become complex, they can take longer to run. To reduce total execution time, use parallel testing techniques where different integration tests are executed simultaneously across multiple environments or containers.

Step 3. Use Mocks and Stubs Appropriately

Mocking external services is a common technique in integration testing to simulate third-party services, databases, or other components that might be unreliable or unavailable during testing. However, mocks should be used wisely.

- **Mock Only Unreliable or Costly Dependencies**: Use mocks for external services such as payment gateways, third-party APIs, or other components that are difficult or expensive to test in real time. Mocking these services allows you to simulate different scenarios, such as timeouts or failures, without depending on actual services.
- **Avoid Over-Mocking**: Mocks should not replace real integrations entirely. Over-mocking can give a false sense of security and fail to expose real-world issues. For critical components, always try to test with actual services in a staging environment to verify real-world behavior.

Step 4. Maintain Production-Like Test Environments

One of the key factors in successful integration testing is having a test environment that closely mirrors the production environment. This allows you to identify issues that may not appear in isolated unit tests but arise due to environment-specific factors such as configuration, scaling, or network issues.

- **Use Containerization**: Tools such as Docker and Kubernetes allow you to replicate production environments in your testing process. Containerization ensures that the same environment is used across all test runs, minimizing inconsistencies.
- **Isolated Test Environments**: Ensure that integration tests are run in isolated environments so they do not interfere with other testing or development activities. Isolated environments also allow you to reset the environment between tests to maintain consistency.

- **Database Reset and Seed Data**: Create a strategy to reset the database or test data between test runs. This prevents leftover data from previous tests from contaminating future tests and causing inconsistent results.

Step 5. Use Contract Testing for Microservices

In distributed systems, particularly microservices architectures, where multiple services interact via APIs, contract testing is an essential practice.

- **Define Consumer-Driven Contracts**: Create contracts that define how services will interact. Use tools such as Pact or Spring Cloud Contract to ensure that services adhere to these contracts when they communicate. This approach ensures that services can be developed and tested independently without risking integration failures.
- **Continuous Validation**: Make contract validation part of your CI/CD pipeline to ensure that services comply with the expected API contracts continuously. This prevents breaking changes from causing failures when services are deployed.

Step 6. Maintain Test Data Integrity

Data integrity is a key consideration in integration testing. Since tests often involve interaction between multiple components, they must have access to reliable and consistent data.

- **Use Synthetic Data**: Avoid using real production data in your integration tests, especially when dealing with sensitive information. Instead, use synthetic data that replicates real-world scenarios but does not pose privacy risks.
- **Reset Data Between Tests**: Ensure that each test starts with a fresh, known state to avoid inconsistent test results. Tools such as Flyway or Liquibase can help reset database schemas between tests.

Step 7. Monitor and Analyze Test Results

Integration tests can become complex, and their results may not always be easy to interpret. Implement tools and techniques to monitor and analyze test results for better insights.

- **Detailed Reporting**: Use reporting tools such as **Allure** or native reporting features of CI/CD tools to generate detailed test reports. These reports should clearly indicate test outcomes, failures, and areas that require further investigation.
- **Log Analysis**: Integration tests often involve multiple services, each with its own logs. Use centralized logging tools such as Elasticsearch, Logstash, Kibana (**ELK Stack**), or **Splunk** to aggregate logs from different components and identify issues quickly.

Common Pitfalls in Integration Testing

Despite the best intentions, integration testing can sometimes fall short due to several common pitfalls. Recognizing and avoiding these pitfalls will help you maintain an efficient and effective testing process.

Step 1. Lack of Test Environment Parity

One of the most common pitfalls is running integration tests in environments that are significantly different from production. This leads to situations where tests pass in the testing environment but fail when deployed to production.

- **Avoiding the Pitfall**: Ensure that your integration test environment mirrors production as closely as possible, from configuration settings to data stores and network conditions. Containerization tools such as Docker make this easier to achieve.

Step 2. Over-Reliance on Mocks

Mocks can simplify integration testing, but over-reliance on them may lead to false positives. If too many components are mocked, you may miss real-world issues that arise from genuine interactions between services.

- **Avoiding the Pitfall**: Use mocks for external services and unreliable dependencies, but ensure that critical internal components are tested with real integrations whenever possible.

Step 3. Skipping Integration Tests for Complex Interactions

In complex systems, there may be a temptation to skip or minimize integration testing due to the perceived difficulty of setting up tests for complex inter-service interactions. However, this is a mistake that can lead to missed defects in production.

- **Avoiding the Pitfall**: Invest the time to develop thorough integration tests, especially for critical components and interactions. Use tools such as **Docker Compose** or **Kubernetes** to simplify the management of complex test environments.

Step 4. Flaky Tests

Flaky tests are those that sometimes pass and sometimes fail without any code changes, leading to confusion and a lack of trust in the test suite. Flaky tests are often caused by unreliable external dependencies, inconsistent data, or environmental differences.

- **Avoiding the Pitfall**: Ensure that your test environment is stable and consistent. Isolate external dependencies using mocks and reset data between test runs to maintain a known state. For external services, implement retry logic in tests to reduce flakiness caused by temporary network issues or service timeouts.

Step 5. Not Updating Tests as the System Evolves

As systems grow and evolve, it is essential to update your integration tests to reflect new functionality, APIs, and interactions between components. Failing to update tests can lead to false negatives, where tests pass despite the system being broken.

- **Avoiding the Pitfall**: Regularly review and update your integration tests to reflect the current state of your system. Keep your contract tests and mock configurations up to date, and ensure that new features or services are covered by integration tests.

Integration testing is a critical part of ensuring that the various components of an application work together seamlessly. By following best practices such as automating tests, using mocks judiciously, maintaining production-like environments, and employing contract testing, you can ensure that your integration tests provide valuable feedback and help maintain system stability. Avoiding common pitfalls, such as over-reliance on mocks and failing to update tests, will help you maintain an effective and reliable integration testing strategy. When done right, integration testing ensures that systems are robust, scalable, and ready for production, helping teams deliver higher-quality software faster.

Conclusion

In this chapter, we explored the vital role that integration testing plays in ensuring the proper interaction between various components of an application. We examined how integration testing fits within the broader context of the test pyramid, emphasizing its significance in validating the communication between modules, services, and external dependencies. By understanding the different types of integration testing—such as the Top-Down, Bottom-Up, Incremental, Big Bang, and Sandwich approaches—we learned how each method can be applied depending on the architecture and complexity of the system.

We also delved into advanced concepts such as **mocking external dependencies**, which allow developers to manage dependencies in a controlled environment. Additionally, we discussed the importance of setting up reliable and production-like test environments, ensuring that integration tests reflect real-world conditions as closely as possible. With practical examples and case studies, we gained insight into how real-world projects have successfully implemented these techniques to ensure the quality and reliability of their software systems.

As we conclude this chapter, the next step in our journey will focus on **API Testing Techniques**. APIs are the backbone of modern applications, especially in service-oriented and microservices architectures. In the upcoming chapter, we will explore the different strategies, tools, and best practices for effectively testing APIs. You will learn how to ensure the correctness, performance, and security of your APIs, which are critical to the success of any application that relies on service-to-service communication.

Key Takeaways

- **Role of Integration Testing**: Integration testing is essential for verifying that different modules and services in an application work together as expected, ensuring that inter-service communication is reliable and accurate.
- **Types of Integration Testing**: Different strategies—such as the Top-Down, Bottom-Up, Incremental, Big Bang, and Sandwich approach—offer varied advantages and are chosen based on the system architecture and complexity.
- **Mocking External Dependencies**: Mocking helps isolate external services that may be unreliable or unavailable during testing, allowing developers to simulate real-world interactions without affecting test reliability.
- **Best Practices in Integration Testing**: Setting up production-like environments, automating integration tests, and using tools such as Docker, WireMock, and Pact ensures consistent and reliable test results.

These key takeaways summarize the critical insights from this chapter, providing a solid foundation for applying integration testing in your projects. Armed with these practices, you will be well-prepared to tackle the next chapter, where we will dive into **API Testing Techniques** and learn how to ensure that your APIs perform well, are secure, and meet functional requirements effectively.

CHAPTER 5
API Testing Techniques

Introduction

In the previous chapter, we explored Integration Testing Approaches, delving into how different modules and services within an application interact with each other. We discussed the critical role of integration testing within the test pyramid and how it helps ensure that individual components, once tested via unit tests, function seamlessly when combined. We also covered several integration testing strategies, including Top-Down, Bottom-Up, and Incremental approaches, along with best practices for setting up reliable test environments using tools such as Docker. By the end of the chapter, you gained a clear understanding of how to validate interactions between services and address integration challenges in complex systems.

In this chapter, we will focus on API Testing Techniques, a key aspect of modern software development. API testing ensures that the backbone of your application—its APIs—are functional, secure, and performant. We will dive into different types of API testing, including functional, performance, and security testing, and explore how to design effective test cases. This chapter will introduce you to tools such as Postman, PyTest, Requests, and Locust, guiding you through the process of automating API tests and integrating them into your CI/CD pipelines. By focusing on testing APIs thoroughly, we can ensure that your application's core services communicate efficiently and reliably.

By the end of this chapter, you will be equipped with the knowledge to implement comprehensive API testing strategies that enhance the robustness and quality of your software. You will gain hands-on experience in designing, automating, and executing API tests, as well as understanding how to catch critical issues early. With practical examples, best practices, and case studies, you will be prepared to develop reliable API tests that ensure your APIs perform optimally under various conditions.

Structure

In this chapter, we will explore the crucial role of API testing in ensuring the reliability, performance, and security of your application's core services. Here is what we will cover:

- Introduction to API Testing
- Importance of API Testing in Modern Applications
- Types of API Tests: Functional, Performance, and Security
- Designing Effective API Test Cases
- Automating API Tests with PyTest and Requests
- Best Practices and Common Pitfalls in API Testing

Introduction to API Testing

Application Programming Interfaces (APIs) are at the core of modern software architecture, acting as the communication bridge between different applications, services, or microservices. From web and mobile applications to cloud platforms and microservices-based architectures, APIs enable data exchange and interaction across disparate systems, ensuring that applications can function as a cohesive whole. In this chapter, we will explore the critical importance of API testing, dive into the different techniques and approaches for testing APIs, and outline how to design, implement, and automate effective API tests. By thoroughly testing APIs, development teams can ensure that their applications remain reliable, secure, and scalable.

The primary goal of API testing is to validate the functionality, reliability, performance, and security of APIs. Unlike UI testing, which focuses on user interaction with the front end, API testing directly targets the backend services. It ensures that these services behave correctly, handle different inputs, and return the expected outputs. API testing is crucial for confirming that the business logic and data-handling processes at the backend are working properly before any user interaction occurs.

In this chapter, we will cover the full spectrum of API testing, from **functional testing**, which validates core functionality, to **performance testing**, which assesses how the API behaves under load, and **security testing**, which ensures the API is protected against potential vulnerabilities. We will also discuss how to design comprehensive and reliable API tests, including strategies for automating these tests with widely used tools such as **Postman**, **PyTest**, **Requests**, and **Locust**. As API testing plays a vital role in CI/CD pipelines, we will also explore how API tests can be integrated into continuous integration systems to provide consistent feedback throughout the development process.

Importance of API Testing in Modern Applications

In today's software landscape, APIs are the backbone of numerous modern applications. Their role has become especially important with the growing adoption of **microservices**, **cloud-based platforms**, and **service-oriented architectures**. In these complex ecosystems, APIs serve as the primary way for different services to interact, exchange data, and perform business functions. Whether it is a mobile app pulling data from a cloud service or a microservice interacting with a payment gateway, APIs drive many critical workflows in software systems.

APIs in Modern Architectures

In traditional monolithic applications, all the code typically resides in one large system, and interactions occur internally. In contrast, modern applications are often split into smaller, more manageable services or components, with each service responsible for a particular business function. These services communicate with each other via APIs, which act as a standardized interface. For example, an online shopping platform might have separate services for handling user accounts, processing payments, managing inventory, and generating order receipts. Each service exposes APIs that allow other services to communicate with it seamlessly.

The proliferation of **Software as a Service (SaaS)** applications has further increased the reliance on APIs. SaaS platforms frequently expose APIs that allow third-party developers to integrate their applications with the SaaS service, extending its capabilities. For instance, a project management SaaS platform might expose APIs for creating tasks, assigning team members, or retrieving project reports. These APIs enable organizations to build custom workflows and enhance productivity by automating tasks that would otherwise require manual intervention.

In these distributed architectures, APIs are not just optional add-ons but are critical components for achieving modularity, scalability, and flexibility. However, their widespread use introduces challenges. Since APIs handle business logic, data processing, and security, any failure or vulnerability within an API can have far-reaching consequences, affecting multiple services, components, or even entire platforms.

The Importance of API Testing

Given the central role APIs play in modern software development, thoroughly testing them is vital. API testing is essential for several key reasons:

- **Ensuring Core Functionality**: APIs serve as the backbone for many business-critical functions. A failure in the API can disrupt important workflows or services. Functional API testing ensures that the API behaves as expected, handles valid and invalid requests appropriately, and returns the correct data in various scenarios. This type of testing helps validate core business logic, data transformations, and error handling.

- **Identifying Issues Early in the Development Process**: API testing often occurs earlier in the development lifecycle than UI testing. This "*shift-left*" approach allows developers to catch issues before they propagate to higher levels of the application. Testing the API layer early helps detect and fix bugs related to logic, data flows, and integrations, reducing the risk of encountering larger issues during later testing phases.
- **Promoting Faster Development Cycles**: Since API tests run faster and are easier to automate compared to full UI tests, they help provide rapid feedback during development. API tests can be executed frequently as part of a continuous integration pipeline, enabling development teams to iterate quickly and deliver features or fixes faster. This speed is crucial in **Agile** and **DevOps** environments where frequent deployments are the norm.
- **Facilitating Microservices and Distributed Systems**: In microservices-based architectures, different services interact through APIs. If one service fails to communicate correctly with another, it can lead to widespread application failure. API testing ensures that each service's interface functions correctly and can interact with other services reliably. This is especially critical when teams are developing services independently and need to ensure that changes do not break existing integrations.
- **Scalability and Performance**: APIs often need to handle thousands or millions of requests under real-world conditions. Performance testing APIs helps ensure that they scale efficiently and maintain responsiveness under varying levels of traffic. By simulating high loads, performance tests help identify bottlenecks and potential areas of improvement, allowing teams to optimize their APIs for better scalability and reliability.
- **Security Assurance**: APIs are often targeted by malicious users attempting to exploit vulnerabilities such as injection flaws, improper authentication, or insufficient data validation. API security testing is necessary to identify and mitigate these threats. As APIs expose sensitive business data, protecting them against unauthorized access, data breaches, and other attacks is crucial for maintaining trust and compliance with industry standards.

Scope of API Testing

API testing encompasses a wide range of techniques, from validating the functionality of individual API endpoints to conducting large-scale performance tests that stress test the API under load. Some of the main types of API testing include:

- **Functional Testing**: Ensures that the API operates according to its specifications and returns the correct response for various requests, including success cases, error cases, and edge cases.

- **Performance Testing**: Measures how well the API performs under varying load conditions, checking response times, throughput, and scalability.
- **Security Testing**: This process verifies that the API is protected from common security vulnerabilities, including unauthorized access, injection attacks, and data breaches. It involves testing authentication and authorization mechanisms, encryption, and validation of inputs/outputs.
- **Reliability and Error Handling**: Ensures that the API handles errors gracefully and consistently, returning proper HTTP status codes, error messages, and fallback options when something goes wrong (for example, database timeout, invalid input).
- **Load and Stress Testing**: This method simulates high traffic to determine how the API behaves under peak load and whether it can handle large numbers of requests without degrading performance or availability.

These various aspects of API testing are all vital for ensuring that the API is robust, scalable, and secure under real-world conditions. By conducting comprehensive tests across these areas, development teams can catch defects early and deliver higher-quality APIs to their users.

API testing is one of the most critical phases in the software development lifecycle, especially as APIs become the standard communication layer in many modern applications. As APIs serve as the backbone for communication in **microservices**, **SaaS**, and **cloud-based architectures**, ensuring their functionality, performance, and security is essential to the success of any system.

Types of API Tests: Functional, Performance, and Security

API testing can be broadly categorized into three major types: **Functional Testing**, **Performance Testing**, and **Security Testing**. Each of these focuses on a different aspect of an API's behavior, and together, they form a comprehensive testing strategy. While they share the common goal of ensuring that the API is reliable and robust, the approaches and techniques used for each type of testing vary significantly. Let us explore each of these categories briefly to understand their importance in the overall API testing process.

Functional Testing: Validating API Behavior

Functional testing is the most fundamental form of API testing and focuses on verifying that the API behaves according to the specified requirements. The goal is to ensure that for any given input, the API returns the expected output. This includes validating the API's business logic, its data processing capabilities, and its adherence to specifications such as request and response formats, HTTP status codes, and error messages.

Functional testing ensures that each endpoint behaves correctly under different scenarios, covering both positive and negative cases. It checks whether the API is capable of handling valid inputs (that is, data that conforms to its expected format and content) and can also gracefully handle invalid inputs (that is, data that does not meet the expected criteria, such as missing fields or incorrect data types).

Examples:

- A **POST** request to create a new user should result in the user being added to the database with the appropriate **201 Created** HTTP status code and a response containing the user's details.
- A **GET** request to fetch a product's details by its ID should return the correct product information, while an invalid product ID should return a **404 Not Found** error.

Functional tests often cover a wide variety of test cases, such as:

- **Input Validation**: Ensuring the API can handle various inputs, including valid and invalid data.
- **Response Validation**: Checking whether the API returns the correct HTTP status codes, headers, and body data.
- **Error Handling**: Validating that the API responds appropriately to error conditions, such as malformed requests, timeouts, or system failures.

By automating functional tests and integrating them into CI/CD pipelines, developers can continuously validate API behavior as part of their development workflow, ensuring rapid feedback and reducing the risk of regression issues.

Performance Testing: Ensuring Scalability and Reliability

Performance testing assesses how well an API performs under various conditions, particularly when subjected to high levels of traffic. The goal is to ensure that the API remains responsive and stable even when handling a large volume of requests. Performance testing often includes both **load testing** and **stress testing**.

- **Load Testing**: Simulates normal traffic to measure how the API performs under expected usage. The goal is to identify bottlenecks and assess the system's ability to handle concurrent requests while maintaining acceptable response times. For example, you might simulate 500 users making simultaneous requests to ensure the API can handle the load without significant slowdowns.

- **Stress Testing**: Pushes the API beyond its normal operating limits to determine how it behaves under extreme conditions, such as traffic spikes or resource exhaustion. The goal is to identify the point at which the API fails and how it recovers from failures (for example, does it crash or degrade gracefully?). For example, stress testing might involve sending thousands of requests per second to an API to determine its breaking point.

Examples:

- **Scenario 1**: A real-time stock trading API must handle hundreds or thousands of simultaneous transactions without latency issues. Performance testing would simulate this traffic and identify any slowdowns or failures in the system.
- **Scenario 2**: An e-commerce platform's API must scale during holiday seasons when there is a spike in user traffic. Load testing ensures the platform can handle large numbers of concurrent users without performance degradation.

Performance testing helps ensure that APIs can meet the demands of real-world usage, especially in high-traffic scenarios where scalability is critical. The insights gained from performance testing are often used to optimize APIs, whether by improving database queries, reducing network latency, or increasing the efficiency of backend processes.

Security Testing: Protecting APIs from Vulnerabilities

APIs, by their nature, often expose sensitive data and core business functions to external systems, making them a prime target for attackers. **Security testing** is a critical aspect of API testing that aims to identify and mitigate vulnerabilities that could be exploited by malicious actors. Ensuring that APIs are secure is vital not only for protecting the system but also for safeguarding user data and maintaining compliance with legal and regulatory requirements.

Security testing typically covers several key areas:

- **Authentication and Authorization**: Ensuring that only authorized users can access the API and that user roles and permissions are enforced correctly. For example, an API used by a healthcare system should allow access to patient records only to authenticated and authorized users.
- **Data Encryption**: Verifying that sensitive data, such as credit card numbers or Personally Identifiable Information (PII), is transmitted securely using encryption protocols such as HTTPS. Security testing ensures that data is not exposed in transit or at rest.
- **Input Validation and Injection Flaws**: Protecting against attacks, such as **SQL Injection**, **Cross-Site Scripting (XSS)**, and **Cross-Site Request Forgery (CSRF)**.

APIs must validate and sanitize inputs to prevent attackers from injecting malicious code or commands.

Examples:

- **Scenario 1**: A banking API that handles account transactions must enforce strong authentication mechanisms (such as OAuth 2.0) to ensure that only authenticated users can access and manipulate account data.
- **Scenario 2**: An API handling Personal Health Information (PHI) in a healthcare app must ensure that all sensitive data is encrypted in transit and stored securely to comply with regulations such as the Health Insurance Portability and Accountability Act (HIPAA).

Security testing also involves validating how the API handles **error states**. For example, when an error occurs (such as a failed authentication attempt), the API should return a generic error message without leaking internal system details that could be useful to attackers.

By breaking down API testing into these three essential types—**functional**, **performance**, and **security**—we gain a comprehensive view of how to test the different aspects of API behavior. Functional testing ensures that APIs operate according to their specifications, performance testing verifies that they can handle expected loads, and security testing protects against vulnerabilities that could compromise data or system integrity. Each type of testing plays a crucial role in building reliable, scalable, and secure APIs.

In the subsequent sections of this chapter, we will explore these types of API tests in greater detail, examining specific examples, best practices, and how to implement them using various tools and techniques. Whether you are validating core functionality, ensuring scalability under load, or securing your API against potential threats, a well-rounded API testing strategy is essential for maintaining a high-quality system.

Designing Effective API Test Cases

Designing effective API test cases is critical for ensuring that your APIs function as expected under various conditions. To do this successfully, it is important to define the correct inputs, validate the outputs, cover all edge cases, and ensure the system responds appropriately under all scenarios.

Defining Inputs and Outputs

The foundation of any API test case is understanding the inputs required by the API and the expected outputs it should return. This is the most basic level of testing but is essential for ensuring that the API functions correctly.

Input Validation: Choosing the Right Data to Test

In API testing, input validation is the process of providing the API with various types of data to see how it responds. Different inputs test different scenarios, including valid, invalid, and edge-case data. Ensuring that the API processes data correctly is crucial for verifying its functionality.

Key Input Types to Test:

1. **Valid Inputs**: Test cases should start by sending valid data that conforms to the API's expected input format. This ensures that, under normal circumstances, the API processes and returns the correct response.
   - **Example**: For a user creation API that expects a **`POST`** request with fields such as **`username`**, **`email`**, and **`password`**, the test should provide valid values such as **`"username": "JohnDoe"`**, **`"email": "john@example.com"`**, and **`"password": "StrongPass123"`**.
2. **Invalid Inputs**: Sending invalid data helps test how well the API handles errors and input validation. Invalid inputs can include missing required fields, incorrect data types, or data that does not meet the format requirements.
   - **Example**: If the **`email`** field requires a valid email address, providing an invalid format such as **`"email": "invalid-email-format"`** should trigger an error response.
3. **Boundary Conditions**: Test cases should include boundary conditions, such as sending data that is at the upper or lower limits of acceptable input values.
   - **Example**: If the API allows usernames with a length between 3 and 15 characters, you should test the minimum (**`"username": "abc"`**) and maximum values (**`"username": "longusername12345"`**), as well as slightly outside those boundaries (for example, **`"username": "a"`** or **`"username": "thisisaverylongusername"`**).
4. **Null and Empty Inputs**: Test cases should account for scenarios where fields are left blank or null. APIs should handle these situations gracefully by either providing a default value or returning an appropriate error message.
   - **Example**: If the **`email`** field is required but not provided (**`"email": ""`**), the API should return an error indicating that the field is missing.
5. **Injection Attacks**: It is important to test inputs that mimic potential security threats, such as SQL injection or Cross-Site Scripting (XSS) attacks, to ensure that the API properly sanitizes inputs.
   - **Example**: Sending a value such as **`"username": "' OR '1'='1";--"`** for an SQL injection test ensures that the API is secure against malicious input.

Output Expectations: Validating Responses, Status Codes, and Headers

After defining inputs, the next step is to validate the API's outputs. This involves checking the returned data, HTTP status codes, and headers to ensure that they align with the expected behavior.

1. **Response Body**: The response body should contain the correct data, formatted according to the API's specification. Depending on the API, the response might be in JSON, XML, or other formats. Test cases should validate both the structure and content of the response.

Example: A successful user creation request might return a JSON response with the new user's details:

```
{
  "id": 123,
  "username": "JohnDoe",
  "email": "john@example.com"
}
```

2. **Status Codes**: HTTP status codes are a crucial part of API responses. They inform the client about the success or failure of the request. Test cases should validate that the correct status codes are returned for each scenario. We will later discuss about different status codes.

3. **Headers**: HTTP headers provide additional information about the response, such as content type, authorization status, or cache settings. Test cases should validate that the necessary headers are present and correct.

   - **Example**: After a successful user creation, the **`Location`** header might indicate the URL of the newly created user resource (**`/users/123`**). Headers such as **`Content-Type`** (for example, **`application/json`**) should also be validated to ensure that the API is returning data in the correct format.

Handling Edge Cases and Error Scenarios

Once the core inputs and outputs of an API are covered, it is essential to consider edge cases and error scenarios. These are situations that go beyond normal operation and might occur due to unusual user behavior, unexpected system conditions, or invalid inputs. Testing these scenarios ensures that the API is robust and can handle all types of interactions, including those that fall outside the "*happy path.*"

Identifying and Testing Edge Cases

Edge cases are typically conditions that occur at the extreme boundaries of input data or system usage. Testing these scenarios helps ensure that the API can handle a wide range of inputs without crashing or behaving unpredictably.

1. **Boundary Conditions**: APIs often have constraints on input data, such as minimum or maximum values, string lengths, or the number of allowed items. Edge case tests should check these boundaries to ensure that the API behaves correctly when inputs are at, near, or beyond these limits.
   - **Example**: For a username field that must be between 3 and 15 characters, edge case testing would include tests for:
     - A username that is exactly 3 characters.
     - A username that is exactly 15 characters.
     - A username that is shorter than 3 characters.
     - A username that exceeds the 15-character limit.
2. The API should handle each of these cases appropriately, either by accepting valid inputs or returning an error for invalid inputs.
3. **Extreme Input Values**: It is important to test the API with extreme but valid input values, such as very large numbers, long strings, or deeply nested data structures. These tests help ensure that the API can handle unusual but valid inputs without performance degradation or failures.
   - **Example**: A test could involve sending a request with a large number of items in a list, such as adding 1,000 products to a shopping cart. This helps verify whether the API can handle large payloads efficiently.
4. **Empty and Null Values**: If input fields are left blank or set to null, they can cause unexpected behavior in some APIs. Edge case testing should include scenarios where required fields are missing or optional fields are left empty or null.
   - **Example**: For a product update API, sending an empty or null value for the product name should trigger a proper validation error instead of allowing the update to proceed with missing or invalid data.
5. **Concurrency and Race Conditions**: In distributed systems or systems that handle multiple requests simultaneously, it is important to test how the API behaves when multiple clients attempt to access or modify the same resource at the same time. These edge cases help identify potential race conditions, which can lead to data inconsistency or unexpected results.
   - **Example**: Testing whether two users can update the same user profile simultaneously helps ensure that the API handles concurrency correctly without data corruption or overwriting.

Designing Tests for Error Conditions and Unexpected Inputs

APIs must be designed to handle errors gracefully. When something goes wrong–whether due to invalid input, external service failures, or other issues–the API should return informative and consistent error messages. Testing these scenarios ensures that the API responds appropriately and provides helpful feedback to users or developers.

1. **Invalid Data Types**: APIs should validate that incoming data is of the correct type (for example, strings, integers, booleans) and return an error when the wrong data type is provided.
    - **Example**: If an API expects a numeric user ID, sending a string value such as `"userID": "abc123"` should trigger an appropriate error, such as `400 Bad Request` with an informative message such as `"User ID must be an integer."`
2. **Missing Required Fields**: When required fields are missing from a request, the API should respond with an error indicating which fields are required and what went wrong.
    - **Example**: For a user registration API, if the request is missing the `email` field, the API should return a `400 Bad Request` error with a message such as `"Email is required."`
3. **Malformed Requests**: Requests that do not conform to the expected structure (for example, missing brackets in JSON, or improperly formatted query parameters) should trigger a clear error response. The API should not crash or behave unpredictably when it encounters malformed requests.
    - **Example**: A malformed JSON request (`{"name": "John, "age": 30}`) should return a `400 Bad Request` error with a message such as `"Malformed JSON in request body."`
4. **Handling Timeouts**: When an API depends on external services (for example, a database or third-party API), these services may experience timeouts or delays. The API should be tested to determine how it handles these situations. For example, if an external service times out, the API should return an appropriate error (for example, `504 Gateway Timeout`) rather than leaving the request hanging indefinitely.
    - **Example**: A weather API that relies on an external weather service should return a `504 Gateway Timeout` error with a clear message such as `"Weather service is currently unavailable."` if the external service does not respond within a reasonable time frame.
5. **Unauthorized Access and Permissions**: APIs often include access control mechanisms that restrict access to certain endpoints or actions. Testing

unauthorized access scenarios helps ensure that sensitive data is protected and that the API properly enforces security measures.

- **Example**: Attempting to access a protected endpoint (for example, viewing a user's private data) without proper authentication should return a **`401 Unauthorized`** or **`403 Forbidden`** error, with a message such as **`"Access denied: You do not have permission to view this resource."`**

By incorporating these edge cases and error scenarios into API test cases, testers can ensure that the API handles various situations correctly. These tests go beyond the basic "happy path" and help uncover potential weaknesses, ensuring that the API is resilient and reliable even when faced with unexpected conditions.

Response Validation, Status Codes, and Error Handling

After testing the inputs and handling edge cases, the next crucial step in designing effective API test cases is validating the **responses**. This includes verifying the **response body**, checking the **status codes**, and ensuring the API handles errors correctly by returning appropriate error messages. Proper response validation is essential to ensure that the API behaves as expected in various scenarios, including successful requests, failures, and unexpected conditions.

Response Validation

The **response body** returned by an API is typically structured in a format such as JSON or XML and contains the data requested by the client. In many cases, the response body will include detailed information, such as user data, product details, or transaction results. It is important to validate not only the structure of the response but also the accuracy of the data.

1. **Verifying the Response Structure**: API responses should follow a consistent structure, especially in RESTful APIs. Test cases should validate that the response body adheres to the expected format, which might include keys such as **`id`**, **`name`**, **`email`**, or other attributes relevant to the resource being requested.

   Example: For a user registration API, a successful request might return the following JSON response:

   ```
   {
     "id": 123,
     "username": "JohnDoe",
     "email": "john@example.com"
   }
   ```

   - The test case should validate that the response includes all the required fields (**id**, **username**, **email**) and that they are in the correct format.

2. **Validating Data Accuracy**: In addition to verifying the structure, test cases should also ensure the accuracy of the data returned. The values in the response should match the expectations based on the input provided.

   Example: If a **GET** request is sent to retrieve the details of a product by its **productID**, the returned product name, price, and stock level should match the expected values based on the system's data.

3. **Handling Nested Data and Arrays**: Many API responses contain nested objects or arrays of data, especially when the API returns multiple items, such as a list of users, products, or orders. Test cases should validate that all items in the array follow the expected structure and that the data in each nested object is accurate.

   Example: For a **GET** request to retrieve all orders for a customer, the response might include an array of order objects:

```
[
  {
    "orderID": 456,
    "totalPrice": 49.99,
    "items": [
      {
        "productID": 123,
        "quantity": 2,
        "price": 24.99
      }
    ]
  }
]
```

   - Test cases should validate that the array of orders and the nested **items** arrays are structured correctly and that the values for **orderID**, **totalPrice**, **productID**, **quantity**, and **price** are accurate.

Status Codes: Validating the Correct HTTP Responses

HTTP status codes play a critical role in API testing. They indicate whether a request was successful, whether the client made an error, or if the server encountered an issue. Each API endpoint should return the correct status code for the situation, and the test cases should verify that the API responds appropriately.

1. **Success Codes**: When a request is successful, the API should return a 2xx status code, with different codes depending on the type of success:

   - **200 OK**: Returned for successful **GET**, **PUT**, or **DELETE** requests.

- **201 Created**: Used when a new resource is created (for example, after a `POST` request).
- **204 No Content**: Returned when a request succeeds, but there is no content to return (for example, after a successful `DELETE` request).
- **Example**: When successfully creating a new user via a `POST` request, the API should return a `201 Created` status code, along with the location of the newly created resource.

2. **Client Error Codes**: When the client sends an invalid request, the API should return a 4xx status code. Common client error codes include:
   - **400 Bad Request**: The request is malformed or contains invalid data.
   - **401 Unauthorized**: The request lacks valid authentication credentials.
   - **403 Forbidden**: The client is authenticated but does not have permission to perform the action.
   - **404 Not Found**: The requested resource could not be found.
   - **Example**: If a request is sent to update a product with an invalid `productID`, the API should return a `404 Not Found` status code, indicating that the specified product does not exist.
3. **Server Error Codes**: When something goes wrong on the server side, the API should return a 5xx status code. These indicate that the server failed to process a valid request:
   - **500 Internal Server Error**: The server encountered an unexpected condition that prevented it from fulfilling the request.
   - **502 Bad Gateway**: The server, acting as a gateway, received an invalid response from an upstream server.
   - **503 Service Unavailable**: The server is currently unable to handle the request due to temporary overloading or maintenance.
   - **Example**: If the database server is down and the API cannot retrieve user data, it should return a `503 Service Unavailable` status code with a message such as `"Database service is temporarily unavailable."`

Error Handling: Ensuring Proper Responses for Failures

When an API encounters an error–whether due to invalid inputs, external service failures, or system overload–it should return informative and consistent error messages. Effective error handling helps the client understand what went wrong and how to resolve the issue.

1. **Descriptive Error Messages**: Error messages returned by the API should be clear and informative. They should explain what went wrong and, where possible, offer suggestions on how to fix the issue.

   Example: For a `POST` request that is missing the `email` field, the API might return a `400 Bad Request` status code with a detailed error message like:

   ```
   {
     "error": "Validation Error",
     "message": "The 'email' field is required."
   }
   ```

2. **Consistent Error Format**: APIs should return errors in a consistent format, regardless of the type of failure. This makes it easier for clients to handle errors programmatically, ensuring that the error structure is predictable.

   Example: Whether the error is due to validation (for example, missing fields) or a server failure, the error response should follow a consistent structure, such as:

   ```
   {
     "error": "Validation Error",
     "message": "Invalid input."
   }
   ```

3. **Graceful Handling of Failures**: When an API encounters an error, it should handle it gracefully without exposing internal system details. For example, if the database crashes, the API should not return raw database errors that could be exploited by attackers.

   Example: Instead of returning a verbose database error message such as `"SQLSTATE[HY000]: General error: 2006 MySQL server has gone away"`, the API should return a `500 Internal Server Error` with a message such as `"An internal error occurred. Please try again later."`

Designing effective API test cases involves a detailed process of validating inputs and outputs and handling edge cases and error scenarios. It is crucial to ensure that the API responds appropriately under various conditions, with proper validation of response structures, status codes, and error-handling mechanisms. By carefully crafting test cases that cover all these aspects, you can build a comprehensive suite of tests that ensures the robustness, reliability, and security of your API.

Automating API Tests with PyTest and Requests

In modern software development, automating API tests is essential to ensure the continuous validation of APIs throughout the development lifecycle. Automating these tests not only speeds up the testing process but also makes it easier to integrate testing into Continuous Integration (CI) and Continuous Delivery (CD) pipelines. In this section, we will focus on using **PyTest**, a popular testing framework for Python, in combination with **Requests**, a simple yet powerful library for making HTTP requests in Python. Together, they form a robust foundation for automating API tests.

Setting Up the Environment

Before we begin writing API tests, let us set up a Python environment with PyTest and Requests installed. Both libraries are widely used and can be easily installed using **`pip`**.

Installing PyTest and Requests

First, create a virtual environment to isolate your project dependencies. Then, install the necessary libraries:

```
# Create and activate a virtual environment (optional but recom-
mended)
python3 -m venv venv
source venv/bin/activate  # On Windows, use venv\Scripts\activate

# Install PyTest and Requests
pip install pytest requests
```

After setting up the environment, you are ready to start writing API tests with PyTest and Requests.

Writing Basic API Test Cases

The most basic form of an API test involves sending a request to an API endpoint and validating the response. With Requests, you can easily send HTTP methods such as **`GET`**, **`POST`**, **`PUT`**, and **`DELETE`** to interact with APIs, and PyTest provides the framework to organize and run the tests.

Let us start by writing a simple test case for a **GET** request to retrieve a user's details.

Example: Testing a Simple GET Request

Assume we are working with a user management API where the **`GET /users/{user_id}`** endpoint returns the details of a user based on the provided user ID.

```
import requests

def test_get_user():
    url = "https://api.example.com/users/123"  # Replace with
actual API URL
    response = requests.get(url)
```

```
    # Assert that the request was successful (status code 200)
    assert response.status_code == 200

    # Assert that the response contains the expected data
    data = response.json()
    assert data["id"] == 123
    assert data["username"] == "JohnDoe"
    assert data["email"] == "john.doe@example.com"
```

In this simple test case:

- We use the **`requests.get()`** method to send a **`GET`** request to the API.
- The **`response.status_code`** is checked to ensure that the API returns a **`200 OK`** status code.
- The response data is converted to JSON using **`response.json()`** and validated to ensure that it contains the correct **`id`**, **`username`**, and **`email`**.

Example: Testing a POST Request

Next, let us test an API endpoint that allows us to create a new user. We will use a **POST** request to send user data in the request body and validate the response.

```
import requests

def test_create_user():
    url = "https://api.example.com/users"  # Replace with actual
API URL
    payload = {
        "username": "JaneDoe",
        "email": "jane.doe@example.com",
        "password": "SecurePass123"
    }

    response = requests.post(url, json=payload)

    # Assert that the user was created successfully (status code
201)
    assert response.status_code == 201

    # Assert that the response contains the newly created user's
details
    data = response.json()
    assert data["username"] == "JaneDoe"
    assert data["email"] == "jane.doe@example.com"
```

Here, we use the **`requests.post()`** method to send the request. The payload (data) is sent in JSON format using the **`json`** parameter. Similar to the previous example, we validate the response code (**201 Created**) and check that the response contains the correct data for the new user.

Handling Authentication and Headers in API Tests

Many APIs require **authentication** to ensure that only authorized users can access or modify resources. Requests make it easy to handle authentication by allowing you to pass credentials and tokens as headers.

Example: Testing an API with Bearer Token Authentication

Let us assume our API requires a **Bearer Token** for authentication. In this case, we will include the token in the request headers.

```
import requests

def test_get_user_authenticated():
    url = "https://api.example.com/users/123"  # Replace with
actual API URL
    headers = {
        "Authorization": "Bearer YOUR_ACCESS_TOKEN"  # Replace
with actual token
    }

    response = requests.get(url, headers=headers)

    # Assert that the request was successful
    assert response.status_code == 200

    # Validate the returned user data
    data = response.json()
    assert data["id"] == 123
    assert data["username"] == "JohnDoe"
```

In this example:

1. The token is included in the **Authorization** header.
2. The test case verifies that only authorized requests succeed (in this case, a **200 OK** response).

For APIs that require **Basic Authentication**, you can use the **auth** parameter in Requests:

```
response = requests.get(url, auth=("username", "password"))
```

Managing Test Data and Parameterization

In API testing, it is common to test multiple variations of requests (for example, testing with different input values, user roles, or data sets). PyTest offers **parameterization** to make this process efficient. Instead of writing separate test cases for each variation, you can use parameterization to run the same test with different input values.

Example: Parameterized API Tests

Suppose you want to test the user retrieval API with different user IDs. Here is how you can use PyTest's **`@pytest.mark.parametrize`** decorator to achieve this:

```
import pytest
import requests

@pytest.mark.parametrize("user_id, expected_username", [
    (123, "JohnDoe"),
    (124, "JaneDoe"),
    (125, "Alice")
])
def test_get_user(user_id, expected_username):
    url = f"https://api.example.com/users/{user_id}"
    response = requests.get(url)

    # Assert the request was successful
    assert response.status_code == 200

    # Validate the user data
    data = response.json()
    assert data["username"] == expected_username
```

In this example:

1. We define a set of test cases using different **`user_id`** and **`expected_username`** values.
2. PyTest runs the test multiple times, once for each set of parameters.

Running Tests and Generating Reports

Once your API tests are written, running them is straightforward with PyTest. You can simply execute the following command in the terminal to run all tests:

```
pytest
```

PyTest also supports detailed output and reporting options. For example, you can use the **`-v`** (verbose) flag to get more detailed information about each test:

```
pytest -v
```

If you want to generate test reports (such as HTML reports) for better visualization of the test results, PyTest can be extended with plugins such as **pytest-html**. To install and use it:

```
pip install pytest-html

# Run tests and generate an HTML report
pytest --html=report.html
```

This will generate a detailed HTML report showing the results of your API tests, which is particularly useful in CI/CD pipelines for tracking the success or failure of tests over time.

Best Practices for Automated API Testing

To ensure your API tests are maintainable, scalable, and reliable, it is important to follow a few best practices:

- **Test Coverage**: Ensure that your tests cover all key API endpoints and scenarios, including edge cases and error handling. Tests should include both positive cases (valid requests) and negative cases (invalid requests or unexpected conditions).
- **Keep Tests Isolated**: Each test should be independent of other tests. Tests should not rely on the state set by previous tests. For example, if a test creates a new user, ensure that the user is deleted or cleaned up afterward to avoid conflicts in subsequent tests.
- **Data Management**: Use consistent and reliable test data. Consider using fixtures or mocking for external dependencies to avoid side effects in your test environment.
- **Run Tests Frequently**: Incorporate automated API tests into your CI/CD pipeline to ensure that every code change is validated against the API. This helps catch regressions early and ensures that the API remains functional as the application evolves.
- **Handle Timeouts and Retries**: For APIs that may occasionally fail due to network issues or service outages, implement retry logic and timeout handling in your tests to account for transient failures.

Automating API tests with PyTest and Requests provides an efficient and flexible approach to validating the behavior, performance, and security of your APIs. By following the aforementioned strategies, you can create a robust suite of automated tests that can be easily integrated into your CI/CD pipelines, ensuring that your APIs are continuously tested throughout the development lifecycle.

Performance Testing APIs with Locust

Performance testing is a crucial aspect of API testing, as it ensures that the API can handle large volumes of requests and perform well under load. One of the most popular tools for performance testing is **Locust**, an open-source load testing tool designed for simulating concurrent users and measuring API performance under stress. Unlike other performance testing tools, Locust allows you to write test scenarios using Python, giving you the flexibility to simulate complex user interactions with your API.

In this section, we will explore how to use Locust for performance testing, including practical examples of simulating multiple users interacting with an API, measuring response times, and identifying potential performance bottlenecks.

Setting Up Locust for API Performance Testing

Before you start using Locust, you need to set up the necessary environment. The installation process is straightforward and can be done using `pip`.

```
# Install Locust
pip install locust
```

Once installed, you can start writing performance test scripts to simulate API usage scenarios.

Writing a Basic Locust Test Script

A Locust test script defines user behavior by simulating how users interact with your API. In Locust, you define users as **tasks**, and these tasks represent actions a user might perform, such as making `GET`, `POST`, `PUT`, or `DELETE` requests to your API.

Let us create a basic Locust test script to simulate multiple users making requests to an API endpoint.

Example: Basic Locust Test Script

```
from locust import HttpUser, task, between

class UserBehavior(HttpUser):
    # Simulate users making requests every 1 to 5 seconds
    wait_time = between(1, 5)

    @task
    def get_user(self):
        # Simulate a user making a GET request to retrieve user
data
        self.client.get("/users/123")

    @task
```

```
    def create_user(self):
        # Simulate a user making a POST request to create a new
user
        self.client.post("/users", json={
            "username": "JaneDoe",
            "email": "jane.doe@example.com",
            "password": "SecurePass123"
        })
```

In this basic test script:

1. **`HttpUser`**: Represents a user interacting with your API. It provides the **`client`** object for making HTTP requests to the API.
2. **`task` decorator**: Defines a user action. In this case, we have two tasks: one for retrieving user data with a **`GET`** request and another for creating a new user with a **`POST`** request.
3. **`wait_time`**: Simulates users waiting between 1 to 5 seconds before making the next request.

When this test is run, Locust will simulate multiple users performing these actions concurrently, allowing you to observe how your API performs under load.

Running the Locust Performance Test

To run the performance test, save the aforementioned script to a file, such as **`locustfile.py`**. Then, you can launch Locust from the terminal using the following command:

```
locust -f locustfile.py
```

This will start the Locust web interface, which you can access by navigating to **`http://localhost:8089`** in your web browser. From there, you can configure the number of users and spawn rate for the test.

- **Number of Users**: The total number of simulated users.
- **Spawn Rate**: The number of users to start per second.

Once the test starts, Locust will simulate concurrent users making requests to the API. The web interface will display live performance metrics, including the number of requests per second, response times, and the success/failure rate of requests.

Measuring Performance Metrics

As your Locust test runs, the web interface will provide real-time insights into the API's performance. The key metrics to pay attention to include:

1. **Response Time (ms)**: The amount of time it takes for the API to respond to a request. Locust breaks this down into percentiles:

- **50th Percentile (Median)**: The response time for 50% of the requests.
- **90th Percentile**: The response time for 90% of the requests.
- **99th Percentile**: The response time for 99% of the requests.

2. **Requests Per Second (RPS)**: The number of requests the API can handle per second. This metric helps assess the scalability of the API as more users interact with it.
3. **Failure Rate**: The percentage of requests that fail (for example, due to timeouts, server errors, or other issues). A high failure rate indicates that the API cannot handle the load properly.
4. **Throughput**: The amount of data processed by the API per second. This is especially useful when testing APIs that return large data sets or handle file uploads/downloads.

Example: Analyzing Response Times

- If the **median response time** remains low (for example, <100ms) even with high concurrency, this suggests that the API is performing well under load.
- If the **90th or 99th percentile** response times increase significantly as the number of users increases, this may indicate performance bottlenecks in your API.

Identifying Bottlenecks and Improving API Performance

One of the main goals of performance testing is to identify bottlenecks in your API that could impact its scalability and reliability. Some common performance bottlenecks that Locust tests can reveal include:

1. **Database Latency**: If API endpoints rely heavily on database queries, slow database response times can cause the entire API to slow down. Look for slow response times on API endpoints that interact with the database.
   Solution: Optimize database queries (for example, by adding indexes, caching, or using more efficient SQL queries).
2. **Network Delays**: Network latency can affect the overall performance of your API, especially if it communicates with external services. High response times for requests to external APIs can reveal issues with the network.
   Solution: Implement retries, optimize API calls, or use a faster networking infrastructure.
3. **High Server Load**: If the server cannot handle the increased number of requests, this can lead to timeouts and failures. Monitor CPU, memory, and other server resources during the test.

Solution: Consider scaling horizontally by adding more servers or moving to a more powerful hosting infrastructure.

4. **Concurrency Issues**: If your API processes concurrent requests inefficiently (for example, locking issues or race conditions), this will affect performance under load.
   Solution: Review how your API handles concurrent connections and adjust locking mechanisms or architecture to handle more requests simultaneously.

Locust helps pinpoint where these issues occur by simulating real-world user behavior at scale. By analyzing Locust's performance metrics, you can identify the bottlenecks and take steps to optimize your API.

Simulating Complex User Behavior

In addition to basic request simulations, Locust allows you to define more complex user behaviors that mimic real-world scenarios. This can be useful when testing APIs that involve multiple actions or dependencies.

Example: Simulating a User Journey

Let us simulate a user journey where a user first logs in, then retrieves their profile and finally logs out. Each step in the journey will be a separate API request.

```
from locust import HttpUser, task, between

class UserJourney(HttpUser):
    wait_time = between(1, 3)

    @task
    def login(self):
        response = self.client.post("/login", json={"username":
"testuser", "password": "testpass"})
        # Store the authentication token for later use
        self.token = response.json()["token"]

    @task
    def get_profile(self):
        # Use the token retrieved from the login request
        headers = {"Authorization": f"Bearer {self.token}"}
        self.client.get("/profile", headers=headers)

    @task
    def logout(self):
        # Log out the user by invalidating the token
        headers = {"Authorization": f"Bearer {self.token}"}
        self.client.post("/logout", headers=headers)
```

In this example:

- The user first logs in, and the authentication token is saved.
- The token is used in the **`Authorization`** header for subsequent requests (retrieving the profile and logging out).
- This simulates a typical user journey, allowing you to test multiple endpoints in a realistic sequence.

Locust is a powerful tool for load and performance testing APIs. By simulating real-world user behavior, you can measure how your API performs under various levels of load, identify bottlenecks, and ensure that it scales efficiently. In this section, we covered how to set up Locust, write test scripts, and measure key performance metrics such as response times, requests per second, and failure rates. We also discussed how to simulate complex user journeys and diagnose performance bottlenecks that could affect your API's scalability.

Security Testing APIs

Security testing is a critical aspect of API testing, as APIs are often the gateways to sensitive data and key functionality in modern applications. Ensuring that APIs are secure involves validating that they handle sensitive data appropriately, prevent unauthorized access, and protect against common vulnerabilities such as injection attacks, broken authentication, and insufficient encryption. Without proper security testing, APIs can become an easy target for attackers, potentially leading to data breaches and other serious security incidents.

Authentication and Authorization Testing

One of the first steps in security testing is to ensure that the API is properly protecting its resources through authentication and authorization mechanisms.

1. **Authentication**: Authentication ensures that users are who they claim to be before allowing access to an API. Many modern APIs use token-based authentication mechanisms such as **OAuth 2.0** or **JSON Web Tokens (JWT)** to secure their endpoints.

Testing Authentication:

- **Valid Credentials**: Test with valid credentials (such as a valid API token or username/password combination) to ensure that the API grants access to authorized users.
- **Invalid Credentials**: Test with invalid or expired credentials to verify that the API correctly denies access and returns an appropriate error response, such as **`401 Unauthorized`**.

- **Token Expiry**: Test how the API handles expired tokens. The API should invalidate expired tokens and require re-authentication.

Example: Testing API Authentication

```
import requests

def test_authentication():
    url = "https://api.example.com/protected-resource"
    token = "INVALID_TOKEN"

    headers = {
        "Authorization": f"Bearer {token}"
    }

    response = requests.get(url, headers=headers)

    # Verify that the API correctly denies access with a 401 Un-
authorized status code
    assert response.status_code == 401
    assert response.json()["error"] == "Invalid or expired token"
```

2. **Authorization**: Authorization testing ensures that authenticated users only have access to the resources and actions they are permitted to perform. Role-Based Access Control (RBAC) and user permissions are critical aspects of authorization testing.

Testing Authorization:

- **Role-Based Access**: Verify that users with different roles (for example, admin, user, guest) can only access the resources allowed for their roles. For example, an admin should be able to view and modify all user data, whereas a regular user should only have access to their own data.
- **Privileged Escalation**: Attempt to perform actions that require higher permissions, such as creating or deleting resources, using a lower-privileged account to verify that the API denies access.

Example: Testing Role-Based Authorization

```
def test_admin_access():
    url = "https://api.example.com/admin/dashboard"
    token = "USER_ROLE_TOKEN"

    headers = {
        "Authorization": f"Bearer {token}"
    }

    response = requests.get(url, headers=headers)
```

```
    # Verify that access is denied with a 403 Forbidden status
code
    assert response.status_code == 403
    assert response.json()["error"] == "Insufficient permissions"
```

Encryption and Data Protection

APIs often handle sensitive information, such as personal user data, financial details, or healthcare records. It is essential to ensure that this data is protected both in transit and at rest through encryption and secure protocols such as **HTTPS**.

- **Encryption in Transit**: All API communications should occur over **HTTPS** to ensure that data is encrypted during transmission. Testing should involve verifying that HTTP requests are redirected to HTTPS and that sensitive data (such as passwords, tokens, or personal information) is never sent over unencrypted channels.

  Testing HTTPS:

  - **Enforce HTTPS**: Ensure that the API rejects requests over plain HTTP and enforces the use of HTTPS for secure communication.
  - **Sensitive Data**: Verify that sensitive data such as passwords, tokens, and personal information is not exposed in URLs, query strings, or logs.

  Example: Testing HTTPS Enforcement

```
def test_https_enforcement():
    url = "http://api.example.com /protected-resource"

    response = requests.get(url)

    # Verify that the API redirects to HTTPS
    assert response.status_code == 301 or response.status_code ==
308
    assert "https" in response.headers["Location"]
```

- **Data Encryption at Rest**: APIs should also ensure that sensitive data stored in databases or file systems is encrypted at rest to protect it from unauthorized access. While encryption at rest is typically managed by the backend systems, API tests can verify that encryption keys and sensitive data are stored securely and not exposed through the API itself.

  Key Management Testing: Test that sensitive data such as encryption keys and tokens are not accessible through the API, either accidentally or through misconfiguration.

Vulnerability Scanning and Common API Security Threats

API security testing also involves checking for common vulnerabilities that attackers might exploit. Some of the most common threats are outlined by the **OWASP Top 10 for APIs**, which provides a framework for identifying API vulnerabilities.

Common Vulnerabilities to Test for:

- **Injection Attacks**: Injection vulnerabilities, such as **SQL Injection** or **Command Injection**, occur when user inputs are improperly handled, allowing attackers to execute arbitrary commands on the server.
  - **Testing**: Send payloads designed to exploit injection vulnerabilities and verify that the API correctly sanitizes inputs.
  - **Example**: Attempt to send SQL commands via API query parameters to verify that the API is not vulnerable to SQL injection.
- **Cross-Site Scripting (XSS)**: XSS vulnerabilities allow attackers to inject malicious scripts into the API's responses, potentially compromising client-side applications or user data.
  - **Testing**: Include malicious script payloads in requests and verify that the API properly escapes and sanitizes user inputs.
- **Rate Limiting and Throttling**: Rate limiting protects APIs from brute-force attacks or Denial-of-Service (DoS) attacks by limiting the number of requests a client can make within a specified time frame.
  - **Testing**: Simulate excessive API requests from a single user or IP address and verify that the API enforces rate limits and throttling.

Security Testing Tools: OWASP ZAP and Postman

Several tools can assist with security testing by automating the detection of vulnerabilities and providing insights into potential security weaknesses. Two commonly used tools for API security testing are **OWASP ZAP** and **Postman**.

- **OWASP Zed Attack Proxy (ZAP):** OWASP ZAP is an open-source security testing tool designed for identifying vulnerabilities in web applications and APIs. It can be used to perform automated vulnerability scans and manual security testing.

Using OWASP ZAP for API Security Testing:

1. **Proxy Requests**: Configure OWASP ZAP as a proxy to intercept and inspect API requests and responses.
2. **Active Scanning**: ZAP can actively scan the API for common vulnerabilities, such as SQL injection, XSS, and misconfigurations.

3. **Passive Scanning**: ZAP performs passive scanning by inspecting traffic and identifying security issues without actively attacking the API.

- **Postman for Security Testing**: Postman, a widely used API development tool, also offers features for security testing, such as running automated collections that check for authentication, authorization, and encryption vulnerabilities. You can integrate Postman with other security tools for more comprehensive testing.

Using Postman for Security Testing:

1. **Environment Setup**: Set up Postman environments for testing different API endpoints with various tokens, roles, and permissions.
2. **Automated Tests**: Write automated tests within Postman to validate security-related aspects such as token expiration, access control, and error handling.
3. **Integration with OWASP ZAP**: Postman can be used in combination with OWASP ZAP to automate vulnerability scanning for your API as part of the testing process.

Security testing for APIs is an essential step in ensuring that your APIs are protected against unauthorized access, data breaches, and other security vulnerabilities. By validating authentication and authorization mechanisms, ensuring proper encryption, and identifying common vulnerabilities, you can safeguard your API from attacks. Tools such as OWASP ZAP and Postman provide powerful capabilities for automating security testing and detecting weaknesses early in the development process.

GraphQL API Testing

While REST APIs remain prevalent, GraphQL APIs are increasingly common in modern applications due to their flexibility in data fetching and strong typing system. Testing GraphQL APIs requires specific tools and approaches that account for their unique characteristics.

- **Tools for GraphQL API Testing:** While traditional REST API testing tools are well-established, GraphQL APIs present unique testing challenges due to their flexible query language and hierarchical data structure. Unlike REST endpoints that have fixed response structures, GraphQL allows clients to specify exactly what data they want, leading to virtually infinite combinations of queries and responses. This flexibility requires specialized tools that can handle schema validation, query testing, and response verification. Let us explore some key tools that make GraphQL API testing more efficient and reliable.
- **GraphQL Playground**: It provides an interactive environment for testing GraphQL queries. It offers features like:
  - Schema exploration

- Query auto-completion
- Real-time documentation
- Query history

Example Query in GraphQL Playground:

```
query GetUserOrders($userId: ID!) {
  user(id: $userId) {
    id
    name
    orders {
      id
      total
      items {
        name
        quantity
      }
    }
  }
}

# Variables
{
  "userId": "123"
}
```

- **Postman GraphQL Support:** It allows you to:
  - Send GraphQL queries as POST requests.
  - Maintain collections of GraphQL queries.
  - Use environment variables.
  - Generate documentation.
- **Automated GraphQL Testing**: Using PyTest for automated GraphQL testing requires the `**gql**` library, which provides a Pythonic interface for GraphQL operations, and `**pytest**` for test organization and execution. The `**gql**` library handles schema introspection, query validation, and request transport, while additional libraries such as `**graphene**` can be used for schema definition and mock server creation. Here is how to set up automated GraphQL testing:

```
import pytest
from gql import gql, Client
from gql.transport.requests import RequestsHTTPTransport

@pytest.fixture
def graphql_client():
    transport = RequestsHTTPTransport(
```

```
            url='https://api.example.com/graphql',
            headers={'Authorization': 'Bearer your-token'}
        )
        return Client(transport=transport, fetch_schema_from_
transport=True)

def test_create_user(graphql_client):
    mutation = gql("""
        mutation CreateUser($input: CreateUserInput!) {
            createUser(input: $input) {
                id
                name
                email
            }
        }
    """)

    variables = {
        "input": {
            "name": "John Doe",
            "email": "john@example.com"
        }
    }

    result = graphql_client.execute(mutation, variable_values=-
variables)
    assert result["createUser"]["name"] == "John Doe"
```

Integrating API Tests in CI/CD Pipelines

API testing is essential for ensuring that your APIs function correctly, but to fully leverage the benefits of automated testing, it is critical to integrate these tests into your Continuous Integration (CI) and Continuous Delivery (CD) pipelines. CI/CD pipelines enable automated testing to occur after each code commit or before a new release, providing immediate feedback on the state of the application. This ensures that potential issues with the API are caught early in the development process, significantly reducing the risk of bugs making it into production.

Integrating API tests into a CI/CD pipeline is critical for maintaining the health and performance of your API as your application evolves. Here are several reasons why this integration is important:

- **Early Detection of Issues**: Automated tests run after every code to commit catch defects early, allowing developers to fix issues before they accumulate.
- **Consistency**: Regular automated testing ensures the consistent validation of API functionality and performance.

- **Efficiency**: Continuous testing in the pipeline saves time and effort by automatically verifying changes, reducing manual testing workloads.
- **Confidence**: Automated tests provide confidence in the stability of the codebase, helping teams deliver new features more rapidly while minimizing risk.

Tools for Running API Tests in CI/CD Pipelines

Several tools make it easy to integrate API tests into a CI/CD pipeline. Let us take a look at some of the most commonly used platforms for this purpose: **Jenkins**, **GitHub Actions**, and **CircleCI**. We will be using GitHub Actions to see how it works.

- **GitHub Actions:** GitHub Actions is a powerful CI/CD tool built into GitHub, making it easy to automate tasks such as running API tests after every commit or pull request. It supports running tests in containers, which allows for isolated test environments.

Setting Up API Tests in GitHub Actions:

1. **Create a Workflow File**: In your repository, create a **`.github/workflows/api-tests.yml`** file to define the workflow.
2. **Define the Job**: Set up a job that installs dependencies and runs the API tests.
3. **Configure Triggers**: You can configure the workflow to run on different triggers, such as push events, pull requests, or a schedule.

Example: GitHub Actions Workflow for API Testing

```
name: API Test Workflow

on:
  push:
    branches:
      - main
  pull_request:
    branches:
      - main

jobs:
  test:
    runs-on: ubuntu-latest
    steps:
      - name: Checkout code
        uses: actions/checkout@v2

      - name: Set up Python
```

```
        uses: actions/setup-python@v2
        with:
          python-version: '3.x'

      - name: Install dependencies
        run: |
          python -m pip install --upgrade pip
          pip install -r requirements.txt

      - name: Run API tests
        run: |
          pytest tests/api_tests --junitxml=report.xml

      - name: Upload test results
        uses: actions/upload-artifact@v2
        with:
          name: test-report
          path: report.xml

      - name: Publish Test Results
        uses: dorny/test-reporter@v1
        if: always()
        with:
          name: "API Tests"
          path: report.xml
```

In this GitHub Actions workflow:

1. The workflow runs on pushes to the `main` branch or when a pull request is opened.
2. It checks the code, installs dependencies, runs the API tests and uploads the test results.

Best Practices for Integrating API Tests in CI/CD Pipelines

To ensure smooth integration and maintain a robust pipeline, here are some best practices to follow:

1. **Run Tests in Parallel**: Running tests in parallel can significantly reduce the time required to complete the API tests. Tools such as Jenkins, GitHub Actions, and CircleCI support parallelism, allowing you to run tests on multiple environments simultaneously.
2. **Use Docker for Test Isolation:** By running API tests inside **Docker containers**, you can ensure that the test environment is isolated and consistent. Docker

makes it easier to simulate production-like environments and eliminates "*it works on my machine*" issues.

3. **Fail Fast, Fail Early:** Configure the pipeline to fail fast if any test fails. This prevents subsequent stages from running when the code is already broken, saving time and resources. Notifying the team immediately when a test fails allows for quicker resolution of issues.

4. **Generate Detailed Reports:** Make sure the pipeline generates detailed reports on test outcomes. Reports help developers understand the exact cause of failures, allowing them to debug and fix issues efficiently. Integrate reporting tools such as pytest-html or JUnit to visualize the results.

5. **Automate Security and Performance Tests:** Extend your CI/CD pipeline to include security and performance tests. By automating these tests, you ensure that every change is validated not only for functionality but also for security and performance.

Integrating API tests into CI/CD pipelines is essential for ensuring the continuous health and reliability of your APIs. Tools such as **Jenkins**, **GitHub Actions**, and **CircleCI** offer robust solutions for automating API tests after each code commit or release. By following best practices such as parallel test execution, using Docker for isolation, and generating detailed test reports, teams can improve their testing efficiency and ensure that APIs remain functional and secure as the application evolves. This continuous feedback loop allows for quicker identification of issues, helping teams deliver more reliable software with confidence.

Best Practices and Common Pitfalls in API Testing

API testing is a crucial aspect of ensuring the reliability, security, and performance of modern applications. While it is essential to design comprehensive test cases and automate API testing as much as possible, following best practices is equally important to maintain the quality and effectiveness of the test suite. At the same time, being aware of common pitfalls can help you avoid issues that may undermine your API testing efforts.

Best Practices in API Testing

- **Prioritize Critical APIs and Endpoints**: Not all APIs and endpoints carry the same importance or risk. Prioritizing critical APIs that handle key business logic or sensitive data ensures that the most important functionalities are tested thoroughly.
- **Ensure Comprehensive Test Coverage**: Strive to cover all API operations,

including **GET**, **POST**, **PUT**, and **DELETE** requests. Additionally, ensure that tests cover all edge cases, error conditions, and boundary values to validate how the API behaves under various conditions.

- **Test for All Types of API Failures**: Test for possible failure scenarios, such as timeouts, incorrect input, network failures, and external service dependencies. This helps identify how well the API handles errors and provides the right feedback to users or systems.
- **Avoid Over-Mocking**: While mocking is useful for isolating API components during testing, over-reliance on mocking can result in tests that do not reflect real-world conditions. Whenever possible, integrate real-world external dependencies, such as databases or third-party APIs, to validate actual interactions.
- **Automate Tests in CI/CD Pipelines**: Automated API tests should be integrated into your CI/CD pipelines to ensure that every code change is automatically tested. This enables fast feedback and ensures that bugs are caught early in the development process.
- **Keep Tests Independent**: Ensure that each test case is independent of others. API tests should not rely on the outcome of previous tests, as this can create dependencies that make it harder to identify the source of failures.
- **Use Realistic Test Data**: Ensure that the test data used in API tests mirrors real-world usage. This improves the validity of your test results and helps ensure that the API performs correctly in actual production scenarios.
- **Validate Performance and Security**: Functional testing alone is not enough. API tests should also include performance and security checks to ensure that the API can handle high loads and is protected against security vulnerabilities such as SQL injection, XSS, and authentication issues.

Common Pitfalls in API Testing

- **Neglecting Edge Cases**: One of the most common mistakes in API testing is focusing solely on the "*happy path*" or normal user flows while ignoring edge cases and unusual inputs. Neglecting edge cases can leave the API vulnerable to unexpected conditions.
- **Over-Reliance on Functional Tests**: Functional testing is essential, but it is only one part of a comprehensive API testing strategy. Over-reliance on functional tests while neglecting performance and security tests can lead to an API that works well in normal conditions but fails under load or is vulnerable to attacks.
- **Not Testing in Real Environments**: Testing only in isolated or mock environments can lead to false confidence. While mocks can simplify testing, they do not always reflect real-world conditions, and issues may arise when the API interacts with actual databases, third-party services, or external systems.

- **Inadequate Error Handling Tests**: A common pitfall is not thoroughly testing how the API handles error conditions. APIs should return meaningful and consistent error responses when things go wrong, such as invalid inputs, unavailable resources, or server-side issues.
- **Skipping Negative Testing**: Negative testing involves deliberately providing incorrect or invalid inputs to check how the API responds. Skipping negative testing can leave the API vulnerable to edge cases and incorrect inputs.
- **Not Maintaining Tests**: As APIs evolve, tests must be maintained to stay relevant. Failing to update API tests after modifying the API structure, endpoints, or logic can lead to false positives (tests passing when they should not) or false negatives (valid functionality flagged as broken).

Conclusion

In this chapter, we delved into the essential aspects of API testing, a fundamental component in modern software development. We began by understanding the importance of API testing within applications that rely heavily on service-to-service communication, such as those using microservices or SaaS architectures. From functional to performance and security testing, we explored the various types of tests necessary to ensure the reliability, efficiency, and protection of APIs. Additionally, we discussed how to design effective API test cases and automate these tests using powerful tools such as PyTest and Requests, which help streamline the testing process and integrate easily into CI/CD pipelines.

We further explored advanced API testing techniques, such as performance testing with Locust to identify bottlenecks and load issues and security testing to validate API protections against potential vulnerabilities. By implementing these strategies, testers can ensure that APIs handle expected and unexpected inputs effectively and remain resilient under load. Through real-world examples and case studies, we saw how different testing strategies are applied in practice, enabling teams to deliver more robust, secure, and reliable APIs that meet business and technical requirements.

As we conclude this chapter on API testing, our next focus will shift to **Contract Testing**, which plays a critical role in validating the interactions between services, especially in a microservices architecture. In the upcoming chapter, we will explore how contract testing ensures that services meet predefined expectations and can communicate reliably. We will discuss the differences between contract testing and integration testing and learn how to implement consumer-driven contract tests using tools such as Pact and Python-based libraries. By mastering contract testing, you will gain the skills needed to catch integration issues early and maintain seamless communication between services in your system.

Key Takeaways

- **Importance of API Testing**: API testing is vital for ensuring the reliability, functionality, performance, and security of the backbone of modern applications, especially those built on microservices architectures.
- **Types of API Testing**: Functional testing verifies correct behavior, performance testing checks how APIs handle the load, and security testing ensures APIs are protected against vulnerabilities such as authentication breaches and injection attacks.
- **Designing Effective API Test Cases**: Thorough test cases must account for all possible inputs, outputs, edge cases, error handling, and response validation to ensure APIs are fully validated under various conditions.
- **Automating API Testing**: Automating API tests using tools such as PyTest and Requests ensures quick feedback, consistency, and ease of integration into CI/CD pipelines for continuous validation of API functionality.
- **API Performance and Security Testing**: Using tools such as Locust for performance testing and OWASP ZAP for security testing helps to detect bottlenecks, vulnerabilities, and areas where APIs need improvement to ensure robustness under real-world conditions.

These key takeaways encapsulate the core lessons from this chapter, providing a solid foundation for API testing in your development workflow. In the next chapter, we will explore **Contract Testing**, focusing on maintaining reliable service-to-service communication in microservices environments and detecting integration issues early in the development process.

CHAPTER 6
Contract Testing

Introduction

In the previous chapter, we explored **API Testing Techniques**, focusing on the core components of API functionality, performance, and security. We covered strategies for designing and automating API tests using tools such as Postman, PyTest, and Requests. Additionally, we explored performance testing using Locust and delved into security testing methodologies to protect APIs from vulnerabilities. By the end of the chapter, you will have gained a solid foundation in building comprehensive API testing frameworks, ensuring that the backbone of modern applications–APIs–is robust, secure, and efficient.

In this chapter, we will shift our focus to **Contract Testing**, a vital technique for validating the agreements between services in a microservices architecture. While integration testing ensures that components work together, contract testing specifically verifies that the communication between services adheres to predefined contracts. We will explore the differences between integration and contract testing, introduce tools such as Pact and Pydantic for writing and managing contracts, and dive deep into the consumer-driven approach to contract testing. This chapter will guide you through the technical process of implementing contract tests in Python and integrating them into CI/CD pipelines.

By the end of this chapter, you will have the skills and knowledge necessary to implement contract testing effectively in your development workflow. You will understand how to create and manage contracts between services, detect potential integration issues early, and ensure seamless communication across your microservices architecture. Through real-world examples and best practices, you will be equipped to build robust, reliable systems that ensure services interact correctly, minimizing the risk of failures in production environments.

Structure

In this chapter, we will explore the fundamental concepts of **Contract Testing**, a critical method for ensuring that services in a microservices architecture communicate correctly and reliably. Here is what we will cover:

- Introduction to Contract Testing
- Importance of Contract Testing in Microservices Architecture
- Differences between Integration Testing and Contract Testing
- Implementing Contract Testing
- Integrating Contract Tests in CI/CD Pipelines
- Best Practices and Common Pitfalls in Contract Testing

Introduction to Contract Testing

In the digital age of software development, where microservices and APIs dominate the architecture of modern applications, ensuring that these services can communicate effectively is crucial. As applications grow in complexity, the interactions between services become more intricate, and managing these dependencies can become a significant challenge. This is where **contract testing** comes into play. Contract testing is a method used to validate the interactions between service providers and consumers, ensuring that they adhere to predefined agreements, or "*contracts*." It guarantees that services can communicate and fulfill the expectations set forth, preventing integration failures that could otherwise be missed until production.

At its core, contract testing verifies that the communication between services is accurate and reliable. Unlike traditional integration testing, which focuses on how services work together at a high level, contract testing narrows its focus to the communication layer. It ensures that the API responses, payload structures, and request formats are in line with what has been agreed upon between a service provider (the service offering the functionality) and a consumer (the service making use of the functionality). This type of testing becomes particularly important when different teams or external providers are responsible for various services, making clear communication vital for smooth integration.

The benefits of contract testing extend beyond simply validating interactions. By catching issues early, contract testing reduces the likelihood of unexpected failures in production, where the cost and effort of fixing integration problems are much higher. It provides confidence to teams working in distributed environments that their services will function as expected, regardless of who owns or maintains the interacting services. Additionally, contract testing aligns well with agile and DevOps practices, allowing for faster development cycles and smoother releases by validating service interactions throughout the development process.

In the modern era of microservices, where services are loosely coupled and independently deployable, contract testing has become an essential practice for maintaining the stability and reliability of distributed systems. It ensures that each service adheres to its defined contract, helping teams build scalable, flexible systems where communication between services is predictable and reliable, even as services evolve independently.

Importance of Contract Testing in Microservices Architecture

As modern software systems move toward microservices-based architectures, ensuring smooth communication between independent services becomes a significant challenge. Microservices are built to be loosely coupled and independently deployable, allowing teams to develop, deploy, and scale services in isolation. However, the independence of these services also introduces a higher risk of integration failures when these services need to communicate with each other. Contract testing addresses this challenge by validating the agreements between services, ensuring that their communication remains seamless, even as they evolve independently.

Challenges in Microservices Communication

In a microservices architecture, services interact with each other via APIs or message queues. These services often rely on predefined data formats, payload structures, and response behaviors. While this separation of services offers great flexibility, it also means that a change in one service can break its interaction with others. This poses a few key challenges:

- **Decoupled Development**: In microservices architectures, different teams may be responsible for developing and maintaining different services. As a result, service updates or changes can be made without direct coordination with the teams responsible for other services. This lack of tight coupling increases the risk of introducing breaking changes, especially if one service changes its API without adequately communicating those changes to the dependent services.
- **Frequent Deployments**: Microservices encourage a continuous deployment culture where services are updated and deployed independently. This means that services are changing regularly, and each deployment has the potential to impact its consumers if the contract between services is not upheld. Traditional end-to-end or integration tests may not be run as frequently due to their complexity or time-consuming nature, leading to potential breakages going unnoticed until much later in the development cycle.

- **Complex Interactions**: As the number of microservices grows, the interactions between services become more intricate, making it difficult to test all possible integration points. While unit tests can verify individual functionality and integration tests validate that services work together, these approaches are often insufficient for ensuring that each service abides by its contract with others. Small changes in response formats, status codes, or data types can cause significant issues, even if the functionality of the individual service remains intact.

Contract testing is specifically designed to overcome these challenges by ensuring that each service meets the expectations of its consumers and follows the agreed-upon contract. It focuses on the boundary between services—the point of communication—and ensures that even as services change independently, they remain compatible with each other.

Benefits of Contract Testing for Microservices

Contract testing is particularly well-suited for microservices because it addresses the specific needs of distributed, independent services. Here are several ways in which contract testing is beneficial to a microservices architecture:

- **Prevents Integration Failures Early**: One of the main advantages of contract testing is that it helps catch potential integration issues before they escalate. By testing the service interactions in isolation, contract testing ensures that any changes made to a service will not inadvertently break the contract with its consumers. This prevents problems from surfacing later in the integration or production stages, where fixing them becomes more difficult and costly.
- **Ensures Backward Compatibility**: As microservices evolve, the services may change their behavior or the structure of their API responses. Contract testing helps maintain backward compatibility by ensuring that even as the service changes, it still meets the expectations defined in its contract with other services. This is critical in environments where different versions of a service may be running simultaneously, and breaking changes could disrupt service communication across the application.
- **Decouples Teams and Speeds Up Development**: In large organizations, different teams are often responsible for different microservices. Contract testing allows these teams to work more independently by providing a clear contract that the teams can rely on. A consumer team can write tests based on the contract, and as long as the provider team adheres to this contract, both teams can continue developing at their own pace without requiring constant communication or coordination. This decoupling leads to faster development cycles and reduces the dependency on full end-to-end tests.

- **Enhances Test Granularity**: Unlike traditional integration tests, which test the overall behavior of services working together, contract tests are more granular. They focus specifically on the interaction between a consumer and a provider. This granularity means that contract tests can be faster to execute and easier to maintain. Instead of testing the entire system's integration, contract testing hones in on individual service contracts, making it easier to detect the root cause of any issue.
- **Supports Agile and DevOps Practices**: Agile and DevOps practices emphasize Continuous Integration (CI) and Continuous Delivery (CD) of software. Contract testing aligns perfectly with these methodologies by offering an automated, reliable way to verify service interactions during every code change. Contract tests can be easily integrated into CI/CD pipelines, where they are run automatically with each commit or pull request, providing immediate feedback on whether a change breaks any contracts. This reduces the risk of deployment failures and supports faster release cycles.

Example in Practice: Contract Testing in Action

Consider a typical e-commerce platform built on microservices. It might have separate services for user management, inventory, payment processing, and shipping. The payment processing service may rely on the inventory service to verify product availability before processing a transaction, while the shipping service needs information from both the payment and inventory services to generate a shipping label. With multiple services interacting, it becomes critical to ensure that their communication remains consistent.

If the inventory service changes its API response format or status codes, it could disrupt the payment processing service, even if the functional change in the inventory service is minimal. Contract testing can be used to validate the interaction between these services. The payment service defines a contract that the inventory service must meet, such as returning specific status codes, maintaining the structure of the product availability response, and providing certain error messages if the product is out of stock. Through contract testing, this agreement is continuously validated, ensuring that updates to the inventory service do not break the expectations of the payment service.

Long-Term Benefits of Contract Testing

By implementing contract testing, development teams can mitigate the risk of inter-service failures, ensuring that their microservices architecture remains reliable and resilient to changes. It allows for the independent evolution of services while providing confidence that service interactions will continue to function correctly. This not only improves the overall stability of the application but also reduces the time spent on debugging integration issues and speeds up the development process.

As microservices become the backbone of modern applications, the importance of contract testing grows. It provides an essential safety net that ensures services continue to work together harmoniously, even as they are updated or scaled. The ability to detect potential integration issues early, before they cause widespread failures, makes contract testing a valuable practice for maintaining the reliability of service-to-service communication in distributed systems.

Contract testing in a microservices architecture acts as the glue that holds service interactions together. By focusing on the boundaries between services and ensuring that contracts are respected, developers can build scalable, resilient systems with confidence, knowing that their services will continue to work together even as the architecture evolves.

Differences between Integration Testing and Contract Testing

In modern software development, testing strategies play a crucial role in ensuring that systems function as expected. Integration testing and contract testing are two distinct but complementary approaches to validating service interactions. While both aim to ensure that the components of an application work together as intended, they do so in different ways and with different scopes. In this section, we will explore the key differences between integration testing and contract testing, highlighting their unique characteristics and when to use each in a microservice or service-oriented architecture.

Scope and Focus

The primary difference between integration testing and contract testing lies in their scope and focus.

- **Integration Testing**: Integration testing is a broader testing approach that focuses on verifying that different modules or services within an application work together as expected. It involves testing the interaction between multiple components, such as databases, APIs, or user interfaces, to ensure that they function correctly when combined. The goal is to validate that the system behaves as expected when these components are integrated. Integration testing often includes setting up test environments that simulate production-like conditions, running end-to-end tests, and ensuring that the various services and components communicate and cooperate effectively.
- **Contract Testing**: Contract testing, on the other hand, is more focused and granular. It verifies the "*contract*" or agreement between a service provider and its consumers. The contract defines the expectations regarding data formats, response structures, status codes, and other communication aspects

between services. Contract testing ensures that both the service provider and the consumer meet these predefined expectations. Unlike integration testing, contract testing does not involve testing the entire interaction chain between multiple components. Instead, it focuses solely on the communication boundary between the two services.

In essence, **integration testing is concerned with the overall behavior of multiple components working together**, whereas **contract testing focuses on the communication between individual services** and ensures that the expectations set by the contract are upheld.

Testing Granularity

Another significant difference between integration testing and contract testing is the level of granularity involved in each approach.

- **Granularity in Integration Testing**: Integration testing is often performed at a higher level of abstraction, testing the interaction between several components or services. This makes integration testing broader in scope, as it aims to test the entire system or a large part of it as a cohesive whole. As a result, integration tests may cover multiple aspects of the system, such as data flow, error handling, and performance under load. However, this also means that integration tests can be complex, time-consuming, and harder to isolate when issues arise since they involve testing multiple moving parts.
- **Granularity in Contract Testing**: Contract testing operates at a much more granular level, focusing specifically on the contract between two services. It does not aim to test the entire system or multiple components working together; instead, it focuses on the interaction between a service provider and its consumer. By validating that the provider adheres to the contract and that the consumer's expectations are met, contract testing isolates communication failures to the boundary between services. This granularity makes contract testing faster, more targeted, and easier to maintain compared to integration testing.

Test Complexity and Maintenance

The complexity of the tests and the effort required to maintain them also differ between integration testing and contract testing.

- **Complexity in Integration Testing**: Integration tests often involve setting up production-like environments with multiple components, such as databases, APIs, and message queues, interacting with each other. This complexity makes integration tests more challenging to implement and maintain. For example, if one component of the system changes, it can potentially break multiple integration tests, requiring significant effort to diagnose and fix the issue.

Additionally, integration tests tend to be slower to execute due to the need to simulate real-world conditions and interactions between components.

- **Complexity in Contract Testing**: Contract testing is simpler in comparison because it only tests the interaction between two services based on their contract. It does not require the setup of complex environments or multiple interacting components. Instead, it focuses on validating that the communication between a service provider and its consumer follows the agreed-upon contract. This reduces the complexity of the tests and makes them easier to maintain. If a contract changes, only the tests related to that specific contract need to be updated, making contract testing more scalable in environments where services are constantly evolving.

Independence from the Full System

One of the key advantages of contract testing is its independence from the full system, which differentiates it from integration testing.

- **Integration Testing Relies on the Full System**: Integration testing requires all components involved in the test to be up and running in a production-like environment. For example, if you are testing the interaction between an API and a database, both must be fully operational for the integration test to run successfully. This reliance on the full system can lead to issues if one component is unavailable or if there are discrepancies between the test and production environments.
- **Contract Testing Works in Isolation**: Contract testing, on the other hand, can be conducted in isolation without requiring the full system to be operational. By using mocks and stubs, contract tests simulate the behavior of a service provider or consumer, allowing teams to verify that the contract is upheld without depending on the actual implementation of the other service. This independence makes contract testing faster and more reliable, as it is not affected by the availability or stability of other components.

For example, in a microservices architecture, if the inventory service is down, contract testing between the order service and the payment service can still be performed using mock responses from the inventory service. This allows teams to continue testing their contracts even in the absence of live services, ensuring continuous feedback during the development process.

Evolution of Services

Both integration testing and contract testing handle service evolution differently, especially in microservices environments where services are frequently updated.

- **Service Evolution in Integration Testing**: In integration testing, when one service changes, it can potentially affect many other services that interact with it. This is because integration tests cover the end-to-end interaction between components. As services evolve, integration tests may need to be updated to accommodate the changes in how services interact. This can result in significant overhead, especially in large systems where multiple services are frequently updated. Moreover, if an integration test fails, it can be difficult to pinpoint which service caused the failure, leading to slower debugging and resolution times.
- **Service Evolution in Contract Testing**: Contract testing is designed to handle service evolution more gracefully. Since contract testing focuses only on the communication between two services, changes to one service only impact the contract tests related to that specific service. As long as the service provider continues to meet the agreed-upon contract, the consumer can continue to function without issue. This makes contract testing particularly useful in environments where services are continuously deployed and updated. By focusing on the contract itself, contract testing ensures that services can evolve independently while still maintaining reliable communication with their consumers.

In a scenario where a service changes its API but maintains backward compatibility, contract tests will validate that the existing contract is still honored. If a breaking change occurs, the contract test will fail, alerting the team to update the contract and make the necessary adjustments. This localized impact of service evolution reduces the risk of widespread failures in the system and allows teams to develop and deploy services independently with greater confidence.

Summary of key differences:

The following table summarizes the differences between integration testing and contract testing through various aspects:

Aspect	**Integration Testing**	**Contract Testing**
Scope	Tests the interaction between multiple components or services.	Tests the communication between two services (provider-consumer).
Focus	Validates overall system behavior when components are integrated.	Validates that services adhere to a predefined contract.
Granularity	It has a broader scope, testing the whole system or multiple services together.	More granular, focusing on specific service interactions.

Complexity	It is complex and requires production-like environments.	Simpler, can be done in isolation using mocks and stubs.
System Dependency	Requires the entire system to be operational.	Can be run without the full system, using mock services.
Handling Service Changes	Affected by changes in multiple components.	Affected only by changes in the specific service contracts.

Table 6.1: *Difference between Integration and Contract Testing*

By understanding these differences, you can make informed decisions about when to use integration testing versus contract testing in your development workflow. While integration testing provides a comprehensive view of how services interact within the system, contract testing offers a faster, more focused approach to ensuring reliable communication between services.

Implementing Contract Testing

Contract testing plays a crucial role in ensuring smooth and reliable communication between services in a microservices architecture. Unlike traditional integration testing, contract testing verifies the interactions between service providers and consumers by validating that they adhere to a predefined "*contract*." This contract specifies the expected data formats, request and response structures, and other communication protocols between services. Implementing contract testing is essential for preventing communication failures, especially in distributed systems where services evolve independently. By focusing on individual service contracts, contract testing allows developers to detect issues early and maintain high-quality service interactions even as the application scales and changes over time.

Writing and Managing Contracts

Writing and managing contracts in a contract testing environment is one of the most critical aspects of ensuring reliable service-to-service communication. A contract acts as a formal agreement between a service provider and its consumers, defining how they should communicate, including the structure of requests and responses, data types, and expected behavior. This section will focus on how to create these contracts, maintain them as services evolve, and ensure that they remain reliable and relevant throughout the lifecycle of the application.

Elements to Include in a Contract

A well-defined contract ensures that both the service provider and the consumer have clear expectations regarding communication. The following elements are typically included in a contract:

- **Request Structure**: This defines the structure of the request that the consumer will send to the provider. It includes the HTTP method (GET, POST, PUT, DELETE), the URL endpoints, headers, and any parameters required in the request body or query string.
- **Response Structure**: The response structure outlines what the consumer can expect to receive from the provider. This includes the status code (for example, 200 OK, 404 Not Found), the response body format (JSON, XML), and any headers that should be returned.
- **Data Types**: Data types specify the format and structure of the data being exchanged. For example, the contract should define whether certain fields are strings, integers, arrays, or objects. This helps ensure that the provider and consumer correctly handle the data in the expected format.
- **Field Validations**: Contracts should include validation rules for fields, such as minimum and maximum lengths, mandatory fields, regular expressions for specific formats (for example, email addresses), and other constraints that ensure the integrity of the data.
- **Error Handling**: It is essential to define how errors will be communicated between services. This includes specifying error status codes, error message formats, and any additional data that might be included in error responses. Consumers need to know how to handle errors when the provider cannot fulfill a request.
- **Versioning Information**: As services evolve, contracts may need to change. Including versioning information in a contract ensures that both providers and consumers know which version of the contract they are using. This is particularly important when rolling out new features or making breaking changes.

By ensuring that these elements are included in every contract, teams can avoid many common communication errors between services.

Versioning and Maintaining Contracts

As services evolve, the contracts between them must also evolve. This requires careful versioning and maintenance to ensure that consumers are not inadvertently affected by changes made to the provider's API. Here are some strategies for versioning and maintaining contracts:

- **Semantic Versioning**: Use semantic versioning (for example, v1.0.0, v2.0.0) to track changes in contracts. Semantic versioning allows for a clear distinction between major, minor, and patch updates:

  - **Major Versions** (for example, v1.x.x to v2.0.0) indicate breaking changes that may affect the consumers and require them to update their code.
  - **Minor Versions** (for example, v1.0.0 to v1.1.0) indicate backward-compatible feature additions.
  - **Patch Versions** (for example, v1.0.0 to v1.0.1) indicate backward-compatible bug fixes or minor adjustments.

  Semantic versioning ensures that consumers can continue using the older version of the contract if they are not ready to adopt the new changes.

- **Backward Compatibility**: One of the key principles in contract management is ensuring backward compatibility. When updating a service, providers should avoid making changes that will break existing consumers. This can be achieved by maintaining older versions of the API while introducing new versions in parallel. For instance, if the provider adds a new field to the response, it should not remove existing fields that consumers may rely on.
- **Deprecating Contracts**: Over time, certain contracts may become obsolete as services evolve. When deprecating a contract, it is important to notify consumers well in advance and provide them with a transition plan. This includes setting a clear timeline for when the deprecated contract will be removed and ensuring that the new version is thoroughly documented.
- **Contract Tests for Versioning**: Contract tests themselves should be versioned along with the contracts. This means writing specific tests for each version of the contract and ensuring that both the provider and the consumer adhere to the correct version during testing. When making changes to a service, ensure that the contract tests for both the old and new versions pass before deployment.

Managing Contracts in a Microservices Environment

Managing contracts becomes more complex in a microservices environment, where multiple services interact and communicate with one another. To effectively manage contracts in such an environment, it is important to establish standardized practices and tools that can streamline the process.

- **Centralized Contract Repository**: In a microservices architecture, it is crucial to have a centralized repository where all contracts are stored and versioned. This repository should be easily accessible to both providers and consumers, allowing them to refer to the contract when developing or updating their services. By centralizing contracts, teams can avoid inconsistencies and ensure that everyone is using the latest version of the contract.
- **Automated Contract Validation**: Automation plays a key role in managing contracts. Providers should continuously validate their services against the

contracts to ensure that they are adhering to the agreed-upon terms. Tools such as Pact can automate this process by running contract tests in the CI/CD pipeline, ensuring that any contract violations are detected early before deployment.

- **Collaboration between Providers and Consumers**: Contract testing is inherently a collaborative process between service providers and consumers. In many cases, it is the consumers who define the contract (consumer-driven contract testing), and the provider must adhere to it. To ensure smooth collaboration, establish clear communication channels between teams that own different services. Regularly review contracts together, and agree on changes before they are implemented.
- **Documentation and Communication**: Proper documentation is essential for managing contracts. Each contract should be thoroughly documented, including details about the request and response structures, error handling, versioning, and any changes made over time. This documentation should be easily accessible to all stakeholders, including developers, testers, and operations teams. Additionally, when making changes to a contract, communicate these changes clearly to all affected teams to avoid confusion and ensure that everyone is on the same page.

Best Practices for Writing and Managing Contracts

- **Start with Consumer Needs**: Always start by considering the needs of the consumer when defining a contract. The contract should reflect the data and functionality that the consumer requires from the provider, without over-complicating the design.
- **Keep Contracts Simple and Concise**: A contract should be as simple and concise as possible while still providing all the necessary information. Avoid including unnecessary fields or data types that are not needed by the consumer, as this can lead to confusion and increased maintenance overhead.
- **Test Contracts Continuously**: Incorporate contract testing into the CI/CD pipeline to ensure that services continue to adhere to the contract as they evolve. This ensures that any violations are caught early and can be addressed before they reach production.
- **Document Everything**: Every change to a contract should be thoroughly documented, including the reasoning behind the change, the impact on consumers, and any necessary migration steps. This will help avoid misunderstandings and ensure that both providers and consumers are aware of any changes.
- **Review Contracts Regularly**: Regularly review and update contracts to ensure that they remain relevant as the application evolves. This is especially

important in a microservices architecture, where services are constantly being developed and updated.

By following these best practices, you can create and manage contracts that are clear, reliable, and easy to maintain, ensuring that communication between services remains smooth and error-free. Managing contracts effectively in a contract testing environment is key to maintaining the stability and performance of your microservices architecture over time.

Types of Contract Testing

When implementing contract testing, it is crucial to understand the different types of contract testing available. These types help ensure that both service providers and consumers maintain a consistent agreement (contract) about how they interact with each other. In this section, we will discuss two primary forms of contract testing: **Consumer-Driven Contract Testing** and **Provider-Driven Contract Testing**. Understanding both will help you select the appropriate strategy based on your application architecture and testing requirements.

Consumer-Driven Contract Testing

Consumer-Driven Contract Testing (CDCT) is the most commonly used approach, especially in microservices architectures. In CDCT, the consumer of a service defines the contract. This means that the consumer specifies its expectations for how the provider service should behave–what inputs it will send, what outputs it expects to receive, and how the service should respond under various conditions.

Key Characteristics of CDCT:

- **Consumer-Centric:** The consumer service defines the contract, focusing on its specific needs and expected interactions with the provider.
- **Greater Collaboration:** It requires effective collaboration between the service provider and the consumer teams, ensuring that the provider service can meet the consumer's expectations.
- **Contract Evolution:** As the consumer evolves and adds new features, the contract can be updated, and the provider must comply with the new version.

Advantages of CDCT:

- **Detecting Breaking Changes Early:** Since the contract is based on the consumer's needs, any breaking change made by the provider that violates the contract is caught early in the development process.
- **Reduced Risk of Miscommunication:** By formalizing the expectations of the consumer, the risk of miscommunication between the development teams is reduced.

- **Faster Feedback Loop:** Contract tests can be executed early in the CI/CD pipeline, providing fast feedback to both the consumer and provider teams when changes are made.

Example of CDCT in Action: Consider an e-commerce system where a payment service (consumer) interacts with an order service (provider). The payment service expects the order service to provide specific data, such as order totals and customer details. By defining the contract upfront, the payment service ensures that any changes in the order service (such as modifying the API response) do not break its integration.

Provider-Driven Contract Testing

In provider-driven contract testing, the contract is defined and maintained by the service provider. The provider specifies the structure and behavior of the service, including the data formats, endpoints, and expected responses. The goal is for the provider to define a stable contract that all consumers can rely on, reducing the likelihood of breaking changes during service upgrades or modifications.

Key Characteristics of Provider-Driven Contract Testing:

- **Provider-Centric:** The service provider controls the contract and ensures that it remains backward-compatible with its consumers.
- **Provider Control:** This type of testing places more responsibility on the provider to ensure that the contract remains stable, especially if multiple consumers rely on the service.

Advantages of Provider-Driven Contract Testing:

- **Centralized Control:** The provider has full control over the contract, making it easier to ensure that the service remains consistent.
- **Backward Compatibility:** By owning the contract, the provider can ensure backward compatibility for all its consumers, reducing the chance of breaking changes.
- **Less Coordination Needed:** Unlike CDCT, which requires close collaboration between the consumer and provider, provider-driven contract testing is more autonomous since the provider sets the standards.

Example of Provider-Driven Contract Testing:

Imagine a payment gateway service that interacts with multiple client applications (such as e-commerce websites). The payment gateway defines the contract that all clients must adhere to, specifying how payments should be processed, which data formats should be used, and what error responses to expect.

Choosing between CDCT and Provider-Driven Contract Testing

Both approaches have their use cases and advantages, but in modern microservices architectures, **Consumer-Driven Contract Testing** is more prevalent. This is because microservices are often independently developed, and the consumer typically knows its requirements better than the provider.

- **CDCT** is beneficial when the focus is on ensuring that the provider service adapts to the evolving needs of its consumers.
- **Provider-Driven Contract Testing** is useful in scenarios where a provider needs to maintain backward compatibility and control over its contracts, especially when interacting with multiple consumers.

In practice, many systems may benefit from a **hybrid approach**, where both consumer-driven and provider-driven contracts are implemented. This ensures a robust testing strategy that validates both consumer expectations and provider stability.

By understanding the different types of contract testing, development teams can make informed decisions on how to implement the best strategy for their specific architecture. These approaches help prevent integration issues by ensuring that services comply with agreed-upon contracts, whether those contracts are driven by consumers or providers.

Implementing Contract Tests in Python

Contract testing with Python enables developers to validate the interactions between services by ensuring that the predefined contracts between them are adhered to. In a microservices environment, where services are distributed and evolve independently, contract testing is essential to detect communication issues early. Python, being a versatile and widely used language in the testing domain, offers several tools and libraries to effectively implement contract tests. In this section, we will explore how to write contract tests using popular libraries such as Pact, Pydantic, and FastAPI, providing practical code examples and guidance on how to automate contract testing in real-world applications.

Introduction to Pact

Pact is a widely used open-source tool for consumer-driven contract testing. It helps ensure that interactions between consumers (clients) and providers (APIs or services) adhere to predefined contracts. Pact allows consumers to define the expected behavior from the provider, and the provider can verify that they meet these expectations. In a Python-based environment, Pact is integrated via the **`pact-python`** library.

Here is how to get started with Pact for contract testing in Python:

Installing Pact-Python:

To install **pact-python**, you can use **pip**:

```
pip install pact-python
```

Example: Setting Up Consumer-Driven Contract Tests

In a consumer-driven contract testing approach, the consumer of a service defines the contract. This contract specifies what the consumer expects from the provider, such as request and response formats. The provider must then implement the contract and verify that it fulfills the consumer's expectations.

Let us assume you are testing an e-commerce service where the consumer needs to fetch product details from a product service API. Here, the contract defines the structure of the request the consumer will send and the expected response from the provider.

Step 1: Define the Contract in the Consumer Test

First, you define the contract in the consumer test. Following is an example of writing a consumer-driven contract test using Pact:

```
import unittest
from pact import Consumer, Provider
import requests

class ProductServiceContractTest(unittest.TestCase):
    def setUp(self):
        self.pact = Consumer('ProductServiceClient').has_pact_
with(Provider('ProductService'))
        self.pact.start_service()
        self.addCleanup(self.pact.stop_service)

    def test_get_product(self):
        expected_response = {
            'id': 1,
            'name': 'Laptop',
            'price': 1000,
            'stock': 50
        }

        # Define the interaction (contract)
        self.pact.given('Product with ID 1 exists').upon_
receiving('a request for product ID 1')\
```

```
            .with_request('get', '/product/1').will_respond_
with(200, body=expected_response)

        # Execute the test
        with self.pact:
            result = requests.get('http://localhost:1234/prod-
uct/1')
            self.assertEqual(result.json(), expected_response)

if __name__ == '__main__':
    unittest.main()
```

In this example, we use **pact-python** to define the contract for fetching a product with a given ID. The **pact.given()** function describes the preconditions for the interaction, and **upon_receiving()** specifies the expected request and response between the consumer and provider. The test then validates that the provider meets the expectations by simulating an API request.

Step 2: Verify the Contract in the Provider

Once the consumer test generates the contract, the provider (API service) needs to verify it. The provider's job is to ensure that it can fulfill the contract's expectations. You do this by running Pact verification tests on the provider.

The provider test will be run against the real implementation of the service, ensuring that it adheres to the contract:

```
from flask import Flask, jsonify

app = Flask(__name__)

@app.route('/product/<int:product_id>', methods=['GET'])
def get_product(product_id):
    if product_id == 1:
        return jsonify({'id': 1, 'name': 'Laptop', 'price': 1000,
'stock': 50}), 200
    return {}, 404

if __name__ == '__main__':
    app.run(port=8080)
```

In this case, the provider offers an API that responds with the product details. You can run Pact verification by feeding it the contract generated by the consumer, ensuring that the provider adheres to it.

```
pact-verifier --provider-base-url=http://localhost:8080 --pact-
url=pacts/ProductServiceClient-ProductService.json
```

If the provider successfully passes the verification, it confirms that it meets the consumer's expectations.

Using Pydantic for Data Validation

While Pact handles the contract between consumer and provider, you can use Pydantic to enforce data validation in Python applications. Pydantic ensures that the data being exchanged between services is of the correct type and format. This is especially important when dealing with complex data structures, as it prevents runtime errors due to mismatched data types.

Example: Pydantic Data Model

Let us enhance the product service with Pydantic for validating request and response data. You define a Pydantic model for the product schema:

```
from pydantic import BaseModel

class Product(BaseModel):
    id: int
    name: str
    price: float
    stock: int
```

You can then use this model in the provider API to validate the data before responding to the consumer:

```
from flask import Flask, jsonify
from pydantic import ValidationError

app = Flask(__name__)

@app.route('/product/<int:product_id>', methods=['GET'])
def get_product(product_id):
    try:
        product = Product(id=1, name="Laptop", price=1000,
stock=50)
        return jsonify(product.dict()), 200
    except ValidationError as e:
        return str(e), 400

if __name__ == '__main__':
    app.run(port=8080)
```

Here, Pydantic ensures that the product data adheres to the defined structure before it is returned to the consumer. If there are any validation errors, the service can return an appropriate error response.

FastAPI for Contract Testing

FastAPI is a modern Python web framework known for its speed and ease of use. It is an excellent choice for building services that need to communicate via well-defined contracts. FastAPI integrates seamlessly with Pydantic, making it easy to validate request and response data against predefined models.

Example: Implementing Contract Testing with FastAPI

Here is how you can implement a simple API using FastAPI that adheres to a contract defined by a consumer:

```
from fastapi import FastAPI, HTTPException
from pydantic import BaseModel

app = FastAPI()

class Product(BaseModel):
    id: int
    name: str
    price: float
    stock: int

@app.get('/product/{product_id}', response_model=Product)
def get_product(product_id: int):
    if product_id == 1:
        return Product(id=1, name="Laptop", price=1000, stock=50)
    raise HTTPException(status_code=404, detail="Product not
found")
```

FastAPI uses Pydantic under the hood to validate the response, ensuring that the provider adheres to the contract.

Implementing contract tests in Python with libraries such as Pact, Pydantic, and frameworks such as FastAPI allows you to validate service interactions efficiently. By ensuring that services adhere to predefined contracts, you can prevent integration issues and maintain seamless communication between them. This approach promotes confidence in the reliability of microservices as they evolve independently, allowing both consumers and providers to continue functioning as expected. Through practical examples and best practices, you can now apply contract testing effectively to ensure smooth inter-service communication in your applications.

Integrating Contract Tests in CI/CD Pipelines

Contract testing becomes even more powerful when integrated into Continuous Integration/Continuous Deployment (CI/CD) pipelines. By automating contract tests within CI/CD pipelines, you ensure that service contracts are validated with each new commit, minimizing the risk of breaking service dependencies. This section explores how to integrate contract tests in your CI/CD pipeline using tools such as Jenkins, GitHub Actions, and CircleCI and how contract testing fits into the broader automated testing lifecycle.

Benefits of Integrating Contract Testing in CI/CD:

In a microservices architecture, where services are independently deployed, the possibility of one service inadvertently breaking another due to contract changes is high. By integrating contract tests into CI/CD pipelines, any discrepancies between service provider and consumer contracts are flagged early in the development process. This reduces the likelihood of breaking changes being deployed to production, thus maintaining smooth and predictable inter-service communication.

The benefits of integrating contract tests into CI/CD include:

- **Immediate Feedback**: Developers receive instant notifications if contract expectations are violated, allowing them to address issues before they reach production.
- **Automated Validation**: No manual intervention is needed to check if services adhere to the contract, as testing is triggered with each change.
- **Preventing Downtime**: Ensuring contract compliance reduces the risk of service failures in production environments.
- **Continuous Monitoring**: Each new release or update can be thoroughly tested to verify that no communication between services is broken.

Setting Up Contract Testing in CI/CD

Integrating contract testing within a CI/CD pipeline can be broken down into a few key steps:

1. **Creating Contracts**: Contract tests are defined based on service expectations, as we discussed in the earlier section on writing and managing contracts. These contracts are shared between both service providers and consumers.

2. **Adding Contract Tests to the Pipeline**: Most CI/CD tools allow you to add steps or jobs to your pipeline that run specific tests. You can configure contract tests to run automatically after a code commit or before deployment to a staging/production environment. Common CI/CD platforms such as Jenkins, GitHub Actions, and CircleCI support this functionality.

3. **Automating Tests with Pact**: Pact is one of the most popular tools for contract testing. You can integrate Pact into your Python project and CI/CD pipeline to run contract tests as part of the pipeline workflow. For example, a new job or step in the pipeline that runs the contract tests can be created if you are using Jenkins. In the case of GitHub Actions or CircleCI, these workflows can be defined in YAML configuration files.

Example: Integrating Contract Tests in GitHub Actions

GitHub Actions allows you to define automated workflows in YAML, and you can add contract testing as part of your build and test steps:

```
name: CI
on:
  push:
    branches:
      - main
jobs:
  test:
    runs-on: ubuntu-latest
    steps:
      - name: Checkout code
        uses: actions/checkout@v2

      - name: Set up Python
        uses: actions/setup-python@v2
        with:
          python-version: '3.x'

      - name: Install dependencies
        run: |
          pip install -r requirements.txt

      - name: Run Contract Tests
        run: |
          pytest --pact-verifier-url=<provider_url> --consumer=-
consumer_service
```

In this example, the **`Run Contract Tests`** step runs Pact-based contract tests during the GitHub Actions CI workflow.

Fit into the Testing Lifecycle

Contract tests should be integrated as part of the broader testing lifecycle, fitting alongside unit, integration, and end-to-end tests. Here is how contract testing fits into the lifecycle:

1. **Pre-Merge Testing**: Contract tests should be part of the automated tests that run on each pull request to ensure changes do not break service contracts before merging into the main branch.
2. **Post-Merge Testing**: Once the code is merged, contract tests should be run again to confirm that the merged code meets contract expectations in the integrated environment.

3. **Pre-Deployment Testing**: Before deploying to staging or production environments, contract tests ensure that the services will communicate properly after deployment.
4. **Periodic Testing**: In long-lived systems, contract tests can be set up to run periodically (for example, nightly builds) to validate the ongoing compatibility of services over time, even without recent changes.

Handling Failures in CI/CD

In the event of a contract test failure, the pipeline should automatically stop, preventing further steps such as deployment. CI/CD tools will typically provide logs and error details, allowing developers to quickly identify and resolve the issue. The team can then either update the service to comply with the existing contract or renegotiate the contract based on the new changes.

Best Practices for CI/CD Integration

- **Automate Everything**: Ensure that contract tests are an automated part of the CI/CD workflow, triggered by every relevant code change.
- **Run Tests in Parallel**: To optimize speed, contract tests can often be run in parallel with other types of tests, such as unit or integration tests.
- **Maintain Test Artifacts**: Store contract test results as artifacts in your CI/CD tool to enable debugging and tracking of issues over time.
- **Version Contracts**: Maintain version control over service contracts, ensuring both consumers and providers are testing against the correct contract version.
- **Use Production-Like Environments**: To ensure reliable results, contract tests should be run in environments as close to production as possible.

By integrating contract tests into your CI/CD pipelines, you automate the validation of service interactions across multiple microservices, ensuring that each service adheres to agreed-upon contracts before deployment. This not only minimizes the risk of service failures but also provides immediate feedback to developers, helping teams address issues early. Whether you are using Jenkins, GitHub Actions, or CircleCI, integrating contract tests can greatly improve the reliability and robustness of your microservices architecture, providing peace of mind as you scale and evolve your services.

Best Practices and Common Pitfalls in Contract Testing

As with any testing strategy, following best practices and avoiding common pitfalls can significantly improve the effectiveness and reliability of contract testing. In this section, we will outline actionable best practices to follow when implementing contract testing and highlight potential pitfalls that teams should be aware of.

Best Practices for Contract Testing

- **Clearly Define the Contract:** A well-defined contract is the foundation of contract testing. Ensure that both the provider and consumer teams agree on the structure and expectations outlined in the contract. This should include request and response formats, required and optional fields, data types, and any constraints or validation rules. Having clear, mutually agreed-upon contracts reduces ambiguity and minimizes communication errors between services.
- **Version Contracts:** As services evolve, it is crucial to version contracts properly to manage backward compatibility. Whenever changes are made to a service, ensure that the contract version is updated to reflect those changes. This prevents outdated services from breaking due to unexpected changes in the contract and allows teams to support multiple versions of service without forcing all consumers to upgrade immediately.
- **Use Consumer-Driven Contracts:** In many cases, using consumer-driven contracts is a best practice. This means that the consumer of a service defines the contract, which the provider must then implement and adhere to. Consumer-driven contracts help to ensure that the provider meets the specific requirements of all its consumers, preventing situations where a provider makes changes that inadvertently break its consumers.
- **Automate Contract Testing in CI/CD:** Contract testing should be fully automated and integrated into the CI/CD pipeline to ensure that contract violations are caught early. By running contract tests with every commit, you can verify that changes in either the provider or consumer do not break the agreed-upon contract. Automation also allows for continuous validation of the contracts as part of your testing lifecycle, providing immediate feedback to developers.
- **Run Tests in Production-Like Environments:** It is essential to run contract tests in environments that closely mirror production. This ensures that the tests reflect real-world conditions and that services interact as expected in the production environment. Using tools such as Docker to replicate production environments for contract testing can help you catch potential issues early and reduce the risk of deploying faulty services.
- **Keep Contracts Lightweight:** Contracts should focus on the essentials. Avoid over-complicating the contract with too many details or edge cases. This will make the contracts easier to manage, maintain, and test over time. Contracts that are too complex can lead to higher maintenance costs and slower testing cycles.

- **Regularly Review Contracts:** Regular contract reviews should be part of your process, especially when there are significant changes to the service or the business requirements. This ensures that the contract remains relevant and up-to-date as services evolve, and it allows both the provider and consumer teams to collaborate and refine the contract as needed.
- **Monitor Test Results and Track Failures:** Ensure that you monitor the results of contract tests closely and track test failures over time. This will help you identify patterns, such as certain services or endpoints that frequently fail, and allow you to address these issues proactively. Maintaining a historical record of contract test results also provides valuable insight into the reliability of inter-service communication over time.

Common Pitfalls in Contract Testing

- **Focusing Solely on Consumer or Provider:** A common mistake is focusing too much on either the consumer or the provider when defining contracts. It is important to maintain a balance where both parties' needs are addressed. If the contract only serves the provider's interests, it may not meet the consumers' functional needs, and vice versa. Successful contract testing requires collaboration and agreement between both sides.
- **Neglecting Versioning:** One of the most dangerous pitfalls in contract testing is failing to version contracts properly. As services evolve, it is critical to maintain backward compatibility and allow multiple versions of a service to coexist. If versioning is neglected, updates to a service could break its consumers, resulting in service failures and downtime. Be sure to establish clear versioning practices and maintain old versions for as long as they are required by consumers.
- **Overcomplicating the Contract:** Trying to account for every possible edge case or scenario in a contract can lead to overly complex contracts that are difficult to maintain. This can also result in slower testing cycles and higher maintenance costs. Instead, focus on the core requirements and keep contracts as simple as possible. Use other types of tests, such as integration or end-to-end tests, to handle more complex scenarios.
- **Ignoring Real-World Conditions:** Running contract tests in isolated or overly simplified environments that do not reflect the real-world conditions of your production environment can lead to false confidence. Ensure that contract tests are run in production-like environments to accurately validate that services will behave as expected when deployed to production.
- **Not Updating Contracts when Changes Occur:** Another common pitfall is failing to update the contract when changes are made to the service or its functionality. This can result in services drifting apart and breaking when they

interact in production. To avoid this, always update the contract to reflect any changes to the provider's API or functionality and ensure that consumers are informed of these changes.

- **Skipping Tests for Minor Changes:** Sometimes, teams may skip contract tests when making what they perceive to be "minor" changes. However, even small changes to a service can have a ripple effect on its consumers. Skipping tests can lead to undetected contract violations that may only become apparent in production. Always run contract tests as part of your CI/CD pipeline, regardless of the size of the change.
- **Relying Solely on Contract Testing:** While contract testing is powerful, it should not be the only testing method used to validate inter-service communication. It is important to complement contract testing with other types of testing, such as integration, unit, and end-to-end tests, to ensure comprehensive coverage of your system. Contract testing focuses on validating service agreements but may not catch all potential issues.

Contract testing plays a crucial role in ensuring reliable communication between services, particularly in a microservices architecture. By following best practices, such as clearly defining and versioning contracts, automating tests, and running tests in production-like environments, you can ensure that contract testing is both effective and scalable. However, it is important to avoid common pitfalls, such as overcomplicating contracts, neglecting versioning, or skipping tests for minor changes. By striking the right balance, contract testing can help you maintain smooth, reliable service interactions and avoid costly service failures in production.

Conclusion

In this chapter, we explored the concept and implementation of Contract Testing, a critical technique for ensuring reliable communication between services, especially in microservices architectures. We started by understanding the importance of contract testing, particularly in distributed systems, where independent services must collaborate seamlessly. Through this, we examined the key differences between contract testing and traditional integration testing, highlighting how contract testing focuses on the service agreements between providers and consumers.

We then dived into the technical aspects of writing and managing contracts, discussing how to define clear contracts, version them effectively, and maintain them over time. By implementing contract tests in Python using libraries such as Pact and Pydantic, we gained insight into how to build and automate robust contract tests for real-world applications. Additionally, we explored best practices and common pitfalls, equipping you with strategies to avoid typical mistakes and ensure your contract testing process remains scalable and reliable.

As we conclude this chapter on Contract Testing, we are now prepared to transition into our next chapter on Distributing Tests Across UI, API, and Backend Layers. In that chapter, we will focus on how to strategically distribute tests across different layers of an application to ensure comprehensive coverage and maintain test efficiency.

Key Takeaways

- **Role of Contract Testing in Microservices:** Contract testing is vital in service-oriented and microservices architectures to ensure smooth, reliable communication between independently developed and deployed services.
- **Differences between Integration and Contract Testing:** Integration testing focuses on the interactions between components, while contract testing validates the specific agreements (contracts) between service providers and consumers.
- **Writing and Managing Contracts:** Effective contract management requires clear definition, proper versioning, and maintaining backward compatibility as services evolve, ensuring that consumer and provider agreements remain intact.
- **Best Practices and Pitfalls:** Following best practices such as automating contract tests, using consumer-driven contracts, and testing in production-like environments helps avoid common pitfalls such as neglecting versioning and skipping tests for minor changes.

These key takeaways offer a comprehensive overview of Contract Testing, emphasizing its significance in maintaining service reliability in modern architectures. Up next, we will delve into distributing tests across different layers—UI, API, and Backend—providing strategies to optimize testing efforts and achieve better test coverage.

CHAPTER 7
Distributing Tests Across UI, API, and Backend Layers

Introduction

In this chapter, we will shift our focus to Distributing Tests Across UI, API, and Backend Layers. Layered testing is a strategic approach that ensures comprehensive coverage of your application by testing each layer—UI, API, and backend—at the appropriate level. We will discuss how to design and implement effective tests for each layer, ensuring that they complement each other and work together seamlessly. By understanding the role each layer plays in the overall testing strategy, you will learn how to distribute tests effectively to avoid redundancy while ensuring maximum test coverage.

By the end of this chapter, you will have a comprehensive understanding of how to strategically distribute tests across different layers of your application, ensuring that your testing strategy is both thorough and efficient. You will be equipped with the tools, techniques, and best practices needed to implement and automate UI, API, and backend tests effectively. Furthermore, you will learn how to integrate these tests into CI/CD pipelines, providing continuous feedback and maintaining high-quality standards across your application's layers.

Structure

In this chapter, we will explore the strategic distribution of tests across the **UI, API, and backend layers,** ensuring comprehensive coverage and efficient testing of each component. By understanding the role of each layer in the testing process, you will learn to build a balanced and effective testing strategy. Here is what we will cover:

- Introduction to Layered Testing Strategies
- Importance of Layered Testing in the Testing Pyramid

- Differences Between UI, API, and Backend Tests
- Designing Effective Test Cases for Each Layer
- Best Practices and Common Pitfalls in Layered Testing

Introduction to Layered Testing Strategies

Layered testing is a strategic approach to software testing that divides the testing process into distinct layers, each targeting a specific aspect of the application. These layers typically include the **User Interface (UI), Application Programming Interface (API), and backend (data and business logic)**. By isolating tests at these levels, layered testing ensures that each component of an application is thoroughly validated in its own context while also addressing interactions between components.

The primary goal of layered testing is to achieve **comprehensive coverage** while minimizing redundancy. Instead of testing every aspect of an application at every layer, this approach allows testers to focus on the areas where a particular type of testing is most effective. For instance, while UI tests validate the user-facing elements and their interaction with APIs, backend tests focus on data processing, business rules, and database operations. API tests, on the other hand, validate the endpoints and communication mechanisms, acting as the bridge between the UI and backend layers.

Layered testing reflects the principles of **efficiency and scalability**. By testing individual components where they are most relevant, teams can identify and resolve issues faster and with fewer resources. It also provides clarity in debugging, as failures can be traced back to specific layers, reducing the time required for root-cause analysis.

This strategy is particularly valuable in modern development practices such as **microservices architectures**, where components are often loosely coupled and independently developed. Layered testing ensures that each service works as expected in isolation and integrates seamlessly with others. It is a cornerstone of **shift-left testing** approaches, promoting early and targeted testing throughout the development lifecycle.

In the following sections, we will explore how layered testing aligns with the **testing pyramid**, its significance in distributed systems, and how it helps in creating robust, maintainable, and efficient testing workflows.

Alignment of Layered Testing with the Testing Pyramid

As discussed in earlier chapters, the **testing pyramid** serves as a guiding framework for structuring and prioritizing tests across various layers of an application. Layered testing aligns seamlessly with this framework by ensuring a balanced and strategic approach to testing each component of an application.

By focusing the bulk of the effort on **unit tests** at the base, layered testing ensures the core logic and backend components of the application are thoroughly validated. Moving upward, **integration and API tests** in the middle layer serve as the backbone for verifying interactions between services and components. These tests remain essential for detecting communication issues or misaligned expectations between dependent systems, as previously emphasized in our discussion of API and contract testing.

At the top of the pyramid, layered testing ensures **UI tests** are limited to critical end-user workflows, avoiding overreliance on slow and flaky tests. This strategic distribution reduces redundancy and improves the overall efficiency of the testing process, aligning with the principles we have already explored in the context of the testing pyramid.

By reinforcing these concepts, layered testing serves as a practical implementation of the pyramid's philosophy, ensuring tests are performed at the most appropriate level, enhancing reliability, and optimizing test execution. This alignment not only supports efficient resource utilization but also ensures comprehensive test coverage tailored to modern application architectures.

Significance of Distributing Tests

Distributing tests across different layers of an application–UI, API, and backend–is a strategic approach that enhances both the efficiency and effectiveness of the testing process. It ensures that each test is executed at the most appropriate layer, reducing redundancy and optimizing resource usage. By assigning specific types of tests to the layers where they are most relevant, teams can focus their efforts on validating functionality where it matters most.

For example, **unit tests** at the backend layer are faster and more cost-effective for validating core business logic compared to running the same validations at the UI level. Similarly, **API tests** serve as an efficient middle ground for verifying service-to-service communication without relying on the overhead of UI tests. Meanwhile, **UI tests** are reserved for critical end-user workflows, ensuring that the application behaves as expected from the user's perspective without overburdening the testing suite with unnecessary UI validations.

This layered distribution aligns with the principles of the **testing pyramid**, emphasizing a bottom-heavy structure with a focus on robust unit and API testing. It also helps mitigate common pitfalls such as flaky tests, slow execution times, and maintenance challenges associated with overly UI-focused testing strategies.

By adopting a distributed testing approach, teams can achieve better **test coverage** while maintaining scalability, reliability, and speed in their testing pipelines. It fosters an agile and systematic approach to identifying and resolving defects early, ensuring a high-quality application that performs seamlessly across all layers.

Importance of Layered Testing in the Testing Pyramid

Layered testing plays a pivotal role in achieving comprehensive test coverage. By distributing tests across UI, API, and backend layers, it ensures that every critical aspect of the application is validated. Each layer has unique responsibilities within the system, and layered testing ensures that these responsibilities are addressed at the most appropriate level.

For instance, **UI tests** validate user workflows and interactions, ensuring that the end-user experience remains seamless. **API tests** focus on service-to-service communication, verifying that endpoints respond correctly and adhere to expected contracts. Meanwhile, **backend tests** delve into the core business logic, database interactions, and data processing to confirm that the application's foundation is reliable.

By strategically layering tests, teams can minimize overlaps while ensuring that no critical functionality is overlooked. This approach not only enhances the depth of testing but also reduces the likelihood of defects escaping into production.

Balancing Efforts Across UI, API, and Backend Layers

A balanced distribution of testing efforts is essential for achieving an optimal testing strategy. Excessive reliance on any one layer can lead to inefficiencies and missed opportunities for defect detection.

For example, heavily focusing on UI testing often results in longer test execution times, flakiness due to environmental dependencies, and higher maintenance costs. Conversely, ignoring UI testing can leave critical end-user scenarios untested. By balancing efforts across layers, teams can leverage the strengths of each testing type.

- **UI Tests** are prioritized for validating critical paths and high-value workflows, but their scope is intentionally limited to reduce test execution overhead.
- **API Tests** handle a majority of integration and functionality testing, providing a reliable middle layer for catching defects in service communication without UI dependencies.
- **Backend Tests** are emphasized for verifying core logic, ensuring that the application functions correctly at its foundation.

This balanced approach aligns with the testing pyramid's principles, emphasizing a heavier focus on fast, reliable backend and API tests while reserving UI tests for high-impact scenarios.

Advantages of Following the Testing Pyramid

Adhering to the testing pyramid's structure amplifies the advantages of layered testing, making it a cornerstone of modern testing strategies.

- **Efficiency and Speed:** Backend and API tests execute significantly faster than UI tests, enabling quicker feedback and faster iteration cycles during development.
- **Cost-Effectiveness:** Running tests closer to the code (at the backend and API layers) reduces the cost of defect detection and resolution compared to finding issues during UI testing.
- **Scalability:** A well-distributed testing approach supports scalability by minimizing bottlenecks in CI/CD pipelines and ensuring that new functionality can be tested rapidly.
- **Reliability:** Backend and API tests are less prone to flakiness caused by UI dependencies, making the testing suite more stable.
- **Comprehensive Validation:** Distributing tests ensure that every layer is validated thoroughly, from foundational business logic to user-facing workflows, leaving no critical gaps.

By emphasizing layered testing within the testing pyramid, teams can strike an optimal balance between speed, cost, and coverage, ensuring that their applications are robust and user-ready. This methodology not only enhances the quality of the software but also fosters confidence in the testing process, enabling smoother development cycles and more reliable deployments.

Differences Between UI, API, and Backend Tests

Understanding the distinctions between UI, API, and backend tests is essential for implementing a layered testing strategy that is efficient and comprehensive. Each layer plays a unique role in validating specific components of the application, ensuring that the system functions as expected at all levels.

Key Distinctions and Objectives of Each Type of Test:

- **UI Tests**
  - **Objective:** Validate user interactions and workflows at the graphical interface level.
  - **Focus:** Ensure the application behaves as expected from the end user's perspective, including visual elements, navigation, and responsiveness.

- **Characteristics:**
  - Involves simulating user actions such as clicks, typing, and scrolling.
  - Verifies UI elements such as buttons, forms, and menus.
  - Susceptible to flakiness due to environmental dependencies.
- **Scope:** Limited to critical user workflows to avoid inefficiencies.

- **API Tests**
  - **Objective:** Validate the communication and data exchange between services through API endpoints.
  - **Focus:** Ensure that APIs function as expected, returning correct responses for various requests and adhering to defined contracts.
  - **Characteristics:**
    - Faster than UI tests, as they bypass the user interface.
    - Validates HTTP methods (GET, POST, PUT, DELETE) and responses.
    - Includes testing edge cases, error codes, and security aspects such as authentication.
  - **Scope:** Covers service-to-service interactions and ensures data integrity across microservices.
- **Backend Tests**
  - **Objective:** Validate the core business logic, database operations, and backend workflows.
  - **Focus:** Ensure that the application's foundation is robust and can handle data processing and storage accurately.
  - **Characteristics:**
    - Verifies algorithms, data transformations, and database queries.
    - Includes unit tests for individual functions and integration tests for components.
    - Detects issues early, often during development.
  - **Scope:** Tests are closest to the code and typically form the largest part of the test suite.

Positioning Layers within the Testing Hierarchy

Each type of test fits into the testing hierarchy at different levels, aligning with the principles of the **Testing Pyramid**:

- **UI Tests:** Occupy the top of the pyramid, representing a smaller portion of the overall testing effort due to their slower execution and higher maintenance cost. These tests focus on validating the user-facing aspects of the application.

- **API Tests:** Form the middle layer of the pyramid. They strike a balance between coverage and efficiency, providing comprehensive validation of service interactions without requiring the UI.
- **Backend Tests:** Reside at the base of the pyramid, forming the largest portion of tests. These tests are the fastest to execute and provide the quickest feedback, focusing on foundational components such as business logic and database interactions.

Examples of Scenarios for Each Layer:

- **UI Test Scenarios:**
  - Validating a login form by entering valid and invalid credentials.
  - Ensuring a shopping cart updates correctly when items are added or removed.
  - Checking that a webpage renders properly on different devices and screen sizes.
- **API Test Scenarios:**
  - Testing a **`GET /products`** endpoint to verify it returns a list of products in JSON format.
  - Validating that a **`POST /orders`** endpoint correctly creates an order when provided with valid data.
  - Ensuring an endpoint returns a 401 error for unauthorized access attempts.
- **Backend Test Scenarios:**
  - Testing a function that calculates shipping costs based on weight and location.
  - Validating a database query that retrieves user data based on a specific condition.
  - Ensuring that a batch job processes transactions accurately and updates records in the database.

UI, API, and backend tests differ significantly in their scope, objectives, and role within the testing hierarchy. By leveraging their strengths and aligning them with the testing pyramid, testers can create a robust test suite that maximizes efficiency, reduces redundancy, and ensures comprehensive coverage. Each layer complements the others, collectively ensuring the reliability and quality of the application.

Designing Effective Test Cases for Each Layer

Effective test design is the foundation of a robust testing strategy. When working across the UI, API, and Backend layers, it is crucial to ensure that test cases are well-structured, targeted, and aligned with the responsibilities of each layer. This section explores how to design test cases that are precise, efficient, and capable of providing comprehensive coverage. By mapping requirements to the correct testing layer and avoiding redundancy, we can maximize the value of each test while minimizing effort.

We begin with guidelines for crafting precise and efficient test cases, followed by strategies for mapping requirements to the appropriate layer and ensuring full coverage without duplication.

Guidelines for Writing Precise and Efficient Test Cases

To create precise, efficient, and maintainable test cases, keep the following in mind:

- **Define Clear Objectives:** Every test case should have a specific goal tied to a requirement or functionality. Avoid vague objectives that lead to poor coverage or redundancy.
  Example: Test the login API by validating responses for valid and invalid credentials rather than testing the "*login functionality*" broadly.
- **Focus on Layer-Specific Responsibilities:** Each layer has distinct roles:
  - **UI Layer**: Test user interactions, workflows, and visual elements.
  - **API Layer**: Validate endpoints, response structures, and inter-service communication.
  - **Backend Layer**: Focus on business logic, computations, and database interactions.
- **Keep Test Cases Atomic:** Each test case should validate one specific behavior, making debugging and maintenance easier.
- **Use Descriptive Names and Details:** Name test cases clearly to reflect their purpose, and include all relevant details, such as preconditions and expected outcomes.
- **Leverage Data-Driven Testing:** Reuse test cases with parameterized inputs for broader coverage without duplicating effort.
- **Include Assertions for Validation:** Explicitly validate outcomes against expectations, ensuring meaningful results for each test case.

Mapping Requirements to the Appropriate Layer

To maximize efficiency, tests should align with application requirements based on their context and purpose:

- **UI-Specific Requirements:** Focus on workflows, layout, responsiveness, and accessibility.

- **API-Specific Requirements:** Target data exchange, endpoint responses, and service communication.
- **Backend-Specific Requirement:** Cover server-side logic, database interactions, and complex computations.

Mapping requirements to the correct layer avoids redundancy and ensures that tests provide meaningful feedback at the most effective level.

Avoiding Redundancy while Ensuring Coverage

Redundant testing inflates execution time and complicates maintenance. To avoid this:

- **Follow the Testing Pyramid Principles:** Emphasize lower-layer tests (Backend and API), reserving UI tests for essential workflows.
- **Apply a Layer-Specific Focus**
    - Backend tests should validate logic in isolation.
    - API tests should confirm data exchange.
    - UI tests should focus on end-user interactions.
- **Use Shared Test Artifacts:** Centralize test data and utilities to maintain consistency and reduce duplication.
- **Ensure Traceability Without Duplication:** Map requirements to layers using traceability matrices, ensuring comprehensive coverage without overlap.

By carefully designing tests to target the appropriate layer and minimizing overlap, testers can maximize test efficiency. This layered approach enhances coverage, reduces execution time, and makes the test suite easier to maintain without compromising quality.

Automating UI Tests

Automating UI tests is an essential part of validating user-facing functionality, ensuring that applications deliver a seamless user experience across various devices and browsers. By leveraging modern UI automation tools such as Selenium and Playwright, teams can execute tests more efficiently, reduce manual effort, and identify UI-specific issues such as layout inconsistencies, broken workflows, or incorrect validations. This section explores writing and executing automated UI tests, determining which tests should or should not be included in UI automation, addressing common challenges, and adopting best practices for framework setup and test design.

Writing and Executing Automated UI Tests

Automated UI testing focuses on simulating user interactions, verifying workflows, and ensuring visual accuracy. The process involves selecting suitable tools, designing test scripts, and executing them across diverse environments.

Example: A Page Object Model implementation for login functionality using Playwright

```
# UI Layer Tests using Playwright
from playwright.sync_api import Page
from typing import Dict

class LoginPage:
    """Page Object Model for Login functionality"""
    def __init__(self, page: Page):
        self.page = page
        self.username_input = page.locator("#username")
        self.password_input = page.locator("#password")
        self.login_button = page.locator("button[type='submit']")
        self.error_message = page.locator(".error-message")

    async def login(self, username: str, password: str):
        """Perform login action"""
        await self.username_input.fill(username)
        await self.password_input.fill(password)
        await self.login_button.click()

    async def get_error_message(self) -> str:
        """Get error message if login fails"""
        return await self.error_message.text_content()

def test_valid_login(page: Page):
    """Test successful login scenario"""
    login_page = LoginPage(page)
    await login_page.login("valid_user", "valid_pass")
    # Verify redirect to dashboard
    assert page.url.endswith("/dashboard")

def test_invalid_login(page: Page):
    """Test login with invalid credentials"""
    login_page = LoginPage(page)
    await login_page.login("invalid", "wrong")
    error = await login_page.get_error_message()
    assert "Invalid credentials" in error
```

Popular UI Automation Tools

Here are some of the popular UI automation tools:

- **Selenium**
  - A widely used open-source framework supporting multiple programming languages such as Python, Java, and C#.
  - Ideal for cross-browser testing, interacting with web elements, and validating dynamic web applications.
  - **Example**: Automating login forms, navigation menus, or search functionalities.
  - **Limitations**: Slower execution due to browser dependency and challenges in handling modern web features such as shadow DOM.
- **Playwright**
  - A modern alternative to Selenium, developed by Microsoft, supports multiple programming languages and provides powerful capabilities for browser automation.
  - **Key Features**:
    - Built-in support for headless execution and parallel testing.
    - Excellent for testing modern web applications, including handling iframes, popups, and network activity.
  - **Example**: Testing the rendering of dynamic content in Single Page Applications (SPAs).
  - **Advantages**: Faster and more reliable than Selenium for UI testing.
- **Cypress**
  - Focuses on front-end testing and offers a developer-centric approach with real-time execution and debugging.
  - **Example**: Testing forms, data submission, or client-side validations.
  - **Limitations**: Limited support for cross-browser testing compared to Selenium and Playwright.
- **Puppeteer**
  - A Node.js library for controlling Chrome or Chromium, widely used for automating Chrome-specific workflows and UI rendering tests.
  - **Example**: Generating screenshots or PDFs of web pages.

Execution and Environment Setup

Let us take a look at the execution and environment setup:

- **Cross-Browser and Cross-Platform Testing:** Automated UI tests should run across different browsers (for example, Chrome, Firefox, Edge) and platforms (for example, Windows, macOS, mobile). Tools such as Selenium Grid or Playwright's inbuilt parallel execution make this feasible.
- **CI/CD Integration:** Running automated UI tests as part of a CI/CD pipeline ensures early detection of UI issues after every deployment. Tools such as Jenkins, GitHub Actions, or CircleCI can be integrated with Selenium or Playwright for seamless test execution.
- **Headless Mode Execution:** Tools such as Playwright and Puppeteer offer headless execution to speed up test runs without rendering a GUI, making it suitable for CI environments.

By choosing the right tool and configuring tests effectively, teams can achieve reliable and scalable UI automation. In the next sections, we will delve deeper into selecting the right test scenarios for UI automation, avoiding pitfalls, and addressing common challenges.

Tests Suitable for the UI Layer

UI tests are crucial for validating workflows and interactions that directly impact user experience. However, due to their higher maintenance cost and longer execution times compared to other types of tests, it is essential to select scenarios that genuinely require UI-level validation. The following are the types of tests that should be included in UI automation, along with examples for each:

- **Core User Workflows:** Tests that validate end-to-end workflows users frequently perform should be included to ensure the application works as expected from the user's perspective.

  Examples:

  - **E-commerce Application**: Automating the purchase flow, including adding items to the cart, proceeding to checkout, and completing payment.
  - **Banking Application**: Testing money transfer functionality, including selecting accounts, entering transfer details, and confirming the transaction.
- **Critical User Interactions**: Scenarios that involve interaction with UI components such as buttons, forms, dropdowns, and modals should be automated to ensure proper functionality and responsiveness.

Examples:

- **Form Validation**: Verifying that required fields show appropriate error messages when left blank.
- **Interactive Elements**: Testing button clicks that trigger modals or navigate to another page.

- **Visual and Layout Validation:** UI tests should include scenarios that validate the correct rendering of key UI components to maintain a consistent user experience across devices and browsers.

  Examples:

  - **Responsive Design Testing**: Ensuring that the application adapts correctly to different screen sizes (for example, mobile, tablet, desktop).
  - **Visual Elements**: Verifying that critical elements such as logos, banners, or buttons are correctly positioned and visible.

- **Multi-Step Navigation Flows**: UI tests are ideal for scenarios where users perform a sequence of actions across multiple pages or states, as they mimic real-world usage.

  Examples:

  - **Job Application Flow**: Testing the sequence of uploading a resume, filling out a form, and submitting an application.
  - **Subscription Flow**: Automating the process of selecting a plan, entering billing details, and confirming a subscription.

- **Browser-Specific Scenarios**: Automated UI tests should cover scenarios that are prone to browser-specific behavior or compatibility issues.

  Examples:

  - **Popups and Alerts**: Testing browser alerts and modals across different browsers.
  - **CSS Rendering**: Ensuring consistent styling, such as font sizes or button shapes, in Chrome, Firefox, and Safari.

- **Accessibility Testing**: Scenarios that validate accessibility features, such as keyboard navigation and screen reader support, should be included to ensure compliance with accessibility standards.

  Examples:

  - Verifying that all actionable elements are accessible via keyboard.
  - Ensuring proper labeling of form fields for screen readers.

- **Integration with Third-Party Services**: UI tests should include scenarios that involve critical third-party integrations directly exposed in the UI, such as payment gateways or social media logins.

  Examples:

  - Validating PayPal or Stripe payment workflows.
  - Testing login functionality using Google or Facebook OAuth.

By focusing on these high-value scenarios, teams can ensure their UI automation efforts deliver maximum impact while maintaining efficient resource utilization. In the next section, we will explore which tests should be avoided in UI automation to reduce redundancy and improve efficiency.

Tests to Avoid in the UI Layer

UI tests, while valuable for end-to-end workflows and user interaction validation, are not suitable for every testing scenario. Due to their slower execution times and higher maintenance effort, certain types of tests are better suited for lower layers, such as API or backend testing. The following are the types of tests that should be avoided in UI automation, along with examples for each:

- **Validations That Belong to Lower Layers:** Tests that primarily validate backend logic or API responses should not be part of UI testing, as these checks can be performed more efficiently at their respective layers.

  Examples:

  - **API Response Validation**: Verifying response codes or payload structures from a REST API is more suitable for API tests.
    - **Avoid**: Testing a user login workflow in UI tests to check whether the login API returns a 200 status code.
    - **Instead**: Validate the API response directly in API tests.
  - **Business Logic**: Testing discount calculations or tax computations in a UI workflow.
    - **Avoid**: Automating UI tests to confirm a discount percentage.
    - **Instead**: Test this logic with backend tests.

- **Extensive Cross-Browser or Visual Testing:** While essential, cross-browser compatibility and visual testing should not be done exhaustively at the UI test level. These scenarios are better handled using specialized tools designed for visual regression or cross-browser testing.

  Examples:

  - **Layout Validation Across All Browsers**: Running the same UI test script on dozens of browser-device combinations unnecessarily increases execution time.

- **Avoid**: Using Selenium to manually automate and execute UI tests for visual alignment across all browsers.
- **Instead**: Use tools such as BrowserStack or Playwright to conduct targeted visual and cross-browser tests.

- **Database or Backend Validations:** UI tests should avoid directly validating database states or backend operations, as these are best handled in backend tests.

  Examples:

  - **Data Integrity**: Verifying that a record is added to the database after form submission.
    - **Avoid**: Writing a UI test that submits a form and then queries the database for data validation.
    - **Instead**: Use a backend test to validate database changes.

- **Performance and Load Testing**: Performance and load testing scenarios are not well-suited for UI automation due to the overhead of browser interactions.

  Examples:

  - **Response Time Testing**: Testing how long a page takes to load after a button click.
    - **Avoid**: Using UI tests to measure response times, as browser operations introduce unnecessary delays.
    - **Instead**: Perform API-level load testing with tools such as JMeter or Locust.

- **Non-Critical Edge Cases:** Tests for edge cases or scenarios with low priority should be omitted from UI automation, as they add unnecessary complexity.

  Examples:

  - **Obscure User Actions**: Testing extremely rare combinations of actions or inputs.
    - **Avoid**: Automating a UI test for a sequence such as selecting invalid options on a rarely used dropdown.
    - **Instead**: Test these cases manually or via other layers where applicable.

- **Redundant Validations Already Covered Elsewhere**: Scenarios that are thoroughly tested in API or backend tests do not need duplication at the UI layer.

Examples:

- **Error Handling**: Validating that an error message displays when submitting invalid form data.
    - **Avoid**: Automating this check in UI tests if API tests already validate the error response.
    - **Instead**: Include a single UI test to confirm that the error message displays correctly in the UI.

- **Flaky or Hard-to-Maintain Tests**: UI tests that rely on unstable factors, such as dynamic content or frequent UI updates, should be avoided to prevent unnecessary maintenance.

  Examples:

  - **Dynamic Content Validation**: Verifying a feed or dashboard that updates constantly with real-time data.
      - **Avoid**: Writing UI tests for components such as live news feeds that change frequently.
      - **Instead**: Use APIs or backend tests to validate data consistency and logic.

By avoiding these scenarios in UI automation, teams can maintain a lean and efficient test suite that focuses on high-value areas. This approach reduces execution time, minimizes maintenance overhead, and ensures that testing efforts are distributed effectively across layers.

Addressing Common Challenges in UI Automation

UI automation can be highly effective but often comes with unique challenges. Addressing these challenges proactively ensures a stable, maintainable, and efficient testing process. Here are some of the most common issues and strategies to overcome them:

- **Flakiness in UI Tests**: Flaky tests produce inconsistent results, often failing due to timing issues, unstable locators, or dependencies.

  Solutions:

  - Use **explicit waits** instead of arbitrary sleep statements to synchronize test execution with the application.
  - Prefer **robust locators,** such as `data-testid` attributes or unique IDs, over brittle locators, such as element indexes.
  - Mock external dependencies to reduce test failures caused by network or third-party service issues.

- **High Test Execution Time**: UI tests are inherently slower due to browser interactions, making it impractical to run a large suite frequently.

  Solutions:

  - Prioritize critical workflows and limit UI tests to end-to-end scenarios while validating lower-level logic at the API or backend layers.
  - Execute tests in parallel using tools such as Selenium Grid or Playwright's built-in parallelization.
  - Use **headless mode** where visual rendering is not required, as it reduces execution time.

- **Frequent UI Changes**: Applications with rapidly evolving UI designs can cause test scripts to break frequently.

  Solutions:

  - Use a **Page Object Model (POM)** to encapsulate UI interactions, so changes in the UI only require updates in one place.
  - Collaborate closely with developers to adopt a **design-first approach**, ensuring testable and stable UI elements.
  - Regularly update locators and selectors during maintenance cycles to align with UI changes.

- **Handling Dynamic Content:** Dynamic elements such as pop-ups, ads, or real-time data can interfere with test execution.

  Solutions:

  - Implement **retry logic** or polling to handle dynamic content that appears or disappears unpredictably.
  - Use tools such as Playwright's **auto-waiting features** to handle dynamic UI states seamlessly.

- **Debugging Failures**: Debugging UI test failures can be complex due to the involvement of multiple layers and dependencies.

  Solutions:

  - Capture **screenshots and logs** during failures to help diagnose issues quickly.
  - Use debugging tools such as Playwright's built-in trace viewer or Selenium's developer tools integration.

Best Practices Related to Framework Setup and UI Test Design

Adopting best practices ensures the effectiveness, maintainability, and scalability of UI automation frameworks. Here are some guidelines for building robust frameworks and designing high-quality tests:

Framework Setup:

1. **Modular Architecture**
    a. Design the framework with a modular structure, separating test scripts, reusable components, utilities, and configurations.
    b. **Example**: Maintain page objects, utilities for test data generation, and reporting modules in dedicated directories.
2. **Use Modern Tools**
    a. Choose tools such as Playwright or Cypress for their support of modern web standards, ease of parallelization, and debugging capabilities.
    b. Leverage Selenium for compatibility with legacy systems or multi-browser testing.
3. **Centralized Configuration Management**
    a. Store browser settings, environment variables, and test configurations in a single file for easy updates.
    b. Use `.env` files or configuration managers such as Python's `ConfigParser` or JavaScript's `dotenv`.
4. **Integrate CI/CD Pipelines**
    a. Automate test execution in CI/CD pipelines using tools such as Jenkins, GitHub Actions, or CircleCI.
    b. Enable parallel execution to optimize test runtime in continuous integration environments.
5. **Use Dependency Injection:** Inject dependencies such as browser instances or test data into test scripts to improve flexibility and maintainability.

UI Test Design:

1. **Follow the Testing Pyramid:** Limit UI tests to critical workflows and reserve validations for lower layers (for example, API, backend) where feasible.
2. **Prioritize Reusability**

   a. Use reusable test steps, setup scripts, and common utilities to reduce duplication.

   b. Example: Implement reusable login functions or pre-configured data setups.

3. **Page Object Model (POM)**

   a. Use POM to abstract UI interactions, making tests easier to maintain and update.

   b. **Example**: Define methods such as `login()` or `searchForProduct()` in the page class and call them from test scripts.

4. **Use Descriptive Test Names and Assertions**

   a. Write test names that clearly explain the intent of the test and include detailed assertions for precise validations.

   b. **Example**: Instead of naming a test "`Check Login`," use "`Verify User Login with Valid Credentials`."

5. **Parallel Execution and Test Isolation**

   a. Ensure tests are independent of one another to allow parallel execution.

   b. Use tools such as Docker containers to create isolated test environments.

6. **Robust Error Handling and Reporting**

   a. Capture screenshots, logs, and stack traces for failed tests to streamline debugging.

   b. Integrate reporting tools such as Allure or HTML reports to generate detailed summaries of test results.

7. **Mock and Stub External Dependencies:** Avoid reliance on third-party APIs or external services by mocking responses in test scenarios.

By addressing common challenges and adhering to these best practices, teams can build resilient UI automation frameworks that are scalable and efficient, ensuring high-quality software delivery.

Automating API Tests

API testing is a critical layer in the testing pyramid, bridging backend functionality with frontend interfaces. Automating API tests ensures the reliability of data exchanges, service integrations, and business logic. This section covers the essential aspects of automating API tests, including writing and executing API tests, determining the tests that should be included, addressing common challenges, and adhering to best practices.

Writing and Executing API Tests

Automating API tests requires selecting the right tools, defining robust test cases, and integrating these tests into the development lifecycle. As discussed in the previous chapter, API testing can encompass various types, including functional, performance, security, and contract tests. Here, we focus on the execution strategies and tooling for automation.

Example: API test classes using PyTest and Requests

```
# API Layer Tests using PyTest and Requests
import pytest
import requests
from typing import Dict

class TestUserAPI:
    """Test suite for User Management API endpoints"""
    BASE_URL = "https://api.example.com"

    @pytest.fixture
    def auth_headers(self) -> Dict[str, str]:
        """Fixture to provide authentication headers"""
        return {"Authorization": f"Bearer {self._get_auth_to-
ken()}"}

    def test_get_user_profile(self, auth_headers):
        """Test retrieving user profile"""
        response = requests.get(
            f"{self.BASE_URL}/users/profile",
            headers=auth_headers
        )

        assert response.status_code == 200
        data = response.json()
        assert "username" in data
        assert "email" in data

    def test_update_user_profile(self, auth_headers):
        """Test updating user profile"""
        update_data = {
            "display_name": "John Doe",
            "bio": "Software Tester"
        }
```

```
        response = requests.put(
            f"{self.BASE_URL}/users/profile",
            headers=auth_headers,
            json=update_data
        )

        assert response.status_code == 200
        data = response.json()
        assert data["display_name"] == update_data["display_
name"]
        assert data["bio"] == update_data["bio"]
```

Selecting the Right Tools

Modern tools simplify API testing with built-in capabilities for making requests, validating responses, and generating test reports. Common tools include:

- **Postman/Newman**: Ideal for creating collections and executing REST API tests.
- **Pytest + Requests**: A Python-based approach offering flexibility for functional and integration testing.
- **RestAssured**: A Java-based library for validating RESTful APIs with expressive syntax.
- **Karate**: A tool combining API testing, mocking, and performance testing into a unified framework.
- **Tavern**: A YAML-based tool tailored for testing APIs with simple configuration.

Each tool offers unique advantages, and the choice depends on the team's language preferences, API complexity, and CI/CD integration needs.

Writing API Test Cases

API test cases should be structured, concise, and designed for maximum reusability.

1. Define the **endpoint**, HTTP method (GET, POST, PUT, DELETE), headers, and payload.
2. Validate **response codes**, payloads, and headers.
3. Assert **business logic** and any data transformations applied.

Example:

For a "**`Login API`**," write test cases to validate:

- Response status codes (200 for success, 401 for unauthorized).
- Response body structure and specific fields such as **`token`** and **`expiry`**.

- Error messages for invalid credentials.

Executing API Tests

API test execution can occur during development, continuous integration, or dedicated testing phases:

- **Local Development**: Execute API tests locally to verify individual endpoints using tools such as Postman or Pytest.
- **Mock Servers**: Use mock servers to simulate external dependencies or endpoints not yet implemented.
- **CI/CD Pipelines**: Integrate tests into CI/CD pipelines for automated execution on every build, using tools such as Jenkins, GitHub Actions, or CircleCI.
- **Environment-Specific Execution**: Run API tests against different environments (dev, staging, production) to validate consistency.

By automating API tests and integrating them with CI/CD workflows, teams can ensure rapid feedback and continuous validation of service-level functionalities.

Tests Essential for the API Layer

Effective API testing requires a strategic selection of tests that align with the functionality, integration, and reliability of the APIs. In the previous chapters, we discussed different types of API tests, such as functional, contract, and performance tests. This section focuses on the specific tests that should be automated and included in your API test suite, ensuring comprehensive coverage without redundancy.

- **Functional Tests**: Functional tests validate that each API endpoint performs as intended based on the provided input and expected output. These tests form the foundation of API testing.

  Examples:

  - **Login API**: Verify that valid credentials return a `200 OK` status with a token, while invalid credentials return a `401 Unauthorized` error.
  - **Search API**: Ensure the correct results are returned for given search parameters, such as keywords or filters.

- **Negative and Boundary Tests**: Testing how the API handles invalid or extreme inputs is crucial to ensure robustness and proper error handling.

  Examples:

  - Submit a payload with missing or invalid fields to ensure the API returns the correct error messages.

  - Test boundary conditions for input fields, such as the maximum allowed length of a string or the range of numeric inputs.
- **Validation of HTTP Status Codes**: APIs must return appropriate HTTP status codes based on the request and its outcome. Testing status codes ensures clarity in API communication.

  Examples:

  - Verify **`200 OK`** for successful requests.
  - Check **`404 Not Found`** for invalid endpoints.
  - Test **`500 Internal Server Error`** handling for unexpected failures.
- **Contract Tests**: Contract testing ensures that APIs adhere to defined specifications, such as OpenAPI or Swagger, and that changes in API structure do not break integrations.

  Examples:

  - Validate that the API response contains all required fields as per the contract.
  - Ensure that no unexpected fields are introduced that could disrupt consumer applications.
- **Data Integrity Tests:** APIs are often the link between the frontend and backend systems, so data integrity must be validated during exchanges.

  Examples:

  - Test that data retrieved by a **`GET`** request matches the data sent in the corresponding **`POST`** request.
  - Ensure the accuracy of calculations or transformations performed on the server-side before returning the response.
- **Security Tests**: APIs are a common attack vector, making security testing essential.

  Examples:

  - Test for unauthorized access by omitting or tampering with authentication tokens.
  - Verify that sensitive data, such as passwords or tokens, is not exposed in the API responses or error logs.
- **Performance and Load Tests**: API performance under normal and peak loads is critical for scalability and user satisfaction.

Examples:

- Measure response times for endpoints under varying loads (for example, 10, 100, or 1,000 concurrent requests).
- Identify bottlenecks by testing how the API performs under stress conditions beyond expected limits.

- **Dependency Tests**: APIs often depend on external services or databases. Testing these dependencies ensures stable integrations.

  Examples:

  - Verify that third-party service integrations return expected responses within acceptable time limits.
  - Ensure database queries triggered by API calls execute correctly and efficiently.

Common Problems in API Tests

While API testing is essential for ensuring the reliability and performance of modern applications, it is not without challenges. Many issues can arise during the design, execution, and maintenance of API tests, potentially undermining their effectiveness. This section highlights common problems in API testing and offers solutions to mitigate them.

- **Inconsistent Test Environments**: API tests often fail due to differences between development, staging, and production environments. These inconsistencies can lead to false positives or negatives, making test results unreliable.

  Example: A test designed for a development environment might fail in staging because of a missing database or incorrect configuration settings.

  Solution:

  - Use Infrastructure as Code (IaC) tools to standardize environments across all stages.
  - Implement environment-specific configurations in your tests to adapt to different setups.

- **Unstable or Changing APIs**: APIs are subject to changes during development, such as modifications in endpoint paths, request/response structures, or authentication mechanisms. These changes can break existing tests, leading to maintenance overhead.

  Example: A renamed field in the API response (`username` to `user_name`) can cause multiple tests to fail.

Solution:

- Adopt contract testing to catch changes in API specifications early.
- Use mocking tools such as WireMock or Postman to simulate stable API responses during testing.

- **Poor Test Coverage**: Focusing only on happy path scenarios can lead to inadequate coverage, leaving edge cases, error conditions, and security vulnerabilities untested.

  Example: Testing only valid user logins without covering invalid credentials, expired tokens, or missing headers.

  Solution:

  - Incorporate negative, boundary, and security tests to cover all possible scenarios.
  - Use code coverage tools such as JaCoCo or Istanbul to identify gaps in test coverage.

- **Overlapping Tests**: Redundant tests across UI, API, and backend layers increase execution time and maintenance efforts.

  Example: Validating API response data in both API and UI tests unnecessarily duplicates effort.

  Solution:

  - Follow the testing pyramid principles, as discussed earlier, to distribute tests effectively across layers.
  - Keep API tests focused on functionality and leave UI validation to UI tests.

- **Inefficient Data Management:** API tests often require specific data setups, and improper data management can lead to flaky tests or execution failures.

  Example: A test dependent on a user account fails because the account has been deleted or modified during another test run.

  Solution:

  - Use dedicated test environments and seed data for consistency.
  - Implement test isolation by creating and tearing down data during test execution.

- **Dependency on External Services**: APIs often rely on third-party services, which may not always be available or may have usage limits during testing.

  Example: An API test fails because a dependent third-party payment gateway is down.

Solution:

- Use mocks and stubs to simulate responses from external services.
- Configure fallback mechanisms for cases where external dependencies are unavailable.

- **Lack of Assertions**: Failing to include detailed assertions in API tests can result in partial validation, where tests pass even if some functionalities are broken.

  Example: A test checks only the HTTP status code (`200 OK`) but overlooks incorrect response payload data.

  Solution:

  - Include comprehensive assertions for all critical aspects of the response, such as status codes, headers, and payload data.

- **Performance Bottlenecks**: API performance issues may go undetected if tests focus solely on functionality.

  Example: Response times are not monitored, resulting in poor user experiences under load.

  Solution:

  - Incorporate performance and load testing tools, such as JMeter or k6, into your API testing strategy.
  - Set performance benchmarks and monitor trends over time.

Best Practices for API Testing

To ensure effective and efficient API testing, adopting industry best practices is crucial. These practices focus on designing robust test cases, maintaining a scalable framework, and achieving high-quality results. This section outlines key principles for creating a successful API testing strategy.

- **Focus on Test Design:**
  - **Prioritize Key Scenarios:** Identify critical API functionalities and prioritize testing based on business requirements and risk analysis.
  - **Example:** For an e-commerce platform, prioritize testing order placement and payment APIs over less critical features such as promotional banners.
  - **Leverage Test Design Patterns:** Utilize patterns such as Data-Driven Testing and Arrange-Act-Assert (AAA) to create reusable, maintainable test cases.

  Refer to *Chapter* 5, API *Testing Techniques*, for detailed explanations of these patterns.

- **Establish Clear API Specifications**:
    - **Use API Documentation:** Comprehensive documentation, such as OpenAPI or Swagger, ensures that test cases align with API specifications.
    - **Validate API Contracts:** Employ contract testing tools such as Pact or Postman to verify adherence to defined request and response structures.
- **Isolate API Tests**:
    - **Avoid Dependence on Other Layers:** Focus API tests on service functionality rather than UI or backend validations.
    - **Use Mocks and Stubs:** Simulate external services or dependencies using tools such as WireMock or Postman to reduce flakiness and improve test reliability.
- **Automate Strategically**:
    - **Automate Critical Tests First:** Start by automating high-priority test cases, such as authentication and data retrieval APIs.
    - **Integrate Automation into CI/CD:** Run automated API tests during every code build to detect defects early. Use tools such as Jenkins, GitHub Actions, or CircleCI for seamless integration.
- **Include Robust Assertions**:
    - **Validate All Aspects of the Response:** Ensure assertions cover:
        - Status codes (for example, **`200 OK`**, **`404 Not Found`**).
        - Headers (for example, **`Content-Type`**, authentication tokens).
        - Payload structure and content.
    - **Example:** For a product search API, assert the presence of required fields such as **`name`**, **`price`**, and **`availability`**.
- Monitor Performance and Scalability:
    - **Incorporate Load Testing:** Use tools such as JMeter, k6, or Gatling to test API performance under stress and monitor response times, throughput, and error rates.
    - **Set Performance Benchmarks:** Define acceptable thresholds for key metrics such as response time and server CPU usage.
- **Ensure Test Data Management**:
    - **Use Clean Test Data:** Prepare test data that is realistic and isolated to prevent conflicts.
    - **Automate Data Setup and Teardown:** Implement scripts for creating and cleaning up test data to maintain consistency across test runs.

- **Version Control for API Tests**:
  - **Maintain Compatibility:** Test APIs for both current and older versions to ensure backward compatibility.
  - **Automate Version-Specific Tests:** Separate test cases for different API versions to avoid confusion.
- **Collaborate Across Teams**:
  - **Involve Developers Early:** Collaborate with developers to understand API requirements and potential edge cases.
  - **Share Test Results:** Provide detailed reports to stakeholders to ensure transparency and continuous improvement.
- **Emphasize Security Testing**:
  - **Test for Vulnerabilities:** Validate APIs for common vulnerabilities such as SQL injection, XSS, and unauthorized access. Use tools such as OWASP ZAP or Burp Suite.
  - **Validate Authentication Mechanisms:** Test API tokens, session expiration, and encryption to ensure secure communication.
- **Implement Logging and Reporting**:
  - **Detailed Logs:** Capture request payloads, response payloads, and error details to facilitate debugging.
  - **User-Friendly Reports:** Generate clear, actionable reports using tools such as Allure, TestNG, or HTML reports in pytest.
- **Keep Tests Maintainable**:
  - **Follow Naming Conventions:** Use consistent and descriptive names for test cases to enhance readability.
  - **Modularize Test Code:** Organize test scripts into logical modules for easier updates.
  - **Example:** Separate tests by functionality, such as `Authentication_Tests` or `Order_Management_Tests`.

Adopting these best practices ensures that API testing is thorough, efficient, and adaptable to changing requirements. By focusing on design, automation, and collaboration, teams can build a reliable and scalable testing strategy that guarantees API quality and performance.

Automating Backend Tests

Backend tests validate server-side logic, database interactions, and the core functionalities of an application. Effective backend testing ensures the reliability of business logic and data consistency, making it critical for application stability. This section outlines key aspects of backend test automation, including writing and executing tests, identifying appropriate tests, addressing challenges, and following best practices.

Writing and Executing Backend Tests

Backend tests typically focus on validating computations, database operations, and other processes not exposed through APIs or the UI. Tools and frameworks designed for backend testing provide flexibility and scalability.

Example: Unit tests for business logic (Order processing)

```
# Backend Layer Tests
from typing import Optional
import pytest
from datetime import datetime
from decimal import Decimal

class Order:
    def __init__(self, user_id: int, items: list):
        self.user_id = user_id
        self.items = items
        self.total = self._calculate_total()
        self.created_at = datetime.now()
        self.status = "pending"

    def _calculate_total(self) -> Decimal:
        """Calculate order total with discounts"""
        subtotal = sum(item["price"] * item["quantity"] for item
in self.items)

        # Apply discount for orders over $100
        if subtotal > 100:
            return subtotal * Decimal("0.9")  # 10% discount
        return subtotal

    def process(self) -> bool:
        """Process the order"""
        if not self._validate_inventory():
            return False

        self.status = "processed"
        return True

    def _validate_inventory(self) -> bool:
        """Check if all items are in stock"""
```

```
        # In real implementation, this would check a database
        return all(item.get("in_stock", True) for item in self.
items)

class TestOrder:
    """Test suite for Order processing logic"""

    @pytest.fixture
    def sample_order(self) -> Order:
        """Create a sample order for testing"""
        items = [
            {"id": 1, "price": Decimal("50.00"), "quantity": 2},
            {"id": 2, "price": Decimal("25.00"), "quantity": 1}
        ]
        return Order(user_id=1, items=items)

    def test_order_total_calculation(self, sample_order):
        """Test order total calculation with discount"""
        # Total should be (50 * 2 + 25 * 1) * 0.9 = 112.50
        expected_total = Decimal("112.50")
        assert sample_order.total == expected_total

    def test_order_processing(self, sample_order):
        """Test successful order processing"""
        assert sample_order.status == "pending"
        success = sample_order.process()
        assert success
        assert sample_order.status == "processed"

    def test_order_with_out_of_stock_items(self):
        """Test order processing with out of stock items"""
        items = [
            {"id": 1, "price": Decimal("50.00"), "quantity": 1,
"in_stock": False}
        ]
        order = Order(user_id=1, items=items)
        success = order.process()
        assert not success
        assert order.status == "pending"
```

Selecting Tools for Backend Automation:

- **Programming Languages:** Python, Java, JavaScript, or Go are commonly used for backend tests. The choice depends on the application stack.
- **Frameworks and Libraries:** Use testing frameworks that suit backend operations, such as:

  - **Python:** Pytest, Unittest, or Nose2
  - **Java:** JUnit or TestNG
  - **JavaScript:** Mocha or Jest
- **Database Testing Tools:** Use libraries such as `pytest-django` or tools such as DBUnit to automate database validation.
- **Mocking Libraries:** Leverage libraries such as Mock (Python) or Mockito (Java) to isolate backend components.

Types of Backend Tests:

- **Business Logic Validation:** Ensure computations, algorithms, and rules execute correctly.
- **Database Testing:** Validate Create, Read, Update, and Delete (CRUD) operations, stored procedures, and triggers.
- **Data Integrity Checks:** Test database constraints, relationships, and consistency.
- **Batch Processing and Jobs:** Validate scheduled tasks such as ETL jobs or periodic reports.

Executing Backend Tests:

- **Isolate Dependencies:** Use mocks or stubs for external systems or APIs to focus on backend logic.
- **Automate in CI/CD Pipelines:** Run tests after every code build to identify regressions early.
- **Leverage Test Data Factories:** Use scripts or tools to create reusable test data for consistent results.

Tests Relevant to Backend Testing

Backend tests should focus on internal processes critical to application functionality. Examples include:

- **Business Logic Validation**

  Example: In an e-commerce system, verify that discount rules apply correctly based on customer type or order volume.

- **Data Processing and Transformation**

  Example: Test ETL jobs to ensure accurate transformation of raw data into usable formats.

- **Database Operations**

  Example: Validate stored procedures for calculating tax or generating invoices.

- **Integration with External Services**

  Example: Test backend logic handling third-party payment gateways or external data feeds.

- **Error Handling and Edge Cases**

  Example: Simulate scenarios such as database downtime or invalid inputs to verify graceful failure.

Common Problems in Backend Testing

Backend testing comes with challenges that require careful strategies to address, including:

- **Complex Dependencies**
  - **Challenge:** Backend systems often depend on databases, APIs, or third-party services.
  - **Solution:** Use mocking and dependency injection to isolate backend logic for testing.
- **Test Data Management**
  - **Challenge:** Managing consistent and reusable test data is difficult.
  - **Solution:** Use version-controlled test data scripts or database snapshots for setup and teardown.
- **Slow Test Execution**
  - **Challenge:** Extensive database operations or integrations can lead to slow test runs.
  - **Solution:** Focus on unit tests for business logic and use integration tests selectively.
- **Debugging Failures**
  - **Challenge:** Backend failures can be hard to trace due to a lack of visibility.
  - **Solution:** Enable detailed logging and use structured error handling in the backend code.

Best Practices for Backend Testing

Adopting the following practices ensures backend tests are efficient, maintainable, and reliable:

- **Focus on Layer-Specific Logic:** Avoid duplicating tests covered at the API or UI layer. For example, validate data formatting at the API layer, leaving backend tests to handle data storage and retrieval.

- **Use Modular Test Design:** Organize tests into modules based on functionality or components (for example, `User Management Tests`, `Order Processing Tests`).
- **Automate Test Data Management:** Automate the setup and teardown of test environments to maintain consistent results.

  Example: Use tools such as FactoryBoy (Python) or Faker to generate test data.
- **Validate Database Transactions:** Test database rollbacks for error scenarios and ensure transaction integrity.

  Example: Verify that incomplete payment transactions do not create inconsistent order records.
- **Mock External Systems:** Use libraries such as WireMock or responses (Python) to simulate interactions with third-party services.
- **Enable Detailed Logging:** Implement comprehensive logs for backend operations to make debugging easier.
- **Integrate with CI/CD Pipelines:** Ensure backend tests run in CI/CD workflows to catch issues early in the development process.
- **Leverage Code Coverage Metrics:** Use tools such as Coverage.py (Python) or Jacoco (Java) to measure test coverage and identify gaps.
- **Monitor Performance:** Integrate performance testing with backend tests to ensure scalability and reliability under load.

  Example: Use JMeter or k6 to simulate high-volume database queries.
- **Regularly Refactor Tests:** Keep tests up-to-date with changes in the application code to avoid maintenance overhead.

Backend testing is a cornerstone of application reliability, focusing on validating core business logic and database interactions. By implementing the best practices outlined in this section, teams can create a robust and scalable testing strategy.

Automating Non-Functional Tests

Non-functional tests evaluate aspects of software that define its quality, such as performance, reliability, scalability, security, and usability. While functional tests focus on verifying *what* the application does, non-functional tests assess *how well* it performs under various conditions. This section explores writing and executing non-functional tests, identifying relevant tests, addressing challenges, and applying best practices.

Writing and Executing Non-Functional Tests

Non-functional tests often require specialized tools and strategies to simulate real-world conditions and measure system behavior.

Types of Non-Functional Tests:

- **Performance Testing:** Evaluates the speed, responsiveness, and stability of an application under load.
- **Load Testing:** Determines how the application performs under expected user loads.
- **Stress Testing:** Pushes the system beyond its limits to identify breaking points.
- **Scalability Testing:** Assesses the application's ability to scale resources dynamically.
- **Security Testing:** Identifies vulnerabilities in the application and ensures data protection.
- **Usability Testing:** Focuses on the ease of use and intuitiveness of the user interface.

Tools for Non-Functional Testing:

- **Performance and Load Testing Tools:** JMeter, Gatling, Locust, and k6.
- **Security Testing Tools:** OWASP ZAP, Burp Suite, and Nessus.
- **Scalability and Reliability Tools:** Kubernetes Horizontal Pod Autoscaler (HPA) and AWS Auto Scaling.
- **Usability Testing Tools:** Crazy Egg and Optimal Workshop.

Setting Up Non-Functional Tests:

- **Define Metrics:** Clearly define success criteria, such as response time, throughput, error rates, or memory usage.
- **Simulate Realistic Scenarios:** Use tools to mimic real-world traffic, user behavior, and environmental conditions.
- **Monitor and Collect Data:** Leverage monitoring tools such as Grafana, Prometheus, or New Relic for data visualization and analysis.

Core Tests for Non-Functional Scenarios:

Non-functional tests should align with system requirements and business goals.

1. **Performance Benchmarks**

   Example: Test an e-commerce site to ensure pages load within 2 seconds under a load of 500 concurrent users.

2. **Security Vulnerability Testing**

   Example: Run OWASP ZAP to identify SQL injection vulnerabilities in a web application.

3. **Disaster Recovery**

   Example: Simulate server failure to test the failover mechanism and ensure minimal downtime.

4. **Resource Utilization Testing**

   Example: Assess CPU, memory, and network usage during a high-traffic event.

Common Challenges in Non-Functional Testing:

- **Complex Test Environment Setup**
  - **Challenge:** Simulating realistic conditions, such as user loads or security threats, can be resource-intensive.
  - **Solution:** Use cloud-based testing platforms such as BlazeMeter or LambdaTest for scalability and ease of setup.
- **Interpreting Results**
  - **Challenge:** Analyzing large volumes of performance or security data is often overwhelming.
  - **Solution:** Define clear KPIs and automate report generation to focus on actionable insights.
- **High Costs of Tools and Infrastructure**
  - **Challenge:** Non-functional testing tools and environments can be expensive to set up and maintain.
  - **Solution:** Opt for open-source tools or leverage SaaS platforms with pay-as-you-go pricing.
- **Lack of Standardized Metrics**
  - **Challenge:** Different teams may use inconsistent benchmarks for success.
  - **Solution:** Establish organization-wide standards for metrics such as response time and uptime.

Best Practices for Non-Functional Testing

- **Define Clear Goals**
  - Determine the quality attributes to test, such as speed, scalability, or security.
  - Work with stakeholders to prioritize tests based on business impact.

- **Automate Repetitive Tasks**
  - Automate load, stress, and security scans to ensure consistency and reduce manual effort.
  - **Example:** Schedule daily automated scans with OWASP ZAP for early vulnerability detection.
- **Test Early and Continuously**
  - Incorporate non-functional tests into CI/CD pipelines to catch issues early.
  - Use synthetic monitoring for continuous performance testing.
- **Monitor During Production**
  - Conduct non-functional tests in production-like environments for more accurate results.
  - **Example:** Use canary deployments to monitor application behavior under real-world traffic.
- **Use Realistic Data and Traffic**
  - Create data sets and traffic patterns that mirror real-world scenarios.
  - **Example:** For an online store, simulate peak sales events such as Black Friday.
- **Focus on Bottlenecks**
  - Identify and optimize bottlenecks in system performance, such as slow database queries or API response times.
- **Leverage Visualization Tools**
  - Use tools such as Grafana or Kibana for real-time monitoring and actionable insights.
- **Perform Regression Testing**
  - Re-run tests after significant changes to ensure no new issues are introduced.

Non-functional testing is indispensable for ensuring an application is performant, reliable, and secure under varying conditions. By employing the right tools, addressing common challenges, and following best practices, teams can deliver robust and scalable systems.

Real-World Examples and Case Studies

Layered testing strategies are instrumental in delivering high-quality software by validating every aspect of an application across its architecture. This section provides practical examples of how these strategies have been applied in real-world scenarios, highlighting the challenges faced, solutions implemented, and lessons learned from diverse projects.

Practical Examples of Layered Testing Strategies

Here are a few Examples of Layered Testing Strategies:

- **E-Commerce Platform Testing:** An e-commerce company implemented a layered testing strategy to ensure a seamless shopping experience.

  UI Layer:

  - Tested critical user workflows such as login, search, adding items to the cart, and checkout.
  - Automated tests using Playwright verified responsiveness on different devices and browsers.

  API Layer:

  - Validated APIs for product search, inventory updates, and payment processing.
  - Used Postman and pytest to create data-driven tests for scenarios such as out-of-stock items and payment failures.

  Backend Layer:

  - Focused on validating pricing logic, discount rules, and database interactions.
  - Used Python with Pytest to ensure that backend calculations, such as total cost with discounts, were accurate under various scenarios.

Outcome: This layered approach reduced defects in production by 60% and significantly improved the reliability of customer transactions.

- **Microservices-Based Banking Application:** A banking app leveraged a microservices architecture, where testing was distributed across layers to validate critical features such as fund transfers and balance checks.
  - **Challenge:** Ensuring seamless communication between microservices for account management, transaction processing, and notifications.
  - **Solution:**
    - **API Layer:** Contract testing using Pact ensured that each microservice adhered to defined communication protocols.
    - **Backend Layer:** Unit tests validated transaction calculations such as interest accrual and penalty deductions.

        - **UI Layer:** End-to-end tests simulated user scenarios such as fund transfers between accounts.
    - **Results:**
        - Early detection of integration issues between services.
        - Faster resolution of errors by pinpointing failures to specific microservices.

Challenges Faced and Solutions Implemented

Now, we will discuss some challenges faced and how they can be solved.

Challenge 1: Overlapping Tests Across Layers

During a project for a logistics company, the team found redundancy between API and UI tests, leading to longer execution times and higher maintenance overhead.

Solution:

- Refined the testing strategy to ensure that API validations, such as response codes and payload structures, were tested exclusively in the API layer.
- UI tests focused only on user workflows and visual validation, reducing the total execution time by 40%.

Challenge 2: Flaky Tests in CI/CD Pipelines

A SaaS company encountered frequent failures in UI tests due to inconsistent loading times in their CI/CD pipeline.

Solution:

- Added lower-layer test cases to lessen the burden on UI tests.
- Introduced dynamic waits in UI tests to handle varying response times.
- Leveraged containerized environments to ensure consistent test setups, resulting in a 70% reduction in false positives.

Challenge 3: Testing Complex Dependencies

For a healthcare application, backend testing was challenging due to dependencies on external APIs and third-party databases.

Solution:

- Implemented mocks and stubs to simulate external dependencies.
- Created integration tests that validated interactions with the actual APIs in a staging environment.
- This strategy ensured that backend logic was thoroughly tested without being hindered by dependency availability.

Lessons Learned from Real-World Applications

- **Layered Testing Reduces Risk:** Dividing responsibilities across layers ensures that issues are caught early and at the appropriate level, minimizing the likelihood of cascading failures.
- **Avoid Over-Testing:** Excessive overlap between layers leads to inefficiency. A clear distinction of responsibilities reduces redundancy while maintaining high coverage.
- **Invest in Automation:** Automation frameworks tailored to each layer, such as Playwright for UI, Postman for API, and Pytest for backend, streamline test execution and improve accuracy.
- **Communication is Key:** Collaboration between developers, testers, and DevOps teams ensures that layered testing strategies are aligned with project goals.
- **Adapt to Project Needs:** Real-world constraints such as tight deadlines or infrastructure limitations require flexibility in test planning and execution.

By applying layered testing strategies effectively, teams can enhance application quality and maintain robust test coverage. These examples and case studies illustrate the value of tailoring testing approaches to the application's architecture and learning from challenges to refine processes.

Best Practices and Common Pitfalls in Layered Testing

A robust layered testing strategy ensures comprehensive application coverage while minimizing redundancy. However, achieving stability, avoiding pitfalls, and maintaining test suites can be challenging. This section outlines best practices for implementing layered testing effectively and highlights common pitfalls to avoid.

Ensuring Test Stability and Reliability

1. **Focus on Clear Test Objectives**

    a. Each test should have a defined goal aligned with the specific layer's responsibility.

    b. Avoid vague assertions or overlapping validations between layers.

    c. Example: UI tests should validate workflows, while API tests confirm data integrity.

2. **Implement Dynamic Waiting Mechanisms**
    a. In UI tests, use dynamic waits instead of fixed delays to handle variable loading times.
    b. **Example**: Use Selenium's `WebDriverWait` to wait for elements to load rather than applying arbitrary sleep intervals.
3. **Use Mocking and Stubbing for External Dependencies**
    a. Simulate external services in API and backend tests to isolate the application logic and ensure consistent results.
    b. **Example**: Mock external payment gateways in API tests to validate the application's handling of responses.
4. **Run Tests in Controlled Environments**
    a. Use containerized or virtualized environments to minimize variability and ensure consistent setups.
    b. **Example**: Run tests in Docker containers to replicate identical environments in local and CI/CD pipelines.
5. **Regularly Review and Update Tests**
    a. Update tests to reflect changes in application features or architecture.
    b. **Example**: When introducing new API endpoints, revise both existing API tests and their corresponding integration tests.

Avoiding Common Mistakes

- **Duplication Across Layers**
    - **Mistake:** Re-validating the same logic at multiple layers unnecessarily.
    - **Impact:** Increases execution time and maintenance overhead.
    - **Solution:** Clearly delineate responsibilities:
        - API layer handles data validation and business rules.
        - UI layer focuses on workflows and user interactions.
        - The backend layer tests internal logic and data processing.
    - **Example:** Avoid testing API response formats in UI tests if they are already covered in API tests.
- **Over-Reliance on UI Tests**
    - **Mistake:** Using UI tests for validations that could be handled at the API or backend layers.

- **Impact:** Leads to flaky tests and longer execution times.
- **Solution:** Limit UI tests to essential workflows and visual validations.
- **Example:** Test error messages for invalid inputs at the API level rather than using UI automation.

- **Ignoring Test Data Management**
  - **Mistake:** Using hardcoded or inconsistent test data across layers.
  - **Impact:** Leads to unreliable tests and difficulties in reproducing failures.
  - **Solution:** Centralize test data management using parameterized tests or test data factories for consistency.
  - **Example:** Use a shared configuration file for environment-specific data such as API URLs or credentials.
- **Neglecting Maintenance**
  - **Mistake:** Allowing obsolete or irrelevant tests to accumulate.
  - **Impact:** Bloats the test suite, leading to longer execution times and reduced clarity.
  - **Solution:** Periodically review and refactor test cases to remove redundancies and outdated scenarios.

Maintaining Test Suites as Applications Evolve

1. **Adopt a Modular Test Design**
   - Create reusable components for common functionalities, such as login steps or database setup.
   - **Example**: A shared `setup_user()` function can be used across API and backend tests.
2. **Use Version Control for Test Code**
   - Store test scripts in version control systems such as Git to track changes and revert if necessary.
   - **Example**: Maintain separate branches for test development and stable versions aligned with the application release cycle.
3. **Integrate with Continuous Integration/Continuous Deployment (CI/CD)**
   - Automate test execution at various pipeline stages to catch defects early.
   - **Example**: Run unit and integration tests on pull requests, with UI tests reserved for staging or pre-release builds.

4. **Monitor and Address Flaky Tests**
    - Identify and resolve tests that fail intermittently due to timing issues, dependencies, or environmental factors.
    - **Example**: Log test failures and analyze patterns to pinpoint recurring flaky tests.
5. **Encourage Collaboration Between Teams**
    - Foster communication between developers, testers, and DevOps to ensure alignment on testing objectives.
    - **Example**: Hold regular discussions on how application changes impact the test strategy.

Common Pitfalls and How to Avoid Them

- **Ignoring Test Coverage Gaps**
    - **Pitfall:** Overlooking critical scenarios due to a lack of traceability.
    - **Solution:** Use a traceability matrix to map requirements to test cases, ensuring no functionality is missed.
- **Testing Non-Critical Features at the UI Level**
    - **Pitfall:** Testing low-priority workflows through UI tests instead of faster, reliable lower-layer tests.
    - **Solution:** Evaluate feature criticality and test accordingly, reserving UI tests for essential user-facing features.
- **Lack of Scalability in Frameworks**
    - **Pitfall:** Designing test frameworks that are hard to extend as the application grows.
    - **Solution:** Build modular and scalable frameworks using design patterns such as Page Object Model (POM) or Factory patterns for UI and API tests.
- **Delayed Feedback Loops**
    - **Pitfall:** Running all tests at the end of the pipeline instead of distributing them.
    - **Solution:** Run faster tests (unit, API) earlier in the pipeline and reserve UI tests for pre-deployment stages.

Layered testing requires balancing thorough validation with efficient execution. By following best practices such as modular test design, dynamic waits, and targeted testing at appropriate layers, teams can maintain stable and reliable test suites. Avoiding pitfalls such as duplication, over-testing, and poor test maintenance ensures streamlined workflows and adaptability as the application evolves. These strategies not only reduce testing overhead but also enhance confidence in the overall quality of the software.

Conclusion

In this chapter, we delved into the practical implementation of layered testing strategies, emphasizing their role in creating efficient and effective testing processes. Starting with an overview of writing and executing tests across different layers–UI, API, and backend–we highlighted the importance of aligning each test with its designated layer to achieve comprehensive coverage. This included identifying which tests are most suitable for each layer and discussing scenarios where tests should be avoided or redistributed to other layers for better efficiency.

We also examined non-functional tests and their role in evaluating system behavior under various conditions, such as load, stress, and security. Furthermore, we introduced integrating layered tests into CI/CD pipelines, outlining the benefits of running tests at appropriate stages to identify issues early in the development lifecycle. Practical case studies and real-world examples illustrate how layered testing strategies are applied, showcasing challenges faced and solutions implemented in diverse scenarios.

The chapter concluded with a detailed discussion of best practices, emphasizing the stability, reliability, and maintainability of test suites. Common pitfalls, such as test duplication, over-testing, and neglecting maintenance, were addressed alongside strategies to mitigate them, ensuring long-term efficiency and scalability of the testing process. As we move forward, the next chapter will focus on the detailed process of integrating layered tests into CI/CD pipelines. It will explore advanced workflows, tools, and techniques for seamless integration, enabling teams to build robust and continuous testing frameworks.

Key Takeaways

- **Layered Testing as a Foundation for Comprehensive Coverage**: Distributing tests across UI, API, and backend layers ensures efficient testing while maintaining the focus on layer-specific validations.
- **Tests to Include and Avoid**: Prioritizing tests based on criticality and execution speed enhances the efficiency of layered testing. Avoiding over-reliance on UI tests and redundancy across layers prevents unnecessary complexity.
- **Role of Non-Functional Tests**: Non-functional testing evaluates system performance, scalability, and security, providing insights into the application's readiness for real-world scenarios.
- **Integrating Layered Tests in CI/CD Pipelines**: Automated workflows in CI/CD pipelines help identify defects early, ensure test reliability, and optimize feedback loops for development teams.

- **Best Practices for Stability and Reliability**: Modular design, dynamic waits, and effective test maintenance strategies are crucial for sustaining robust test suites as applications evolve.
- **Common Pitfalls and How to Avoid Them**: Avoiding duplication, over-testing, and poorly managed test data ensures an efficient and reliable testing strategy across all layers.

This chapter equips you with actionable strategies to implement and optimize layered testing in your projects. In the upcoming chapter, we will delve deeper into CI/CD pipelines, exploring how to seamlessly integrate automated testing at every stage of the development lifecycle to achieve faster, more reliable releases.

CHAPTER 8

Integrating Tests into CI/CD Pipelines

Introduction

In this chapter, we will explore the integration of automated tests into Continuous Integration and Continuous Deployment (CI/CD) pipelines, a cornerstone of modern software delivery practices. CI/CD pipelines automate the process of building, testing, and deploying code, enabling teams to deliver high-quality software at speed. By incorporating automated tests at various stages of the pipeline, from unit tests to UI tests, we ensure that every code change is validated for correctness, reliability, and performance.

We will discuss the strategies and techniques for integrating layered tests–unit, API, backend, and UI–into CI/CD workflows, leveraging popular tools such as GitHub Actions, Jenkins, CircleCI, and GitLab CI/CD. Additionally, we will cover key considerations such as managing test environments, handling test data, and maintaining pipeline efficiency.

By the end of this chapter, you will be equipped to design robust CI/CD pipelines that incorporate automated tests seamlessly, ensuring continuous feedback and fostering a culture of high-quality, rapid delivery. This foundational understanding will prepare you for scaling these practices in more advanced scenarios, discussed in future chapters.

Structure

In this chapter, we will explore the integration of **automated tests into CI/CD pipelines**, highlighting strategies for ensuring consistent and reliable testing across all stages of the software delivery process. Here is what we will cover:

- Introduction to CI/CD Pipelines
- Importance of Test Automation in CI/CD
- Overview of Popular CI/CD Tools

- Designing CI/CD Pipelines for Automated Testing
- Best Practices and Common Pitfalls in CI/CD Test Integration

Introduction to CI/CD Pipelines

Continuous Integration and Continuous Deployment/Delivery (CI/CD) pipelines are foundational to modern software development practices. They represent an automated workflow that integrates and deploys code changes efficiently, ensuring a seamless and reliable software delivery process. At their core, CI/CD pipelines aim to reduce manual intervention, minimize errors, and deliver updates rapidly without compromising quality.

The Purpose of CI/CD Pipelines

The primary goal of a CI/CD pipeline is to enable teams to release high-quality software at speed. CI/CD pipelines achieve this by automating tasks such as building, testing, and deploying code, ensuring that each change made by developers is verified through a consistent process. This approach significantly reduces the risk of introducing bugs into production environments and facilitates frequent, incremental updates.

For example, in a traditional development process, integrating code changes from multiple developers often led to "*integration hell*," where the merging of code caused unexpected issues. CI/CD pipelines address this by integrating code frequently and validating it through automated tests, catching problems early in the development lifecycle.

Key Components of CI/CD Pipelines

The following are the key components of CI/CD pipelines:

- **Continuous Integration (CI):** CI focuses on automating the process of merging code changes into a shared repository multiple times a day. Each change triggers an automated workflow that includes:
  - **Code Compilation:** Ensuring the codebase is buildable after integration.
  - **Unit and Integration Testing:** Validating that new changes do not break existing functionality.
  - **Static Code Analysis:** Checking for potential bugs, vulnerabilities, and adherence to coding standards.
- The frequent feedback provided by CI helps developers address issues quickly and maintain a stable codebase.

- **Continuous Deployment/Delivery (CD):** Continuous Deployment and Continuous Delivery build on CI by automating the deployment of code to production or staging environments. The two terms differ slightly:
    - **Continuous Delivery** involves automating the deployment process up to a staging environment, with manual approval for production deployment.
    - **Continuous Deployment** takes it further by automating the entire deployment process, delivering updates directly to production without manual intervention.
- Both practices emphasize delivering value to users faster while maintaining high reliability and reducing downtime.

Evolution of CI/CD Pipelines

CI/CD pipelines have evolved from simple build-and-test scripts to sophisticated workflows capable of handling complex requirements. Early CI/CD systems required custom scripts and manual setups. However, advancements in tooling have transformed these pipelines into highly configurable systems integrated with version control, cloud platforms, and testing frameworks.

Modern CI/CD pipelines leverage containerization technologies, such as Docker, and orchestration platforms, such as Kubernetes, to ensure consistency across environments. They also integrate with various third-party tools to enable comprehensive testing, monitoring, and deployment capabilities.

The Role of CI/CD Pipelines in Fast and Reliable Delivery Cycles

In today's fast-paced development environments, CI/CD pipelines play a critical role in maintaining a competitive advantage. They enable teams to:

- **Deliver Faster:** Automating repetitive tasks accelerates the development process.
- **Ensure Reliability:** Rigorous automated testing ensures only high-quality changes reach production.
- **Improve Collaboration:** CI/CD fosters a culture of shared responsibility, encouraging frequent code sharing and collaboration among team members.

For instance, a team adopting CI/CD pipelines can achieve daily or even multiple deployments per day compared to traditional release cycles of weeks or months. This agility is essential for responding to user feedback, fixing bugs, and rolling out new features efficiently.

CI/CD pipelines are more than just a toolset; they represent a philosophy of continuous improvement and delivery. As we explore the subsequent sections of this chapter, we will delve deeper into the strategies, tools, and best practices for integrating tests into these pipelines to enhance software quality and delivery speed.

Importance of Test Automation in CI/CD

Test automation is a cornerstone of effective CI/CD workflows, enabling teams to deliver high-quality software at speed. By integrating automated testing into the CI/CD pipeline, organizations can ensure consistent validation of code changes, reduce manual effort, and minimize the risk of defects making their way into production environments. It aligns perfectly with the goals of DevOps, fostering collaboration, efficiency, and reliability across the software development lifecycle.

Consistent Validation of Code Changes

In a CI/CD workflow, code changes are integrated frequently, sometimes multiple times a day. Each integration triggers a series of automated processes, including builds, tests, and deployments. Automated testing ensures that these changes are continuously validated against predefined criteria, such as:

- **Unit Tests:** Verifying individual components of the application.
- **Integration Tests:** Ensuring that different modules or services work together as expected.
- **Functional Tests:** Validating end-to-end functionality from a user's perspective.

The consistency provided by automated testing eliminates the variability inherent in manual testing, ensuring that every change undergoes the same rigorous validation process. This approach reduces the likelihood of defects slipping through due to human oversight or fatigue.

For example, automated regression tests can instantly check whether a new feature breaks existing functionality, providing immediate feedback to developers. This rapid feedback loop enables teams to address issues early, reducing the cost and complexity of fixes.

Reduction of Manual Effort

Manual testing, while valuable in exploratory and usability contexts, is time-consuming and resource-intensive when applied to repetitive tasks. Automating repetitive test cases allows QA teams to focus on more complex and creative testing scenarios that require human insight.

In CI/CD pipelines, automated tests can be executed concurrently across multiple environments, dramatically reducing the time required for validation. This is particularly crucial for large applications with extensive test suites, where manual execution would be impractical.

For example:

- Automated smoke tests can quickly verify whether a build is stable enough for further testing.
- Performance tests can simulate high user loads without manual intervention, ensuring the system meets performance benchmarks.

By reducing manual effort, teams can allocate their resources more efficiently, improving productivity and overall software quality.

Minimizing Risk of Defects in Production

A critical advantage of test automation in CI/CD pipelines is its ability to catch defects before they reach production. Automated testing enables the early identification of issues in areas such as:

- **Code Quality:** Static analysis tools can detect code smells and vulnerabilities before the code is even compiled.
- **Functionality:** Automated functional tests ensure that new features behave as expected across various scenarios.
- **Security:** Tools such as Dynamic Application Security Testing (DAST) can identify vulnerabilities in real time during deployment.

By identifying and addressing issues early in the pipeline, organizations can significantly reduce the risk of costly production failures, data breaches, or service downtime.

Test Automation and DevOps Practices

Test automation is a key enabler of DevOps, the cultural and technical movement focused on unifying development and operations teams to deliver software faster and more reliably. DevOps emphasizes automation as a fundamental principle, and test automation plays a pivotal role in achieving its objectives.

- **Continuous Feedback:** Automated tests provide immediate feedback on the impact of code changes, allowing teams to make informed decisions quickly.
- **Shift Left Testing:** Test automation encourages testing early in the development cycle, catching issues before they escalate.
- **Collaboration:** Automated test results are accessible to all stakeholders, promoting transparency and fostering collaboration across teams.

For instance, a DevOps team using automated testing can seamlessly integrate security testing into their CI/CD pipeline, identifying vulnerabilities as part of their daily workflows rather than during a separate testing phase. This integrated approach reduces silos and streamlines the path to production.

Supporting Rapid and Reliable Releases

In an environment where speed to market is a competitive advantage, test automation is indispensable. It enables organizations to achieve:

- **Faster Deployment Cycles:** Automated tests eliminate bottlenecks, allowing for frequent and rapid releases.
- **Reliable Updates:** Every release is accompanied by a suite of validated tests, ensuring reliability and stability.
- **Scalability:** As applications grow, automated tests can scale alongside them, providing consistent coverage without additional manual effort.

By embedding automated testing into CI/CD workflows, teams not only improve their software's quality and reliability but also create a robust foundation for innovation and agility. As we progress through this chapter, we will explore how specific types of tests (unit, API, and UI) can be integrated into CI/CD pipelines to maximize these benefits.

Overview of Popular CI/CD Tools

The choice of a CI/CD tool can significantly impact the efficiency and reliability of software delivery pipelines. Each tool has unique strengths tailored to specific use cases, from straightforward configuration to extensive customization and scalability. We shall now explore some of the most widely used CI/CD tools: GitHub Actions, Jenkins, CircleCI, and GitLab CI/CD.

GitHub Actions

GitHub Actions is a built-in CI/CD tool for repositories hosted on GitHub, enabling developers to automate workflows directly within the platform. It allows you to define workflows in YAML files stored in your repository, making the setup intuitive and closely integrated with version control.

Key Features:

- **Tight GitHub Integration:** Seamlessly integrates with GitHub's pull requests, issues, and events, enabling trigger-based workflows.
- **YAML Configuration:** Workflows are defined using YAML files (`.github/workflows/`), making them easy to version and share.
- **Prebuilt and Custom Actions:** Access to thousands of community-contributed actions and the ability to create custom ones.

- **Scalability:** Supports both GitHub-hosted runners for quick setups and self-hosted runners for customized environments.
- **Cost-Efficiency:** Free tier available for public repositories, with paid plans for private repositories.

Use Cases: GitHub Actions is ideal for small to medium-sized teams using GitHub as their primary version control platform. Its seamless integration ensures smooth workflows for tasks such as:

- Running unit tests on every pull request.
- Deploying applications to cloud platforms such as AWS, Azure, or Google Cloud.

Limitations: While it excels in GitHub-centered workflows, GitHub Actions might not be as feature-rich for teams needing extensive integrations outside of GitHub.

Jenkins

Jenkins is one of the most mature and widely adopted CI/CD tools. An open-source solution, it is known for its flexibility, extensive plugin ecosystem, and ability to cater to diverse automation needs.

Key Features:

- **Plugin Ecosystem:** Over 1,800 plugins enable integration with various tools, platforms, and services.
- **Customizability:** Jenkins can be tailored to meet specific requirements, from basic CI/CD tasks to complex workflows.
- **Self-Hosting:** Runs on-premises or on cloud servers, giving teams control over their CI/CD infrastructure.
- **Pipeline-as-Code:** Jenkins pipelines can be defined using the Groovy scripting language, allowing for complex automation.
- **Community Support:** A large user community provides extensive documentation and troubleshooting resources.

Use Cases: Jenkins is well-suited for large organizations or teams requiring extensive customization, such as:

- Multi-stage deployment pipelines for enterprise-grade applications.
- Integration with legacy systems using custom plugins.

Limitations: Jenkins has a steeper learning curve compared to modern cloud-based tools. Additionally, maintaining and scaling Jenkins servers can be resource-intensive.

CircleCI

CircleCI is a cloud-based CI/CD tool designed for simplicity and high performance. It offers streamlined workflows and minimal setup, making it an excellent choice for teams that value speed and usability.

Key Features:

- **Ease of Use:** Intuitive configuration and minimal infrastructure overhead make it accessible for new users.
- **Parallelism:** Efficiently runs tests and tasks in parallel, reducing build times.
- **Environment Flexibility:** Supports Docker, virtual machines, and macOS environments for diverse build requirements.
- **Insights Dashboard:** Provides detailed metrics and visualizations of build performance.
- **Scalability:** Cloud-native, enabling effortless scaling for growing teams.

Use Cases: CircleCI excels in scenarios requiring rapid development cycles, such as:

- Continuous delivery for mobile and web applications.
- Agile workflows where frequent integrations and deployments are critical.

Limitations: While CircleCI is highly efficient for standard workflows, advanced customizations may require additional effort compared to tools such as Jenkins.

GitLab CI/CD

GitLab CI/CD is an integrated solution built into GitLab repositories, offering a seamless code-to-deployment pipeline. It provides end-to-end capabilities from version control to deployment, reducing the need for additional tools.

Key Features:

- **Integration with GitLab:** Deep integration with GitLab's issue tracking, merge requests, and version control.
- **YAML Configuration:** Pipelines are defined using **`.gitlab-ci.yml`** files, keeping the configuration in the same repository as the codebase.
- **Built-in Docker Support:** Simplifies containerized builds with native Docker support.
- **Self-Hosted and Cloud Options:** Available as part of GitLab's cloud service or as a self-hosted solution for greater control.
- **Security Scanning:** Built-in security scanning for vulnerabilities, enhancing DevSecOps practices.

Use Cases: GitLab CI/CD is an excellent choice for teams already using GitLab as their version control system. Common applications include:

- Automating build, test, and deployment workflows for DevOps teams.
- Integrated security and compliance workflows for regulated industries.

Limitations: GitLab CI/CD's features are tied closely to the GitLab ecosystem, which may be limiting for teams using other platforms or tools.

Each of these tools–GitHub Actions, Jenkins, CircleCI, and GitLab CI/CD–has distinct strengths, making them suitable for different teams and projects. Whether your priority is tight version control integration, extensive customization, ease of use, or a comprehensive end-to-end solution, these tools provide robust options for building and optimizing CI/CD pipelines. As we progress through this chapter, we will explore how these tools can be leveraged to integrate automated tests across various layers, enhancing the effectiveness of your CI/CD strategy.

Designing CI/CD Pipelines for Automated Testing

A well-structured CI/CD pipeline is essential for ensuring consistent validation of code changes, streamlining development, and maintaining high software quality. By integrating testing at multiple stages, teams can catch defects early, validate functionality, and ensure a smooth deployment process. This section explores the design principles of effective CI/CD pipelines, the structure of stages and jobs, and a high-level example tailored to a Python project.

Key Components of a CI/CD Pipeline:

- **Pipeline Stages:** Stages are distinct phases of a CI/CD pipeline, each representing a group of related tasks. Stages are executed sequentially or in parallel, depending on their dependencies. Common stages include:
    - **Code Checkout:** Fetching the latest changes from version control.
    - **Build/Compile:** Preparing the application or environment.
    - **Testing:** Running various automated tests (unit, integration, API, and UI).
    - **Deployment:** Deploying the application to staging or production environments.
- **Jobs:** Jobs are the tasks executed within a stage. For example, in a "*Testing*" stage, one job may run unit tests, while another runs API tests. Jobs can be run in parallel to optimize pipeline execution time.
- **Dependencies:** Dependencies define the order in which jobs or stages must be executed. For example, unit tests may depend on the environment being

set up, while integration tests depend on the successful completion of unit tests.

- **Artifacts and Cache:** Artifacts are files or outputs generated during a job (for example, test reports), while caching stores reusable files (for example, dependencies) to reduce execution time in subsequent runs.

Design Principles for an Effective Pipeline

Here are the design principles for an effective pipeline:

- **Automated Validation at Every Stage:** Ensure testing is seamlessly integrated at every critical stage of the pipeline to catch defects early.
- **Parallel Execution:** Use parallel jobs to reduce overall execution time.
- **Fail Fast:** Configure the pipeline to stop execution when critical tests fail, avoiding unnecessary resource consumption.
- **Scalability:** Design the pipeline to handle increasing workloads as the project grows.
- **Environment Parity:** Ensure test and staging environments closely mimic production for accurate results.

High-Level Example of a Python CI/CD Pipeline

Here is an example of a CI/CD pipeline for a Python project, demonstrating the integration of testing at multiple stages:

Stage 1: Code Checkout

a. **Purpose:** Fetch the latest code from version control (for example, GitHub).

b. **Tasks:**

   i. Clone the repository.

   ii. Checkout the desired branch or commit.

   iii. Verify repository integrity.

Example YAML:

```
stages:
  - checkout
jobs:
  code_checkout:
    stage: checkout
    script:
      - git clone https://github.com/user/repo.git
      - cd repo
```

Stage 2: Environment Setup

a. **Purpose:** Install dependencies and prepare the runtime environment.

b. **Tasks:**

   i. Install Python and necessary libraries (for example, using **`requirements.txt`**).

   ii. Set up virtual environments or Docker containers.

Example YAML:

```
stages:
  - setup
jobs:
  setup_environment:
    stage: setup
    script:
      - python -m venv venv
      - source venv/bin/activate
      - pip install -r requirements.txt
```

Stage 3: Static Code Analysis

a. **Purpose:** Perform linting and static code analysis to ensure code quality.

b. **Tasks:**

   i. Run tools such as **`flake8`** or **`pylint`**.

   ii. Generate reports on code quality.

Example YAML:

```
stages:
  - analysis
jobs:
  static_analysis:
    stage: analysis
    script:
      - flake8 src/ > flake8_report.txt
```

Stage 4: Unit Test Execution

a. **Purpose:** Validate individual components or functions of the application.

b. **Tasks:**

   i. Run unit tests using PyTest.

   ii. Generate test coverage reports.

Example YAML:

```yaml
stages:
  - test
jobs:
  unit_tests:
    stage: test
    script:
      - pytest --cov=src
```

Stage 5: Integration and API Test Execution

a. **Purpose:** Verify the integration between components and the functionality of APIs.

b. **Tasks:**

   i. Run integration tests.

   ii. Use tools such as **`requests`** or **`Postman`** collections for API testing.

Example YAML:

```yaml
jobs:
  api_tests:
    stage: test
    script:
      - pytest tests/integration/
```

Stage 6: UI Test Execution

a. **Purpose:** Validate the user interface and end-to-end flows.

b. **Tasks:** Execute tests using Selenium or Playwright.

Example YAML:

```yaml
jobs:
  ui_tests:
    stage: test
    script:
      - playwright test
```

Stage 7: Deployment to Staging

a. **Purpose:** Deploy the application to a staging environment for further validation.

b. **Tasks:**

   i. Push the built application or container to a staging server.

   ii. Run smoke tests to ensure deployment success.

Example YAML:

```
stages:
  - deploy
jobs:
  deploy_to_staging:
    stage: deploy
    script:
      - docker build -t my-app:staging .
      - docker run -d -p 8080:8080 my-app:staging
```

This structured pipeline ensures comprehensive testing at every critical stage of development, from checking code quality to validating user-facing features. By automating these steps, teams can achieve faster feedback cycles, minimize risks, and streamline deployments, paving the way for reliable and efficient software delivery.

Example of a CI/CD Pipeline with Layered Testing

Layered testing in a CI/CD pipeline ensures that each layer of the application is thoroughly validated through the appropriate type of testing. The goal is to catch issues early and progressively validate functionality, integration, and performance as the application moves closer to production.

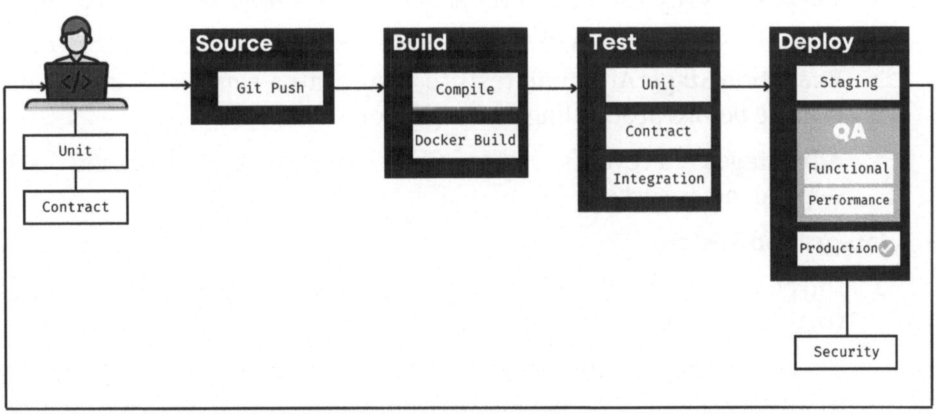

Figure 8.1: *Example of a CI/CD Pipeline with Layered Testing*

Let us analyze the image of the CI/CD pipeline:

Stages of the CI/CD Pipeline

The following are the three stages of the CI/CD pipeline:

1. **Source**: The pipeline begins when changes are pushed to the version control system (for example, Git). This triggers the pipeline and ensures the source code meets the initial quality gates.

2. **Build**: Code compilation and artifact generation occur at this stage. This might include creating binaries or building Docker images. It ensures the codebase is in a deployable state.

3. **Test**: A comprehensive suite of tests is run across different layers to validate the functionality, security, and performance of the application. The following types of tests are performed at different stages:

Types of Tests in the Pipeline

Here is a list of the types of tests in the pipeline:

- **Unit Tests**:
    - **Purpose**: Validate individual components or functions in isolation.
    - **Execution Stage**: Immediately after the code compilation to catch basic issues.
    - **Advantages**: Fast execution time and precise identification of problems in small code units.
- **Contract Tests**:
    - **Purpose**: Verify the interactions between services by ensuring that they meet the agreed-upon APIs or data contracts.
    - **Execution Stage**: After unit tests to ensure inter-service communication is reliable before proceeding to integration.
    - **Advantages**: Prevents integration failures by validating service dependencies early.
- **Integration Tests**:
    - **Purpose**: Test combined components or services to ensure they work together as expected.
    - **Execution Stage**: After contract tests, in an isolated environment such as a Docker container or staging environment.
    - **Advantages**: Detects defects in how components interact, complementing unit tests.
- **QA Tests (Functional)**:
    - **Purpose**: Validate the end-to-end workflows and functionality as experienced by the end-user.
    - **Execution Stage**: Post-integration in a staging environment to mimic production scenarios.
    - **Advantages**: Ensures the application meets functional requirements and business needs.

- **Performance Tests**:
  - **Purpose**: Assess the application's performance, including responsiveness and load handling.
  - **Execution Stage**: Usually in a staging or pre-production environment.
  - **Advantages**: Identifies bottlenecks and scalability issues before deployment.
- **Security Tests**:
  - **Purpose**: Analyze the application's security to uncover vulnerabilities and ensure compliance.
  - **Execution Stage**: Integrated after contract or integration tests.
  - **Advantages**: Strengthens security posture and prevents breaches.

Deployment Stages

Let us take a brief look at the deployment stages:

1. **Staging**: A near-production environment where the application is deployed after passing QA and performance tests. Additional manual or exploratory testing may occur here.
2. **Production**: The final step is where the validated application is deployed to the live environment, accessible by end-users.

By integrating these layers of testing into the CI/CD pipeline, teams can ensure a robust, scalable, and secure application while maintaining a fast release cycle.

Handling Test Data and Environments

In a CI/CD pipeline, managing test data and environments effectively is crucial to ensure that tests are reliable, reproducible, and consistent. As part of the automation process, it is essential to have a well-defined strategy for generating, seeding, and handling test data, setting up consistent test environments, and securely managing environment variables and secrets. This section covers techniques for managing test data and environments in CI/CD pipelines, focusing on test data generation, using Docker for consistency, and securely handling environment variables and secrets.

Test Data Generation and Seeding

Test data plays a critical role in validating the functionality of your application during testing. Without appropriate test data, automated tests could fail to mimic real-world scenarios, leading to incomplete or inaccurate results.

Techniques for Test Data Generation:

- **Automated Data Generation:**
  - For unit and integration tests, it is often useful to generate mock data or use fixtures. Frameworks such as **`pytest`** provide ways to generate dynamic test data before tests are run.
  - In Python, libraries such as **`Faker`** can be used to generate random data (for example, names, emails, addresses), making the tests more representative of real-world data.

Example:

```
from faker import Faker
fake = Faker()

def test_create_user():
    user_data = {
        'name': fake.name(),
        'email': fake.email(),
        'address': fake.address(),
    }
    # Proceed with test using the generated user_data
```

- **Database Seeding for Integration Tests:**
  - When testing applications that interact with databases, it is essential to seed the database with known test data. Automated seeding scripts can populate the database with valid data before each test run.
  - For example, you can write a Python script to insert a predefined set of users, products, or other entities into the database to simulate various test scenarios.
  - This approach ensures that each test starts with the same data, creating consistency and repeatability.
- **Use of Mocking Frameworks:**
  - For API and service-level testing, you can mock the data returned by external services. This is particularly important for tests that rely on external APIs, where using live data might be expensive, slow, or unreliable.
  - Frameworks such as **`unittest.mock`** in Python, or tools such as **`WireMock`**, allow you to simulate responses from external APIs, ensuring your tests remain isolated and focused on the application logic.
- **Data Management in Load Testing:**
  - In performance testing, managing large datasets is crucial. Tools such as **`Locust`** or **`JMeter`** can be used to simulate a large number of users and

generate high volumes of test data dynamically to simulate real-world load on the system.

Using Docker for Consistent Environments

One of the most effective ways to ensure consistency across environments in a CI/CD pipeline is to use Docker containers. Docker allows developers and testers to define the entire application stack, including the application code, libraries, dependencies, and configurations, as a set of containerized services. This consistency eliminates the "*it works on my machine*" problem and ensures that tests run the same way in development, staging, and production environments.

Benefits of Docker in CI/CD Pipelines:

- **Reproducible Environments:** By using Docker, you can define your test environments with Dockerfiles, which specify exactly what should be included in the environment. This ensures that the same environment is used across all stages of the pipeline. For example:

```
# Use official Python image
FROM python:3.9

# Set working directory
WORKDIR /app

# Install dependencies
COPY requirements.txt .
RUN pip install -r requirements.txt

# Copy the application code
COPY . /app

# Run tests
CMD ["pytest"]
```

- **Isolation:** Docker containers allow you to isolate services and applications, which is particularly useful for running multiple tests in parallel without interfering with each other. For example, you can run a database service in one container, your application in another, and your test suite in a third container.
- **Easy Cleanup and Reset:** After each test run, Docker containers can be destroyed, ensuring a clean state for the next test run. This is especially important in integration tests, where database states, files, and configurations may need to be reset.
- **Docker Compose for Multi-Service Environments:** For applications that require multiple services (for example, a database, a cache server, and the application itself), Docker Compose is a powerful tool. It allows you to

define and run multi-container Docker applications, making it easier to spin up complex environments with just a few commands. For example, **docker-compose.yml**:

```
version: '3'
services:
  app:
    build: .
    ports:
      - "8000:8000"
  db:
    image: postgres:latest
    environment:
      - POSTGRES_USER=test
      - POSTGRES_PASSWORD=test
      - POSTGRES_DB=test_db
```

- **Consistency Across Local, Staging, and Production:** With Docker, you can ensure that your local development, staging, and production environments are identical. This helps reduce discrepancies between environments, minimizing the risk of errors related to environment misconfiguration.

Managing Environment Variables and Secrets Securely

When running tests in a CI/CD pipeline, it is important to handle sensitive data such as environment variables, API keys, database credentials, and other secrets securely. Exposing these secrets in source code or version control is a significant security risk. Therefore, securing secrets is a critical aspect of managing test environments.

Best Practices for Managing Secrets:

- **Environment Variables:**
  - Use environment variables to store sensitive data such as API keys and database credentials. This method allows you to inject secrets into your CI/CD pipeline at runtime, avoiding hard-coding them into source code.
  - For example, in a CI/CD pipeline configuration file (for example, **.gitlab-ci.yml** or **.github/workflows**), environment variables can be set securely using the platform's secret management features.
- **Secrets Management Tools:**
  - Use secrets management tools to store and access sensitive information securely. For example, AWS Secrets Manager, Azure Key Vault, and HashiCorp Vault offer secure storage and management of secrets and credentials.

   - These tools provide controlled access to secrets, audit logs, and automated secret rotation, ensuring that your credentials remain secure over time.
- **CI/CD Platform Secret Storage:** GitHub Actions, GitLab CI/CD, and other platforms offer built-in support for managing secrets. For example, GitHub allows you to store secrets securely in the repository settings, which can then be accessed during pipeline execution. Example (GitHub Actions):

```
jobs:
  test:
    runs-on: ubuntu-latest
    env:
      DB_PASSWORD: ${{ secrets.DB_PASSWORD }}
```

- **Docker Secrets:** Docker provides a native mechanism for managing secrets in a secure way when working with Docker Swarm or Docker Compose. Secrets stored this way are encrypted and can be securely accessed by containers during runtime.
- **Environment Segmentation:** Ensure that different environments (development, staging, production) have their own isolated sets of environment variables and secrets. This practice limits the scope of access and reduces the risk of accidental exposure or misuse.

Managing test data and environments in CI/CD pipelines is a crucial aspect of automated testing. Using techniques such as automated data generation, Docker for environment consistency, and secure management of secrets ensures that tests are reliable, secure, and scalable. By implementing these strategies, teams can achieve a seamless and secure automated testing process, minimizing the risk of defects and ensuring that the software is ready for deployment.

Best Practices and Common Pitfalls in CI/CD Test Integration

Incorporating tests into CI/CD pipelines ensures the reliability and quality of the software throughout the development lifecycle. However, integrating tests effectively requires adherence to best practices and awareness of potential pitfalls. This section highlights essential best practices for maintaining efficient pipelines and avoiding common challenges, ensuring a streamlined and robust CI/CD process.

Best Practices for CI/CD Test Integration

- **Maintain Pipeline Efficiency:** Efficient pipelines ensure quick feedback loops, enabling developers to identify and address issues promptly. Key strategies for maintaining efficiency include:

- **Run Only Necessary Tests at Each Stage:** Structure the pipeline to run different sets of tests depending on the stage. For example:
  - **Unit Tests:** Run during the build phase to validate individual components.
  - **Integration Tests:** Execute after successful unit tests to ensure modules interact correctly.
  - **UI Tests:** Reserve for later stages to validate the end-to-end functionality.

  Running all tests at every stage can slow down the pipeline unnecessarily.
- **Optimize Test Dependencies:** Avoid redundant dependencies by carefully analyzing which tests need to run after code changes. Tools such as Jest and PyTest offer mechanisms to run only impacted tests based on code changes.

- **Regularly Update and Refactor Test Suites:** As applications evolve, test suites need to keep up to avoid outdated or irrelevant tests.
  - **Remove Redundant Tests:** Overlapping tests can consume resources unnecessarily. Regular audits help identify and eliminate such redundancies.
  - **Adapt to Feature Changes:** Modify test cases to align with updates in application features or architecture. Neglecting this can lead to irrelevant or failing tests that waste time and obscure real issues.
  - **Refactor Tests for Maintainability:** Regularly review and refactor test code to ensure it is clean, efficient, and adheres to the latest coding standards. Employ test design patterns such as Data-Driven Testing or the Page Object Model (POM) for scalability and maintainability.
- **Use Caching and Parallelization:** Efficient resource utilization is essential for speeding up pipelines.
  - **Caching Dependencies:** Caching frequently used dependencies (for example, package installations and build artifacts) reduces setup time. Most CI/CD tools support caching mechanisms.

Example: GitHub Actions allows caching with a simple configuration.

```
steps:
  - name: Cache dependencies
    uses: actions/cache@v3
    with:
      path: ~/.cache
      key: ${{ runner.os }}-dependencies-${{ hashFiles
('**/requirements.txt') }}
```

- **Parallelizing Tests:** Running tests in parallel reduces execution time significantly. Tools such as PyTest (`pytest-xdist`), Jest, and CircleCI support parallelization to divide tests into smaller subsets and execute them concurrently.
- **Divide Tests by Complexity and Priority:** Split tests into groups based on complexity and runtime. For example:
  - Fast-running unit tests can execute first.
  - Longer-running integration and UI tests can run on separate threads or after quick feedback cycles.

- **Securely Integrate Testing into CI/CD Pipelines**
  - **Implement Environment Segmentation:** Use distinct environments for development, testing, and production. This segmentation minimizes the risks of production-related issues during testing.
  - **Automate Secrets Management:** Use tools such as AWS Secrets Manager, HashiCorp Vault, or the built-in secret management features of CI/CD platforms to securely handle sensitive credentials.
  - **Monitor and Audit Pipelines:** Regularly monitor pipeline performance and test results. Automated notifications for failures ensure issues are identified and resolved quickly.

Common Pitfalls in CI/CD Test Integration

Despite the best intentions, certain pitfalls can hinder the efficiency and reliability of CI/CD pipelines.

- **Neglecting Flaky Test Resolution:** Flaky tests–those that fail intermittently without any code changes–can undermine the credibility of your test suite.
  - **Impact of Flaky Tests:**
    - They erode developer confidence in test results.
    - They increase build failure rates, disrupting the development process.
  - **Addressing Flaky Tests:**
    - Identify flaky tests by tracking their failure patterns over multiple runs.
    - Resolve root causes, such as dependency on timing, environmental inconsistencies, or poor test design.
- **Overloading Pipelines with Unnecessary Jobs:** Adding too many steps or unnecessary tests to pipelines can slow down execution and frustrate developers.
  - **Avoid Running Unused Tests:** Disable or remove outdated tests that no longer add value to the testing process.

  - **Streamline Job Dependencies:** Review job dependencies in your pipeline to eliminate redundant or overlapping steps.
- **Ignoring Pipeline Optimization Opportunities:** Pipelines that lack optimization can become bottlenecks.
  - **Missed Opportunities:**
    - Not using caching or parallelization results in longer execution times.
    - Failing to adapt pipelines for resource efficiency wastes computational power and increases costs.
  - **Solution:** Continuously monitor pipeline performance metrics, such as runtime duration and resource usage, and refine configurations to achieve optimal performance.
- **Inadequate Test Coverage for Critical Areas:** Skipping or under-prioritizing tests for high-risk areas can lead to undetected bugs in production.
  - **Best Practices:**
    - Prioritize tests for business-critical components and high-risk areas identified during risk assessments.
    - Use code coverage tools to identify untested areas and improve coverage over time.
- **Neglecting Cross-Environment Consistency:** Test environments that differ significantly from production can result in false positives or negatives.
  - **Pitfall:** Variations in dependencies, configurations, or data between environments can cause tests to pass in one environment but fail in another.
  - **Solution:** Use tools such as Docker to create consistent environments across all pipeline stages, ensuring that tests behave uniformly in development, staging, and production.

By following these best practices and addressing common pitfalls, teams can integrate tests into CI/CD pipelines effectively. This approach enhances pipeline efficiency, improves software quality, and fosters a culture of continuous improvement in development and testing processes.

Conclusion

In this chapter, we explored the integral role of CI/CD pipelines in modern software development, focusing on their contribution to faster and more reliable software delivery. We began with an introduction to CI/CD pipelines, outlining their purpose and evolution in streamlining code integration and deployment. This foundation set the stage for discussing the importance of test automation within CI/CD workflows, emphasizing its ability to provide consistent validation, minimize manual effort, and enhance overall quality.

A comprehensive overview of popular CI/CD tools—GitHub Actions, Jenkins, CircleCI, and GitLab CI/CD—highlighted their features, strengths, and ideal use cases, enabling teams to choose the right tool for their specific requirements. We also delved into designing CI/CD pipelines with testing in mind, presenting a structured approach for integrating testing stages such as static analysis, unit tests, and integration tests into the pipeline.

The chapter further addressed critical aspects of handling test data and environments, focusing on techniques such as data seeding, environment consistency through Docker, and secure management of secrets. Best practices and common pitfalls in CI/CD test integration provided actionable strategies for maintaining efficient pipelines while avoiding challenges such as flaky tests, redundant jobs, and inadequate test coverage.

Through these discussions, this chapter serves as a comprehensive guide for incorporating robust testing practices into CI/CD pipelines, fostering a culture of continuous integration, delivery, and improvement. In the next chapter, we will explore advanced strategies for CI/CD pipelines, including techniques for parallel test execution, pipeline optimization, enhanced monitoring, and deployment strategies such as blue-green and canary deployments, ensuring high efficiency and reliability in your software delivery process.

Key Takeaways

- **Role of CI/CD Pipelines in Modern Development:** CI/CD pipelines are essential for streamlining code integration, testing, and deployment, ensuring rapid and reliable delivery cycles.
- **Test Automation as a Pillar of CI/CD:** Automated testing validates code changes consistently, reduces manual intervention, and supports DevOps practices by fostering collaboration and reliability.
- **Selecting the Right CI/CD Tools:** Tools such as GitHub Actions, Jenkins, CircleCI, and GitLab CI/CD offer diverse capabilities. The choice depends on factors such as integration needs, scalability, and workflow preferences.

- **Designing Effective Pipelines:** Structuring pipelines with stages such as static code analysis, unit tests, integration tests, and deployment ensures efficient validation at every step.
- **Managing Test Data and Environments:** Test data generation, environment consistency via Docker, and secure handling of secrets are critical for maintaining pipeline reliability and security.
- **Optimizing Pipelines with Best Practices:** Practices such as running only necessary tests, leveraging caching and parallelization, and regularly updating test suites enhance pipeline efficiency.
- **Avoiding Common Pitfalls:** Addressing flaky tests, avoiding overloaded pipelines, and ensuring consistent test environments prevent disruptions and maintain trust in the pipeline.

CHAPTER 9
Advanced CI/CD Strategies

Introduction

In this chapter, we will delve into advanced strategies for optimizing and scaling Continuous Integration and Continuous Deployment (CI/CD) pipelines, a critical aspect of modern software delivery workflows. As software systems grow in complexity, ensuring the efficiency, reliability, and observability of CI/CD pipelines becomes essential for maintaining high standards of quality and delivery speed.

We will explore advanced techniques such as parallel test execution, pipeline performance optimization, and sophisticated test orchestration to minimize execution time and improve feedback loops. Additionally, we will discuss deployment strategies such as Blue-Green and Canary deployments, which enable safer and more controlled releases. Integration of Infrastructure as Code (IaC) will be covered to automate environment provisioning, while monitoring and observability tools will help you maintain pipeline health and detect bottlenecks in real time.

To enhance test reporting and stakeholder visibility, we will introduce Allure Reports for advanced test result visualization. By the end of this chapter, you will have the knowledge to build, scale, and monitor advanced CI/CD pipelines, ensuring that your development processes are optimized for speed, reliability, and maintainability. This advanced understanding will empower you to tackle complex delivery challenges and elevate the efficiency of your software development lifecycle.

Structure

In this chapter, we will explore advanced strategies for optimizing and scaling CI/CD pipelines, focusing on techniques to improve efficiency, reliability, and observability. Here is what we will cover:

- Introduction to Advanced CI/CD Strategies
- Parallel Test Execution

- Optimizing CI/CD Pipelines
- Advanced Test Orchestration and Management
- Implementing Security and Compliance in CI/CD
- Continuous Delivery and Deployment Strategies
- Monitoring and Observability in CI/CD Pipelines
- Best Practices and Common Pitfalls in Advanced CI/CD

Introduction to Advanced CI/CD Strategies

As software development teams scale and projects grow in complexity, the need for optimized, reliable, and highly efficient CI/CD pipelines becomes increasingly critical. In modern software delivery workflows, CI/CD pipelines are no longer limited to basic integration and deployment processes. They now serve as the backbone of automation, enabling teams to deliver software quickly, consistently, and with confidence. However, as pipelines expand to accommodate larger codebases, complex test suites, and diverse deployment environments, teams face challenges in maintaining speed, reliability, and observability.

This chapter introduces advanced CI/CD strategies designed to overcome these challenges. While traditional CI/CD workflows focus on automating the build, test, and deployment process, advanced strategies optimize pipelines for performance, scalability, and visibility into system health. By leveraging techniques such as **parallel test execution**, **advanced test orchestration**, and **infrastructure as code**, teams can streamline workflows and reduce bottlenecks. Similarly, advanced deployment strategies such as **Blue-Green Deployments** and **Canary Releases** allow organizations to ensure safe and gradual rollouts while minimizing downtime and risks.

Key Challenges Addressed by Advanced CI/CD Strategies:

- **Speed:** As software teams grow, CI/CD pipelines may experience significant delays due to large test suites, resource constraints, and inefficient workflows. Advanced strategies such as **parallel execution** and **caching** can drastically reduce build and test times, improving developer productivity and reducing feedback cycles.
- **Reliability:** Ensuring that pipelines produce consistent and accurate results is essential for trust in automated workflows. Advanced orchestration methods, optimized tests, and strategies for identifying and addressing flaky tests help improve the reliability of pipelines, ensuring that builds fail for legitimate reasons and deployments succeed without errors.
- **Monitoring and Observability:** Modern pipelines must provide visibility into

their health, performance, and outputs to allow teams to diagnose issues quickly and prevent failures. By incorporating **monitoring tools** and advanced reporting, teams can gather critical insights into pipeline performance, test results, and deployment status. Observability tools allow real-time tracking and enable teams to optimize their processes continuously.

- **Scalability:** Scaling CI/CD pipelines to accommodate growing workloads, larger teams, and diverse testing environments can pose significant challenges. Strategies such as **Infrastructure as Code (IaC)**, cloud-based CI/CD tools, and containerization (for example, Docker) help build scalable pipelines capable of managing complex workflows while maintaining performance.

Importance of Advanced CI/CD Strategies

In today's competitive software landscape, organizations must deliver updates, fixes, and features faster while maintaining the highest levels of quality. Basic CI/CD processes alone cannot meet these demands when projects scale in complexity. Advanced CI/CD strategies provide the tools and methodologies needed to optimize workflows, reduce risks, and gain visibility into the delivery pipeline.

By addressing the challenges of speed, reliability, and observability, advanced strategies empower teams to build pipelines that are not only faster and more efficient but also resilient and adaptable to changing business needs. This chapter will provide a comprehensive overview of techniques, tools, and real-world examples that demonstrate how organizations can implement and benefit from advanced CI/CD practices.

Parallel Test Execution

Parallel test execution refers to running multiple tests simultaneously across multiple processors, threads, or machines instead of sequentially. In a CI/CD pipeline, this technique plays a pivotal role in reducing the overall test execution time, enabling faster feedback loops, and improving the efficiency of the development workflow.

As software projects grow, test suites become larger, leading to longer execution times. Running tests sequentially becomes impractical as teams aim for rapid iterations and deployments. Parallel execution allows teams to split the workload across available resources, ensuring that tests are completed faster without compromising the scope or quality of validation.

For modern CI/CD pipelines, reducing pipeline duration is essential to:

- Minimize developer wait times for test feedback.
- Accelerate the delivery of code changes to production.
- Enable faster detection and resolution of issues in the pipeline.

While parallel execution provides significant time savings, it also introduces challenges related to resource utilization, test dependencies, and flaky tests. This section explores how to configure parallel test execution in popular tools such as **PyTest** and **GitHub Actions**, along with strategies to manage common trade-offs and challenges.

Techniques to Configure Parallel Execution

PyTest, one of the most widely used testing frameworks in Python, supports parallel execution using the `pytest-xdist` plugin. This plugin allows tests to run concurrently across multiple CPUs or distributed environments.

Steps to Configure Parallel Execution in PyTest:

1. **Install the `pytest-xdist` Plugin**:

   ```
   pip install pytest-xdist
   ```

2. **Run Tests with Parallel Workers**: Use the `-n` option to specify the number of workers. For example, to run tests on 4 parallel workers:

   ```
   pytest -n 4
   ```

3. PyTest will automatically distribute tests across the specified number of CPU cores.

4. **Run Tests across Multiple Environments**: `pytest-xdist` supports distributed execution across multiple machines using a master-slave setup. This allows larger test suites to be executed across a cluster of machines.

5. **Avoiding Resource Conflicts**: When tests share resources such as databases, files, or external APIs, conflicts may arise. Using isolated test data and fixtures ensures that parallel execution does not interfere with test results.

Configuring Parallel Execution in GitHub Actions

GitHub Actions, a widely adopted CI/CD platform, enables parallel test execution using **matrix builds**. Matrix builds allow developers to define jobs that execute simultaneously with different configurations. This is particularly useful for running tests across different environments, Python versions, or operating systems.

Steps to Configure Parallel Execution in GitHub Actions:

1. **Define a Matrix Strategy** in the workflow YAML file: Example configuration:

   ```
   name: Parallel Test Execution

   on: [push, pull_request]
   ```

```
jobs:
  test:
    strategy:
      matrix:
        python-version: [3.8, 3.9, 3.10]
        os: [ubuntu-latest, windows-latest]
    runs-on: ${{ matrix.os }}

    steps:
    - name: Check out code
      uses: actions/checkout@v3

    - name: Set up Python
      uses: actions/setup-python@v3
      with:
        python-version: ${{ matrix.python-version }}

    - name: Install dependencies
      run: pip install -r requirements.txt

    - name: Run tests
      run: pytest -n 4
```

2. **Matrix Strategy Explanation**:
   a. The matrix runs tests concurrently across multiple Python versions (**`3.8`**, **`3.9`**, **`3.10`**) and operating systems (**`ubuntu-latest`**, **`windows-latest`**).
   b. Within each job, PyTest runs with parallel workers (**`-n 4`**), ensuring even faster execution.
3. **Benefits of Matrix Builds**:
   a. Allows concurrent testing across diverse configurations.
   b. Identifies environment-specific issues early in the pipeline.
4. **Optimizing GitHub Actions Performance**:
   a. Use caching to avoid redundant downloads and installations.
   b. Limit parallelism if resource consumption becomes excessive.

Benefits and Trade-Offs of Parallel Test Execution

Benefits:

- **Significant Time Savings**: Parallel execution reduces test duration, enabling rapid feedback and shorter CI/CD pipeline runs.

- **Increased Developer Productivity**: Developers receive faster test results, allowing them to iterate on code changes efficiently.
- **Optimized Resource Utilization**: Modern CI/CD tools and cloud-based infrastructure scale resources dynamically to accommodate parallel workloads.
- **Scalable Test Execution**: Supports execution of large test suites by distributing workloads across machines or cores.

Trade-Offs:

- **Increased Resource Consumption**: Running tests in parallel requires additional CPU, memory, or virtual machines, leading to higher costs in cloud environments.
- **Dependency Conflicts**: Tests relying on shared resources (for example, databases and files) may fail due to concurrent access.
- **Flaky Tests**: Tests that behave inconsistently may become more frequent in parallel execution. Proper isolation and retries are necessary to address flakiness.
- **Complex Debugging**: Parallel execution makes it harder to debug issues because test outputs may be interleaved, and identifying failed tests requires proper reporting.

Handling Dependencies and Flaky Tests in Parallel Executions

Effectively managing test dependencies and addressing flaky tests are critical for ensuring reliability during parallel executions. These practices help maintain consistent results and optimize test pipeline efficiency.

- **Managing Test Dependencies:**
  - **Use Isolated Fixtures**: Ensure tests use isolated environments, such as temporary databases or file directories. PyTest fixtures with **`scope="function"`** help reset the state between tests.
  - **Containerize Tests**: Run tests in isolated containers (for example, Docker) to eliminate resource conflicts.
  - **Mock Shared Resources**: Replace external dependencies with mocks or stubs to prevent interference.
- **Dealing with Flaky Tests:**
  - **Identify Flaky Tests**: Tools such as **`pytest-rerunfailures`** help rerun tests that intermittently fail to verify their reliability. Example:

    ```
    pytest --reruns 3 --reruns-delay 5
    ```

- **Retry Logic**: Add retry mechanisms in CI/CD workflows to handle transient issues.
- **Use Test Reporting**: Leverage tools such as Allure Reports to identify patterns in flaky tests and address root causes.

By incorporating parallel test execution into CI/CD pipelines using tools such as PyTest and GitHub Actions, teams can achieve significant time savings while maintaining efficient test workflows. Addressing trade-offs such as resource utilization and flaky tests ensures that parallel execution remains a robust and scalable solution for optimizing pipeline performance.

Optimizing CI/CD Pipelines

Optimizing CI/CD pipelines is essential to ensure that software delivery remains efficient, fast, and reliable. As pipelines grow in complexity, certain bottlenecks can hinder performance and slow down feedback cycles. The key factors affecting pipeline performance include:

- **Test Execution Time**: Long-running test suites increase pipeline duration, delaying feedback for developers. Optimizing test execution through strategies such as parallel execution, test selection, and caching can reduce this time significantly.
- **Job Dependencies**: Pipelines often include multiple interdependent jobs (for example, building, testing, deployment). Unnecessary or poorly ordered dependencies can create idle time and increase overall pipeline duration.
- **Resource Usage**: CI/CD pipelines consume CPU, memory, and storage resources. Inefficient resource management can lead to slower pipelines, failed jobs, or higher infrastructure costs, especially in cloud environments.

Techniques for Pipeline Optimization

To overcome the challenges of test execution time, job dependencies, and resource utilization, we can implement several optimization techniques in CI/CD pipelines.

Test Caching to Reuse Results

Test caching involves storing and reusing test results or dependencies to avoid redundant computation in subsequent runs. It is particularly useful when tests or processes do not change frequently, as they can leverage cached data to save time.

PyTest Caching: PyTest supports caching to speed up test runs by reusing data such as previous test results or pre-computed dependencies. The **`pytest --cache-show`** and **`pytest --cache-clear`** options allow developers to manage cached data.

Enabling Caching in PyTest: PyTest automatically creates a **`.pytest_cache`** directory during test execution. To reuse test results:

```
pytest --last-failed
```

- The **`--last-failed`** option reruns only the tests that failed in the previous run, reducing execution time for large test suites.
- **Caching Dependencies**: Cache dependencies (for example, test environments and packages) using CI/CD tools to avoid reinstalling or rebuilding dependencies unnecessarily. For instance:

GitHub Actions Caching:

```
steps:
  - name: Cache Python dependencies
    uses: actions/cache@v3
    with:
      path: ~/.cache/pip
      key: ${{ runner.os }}-pip-${{ hashFiles('**/requirements.
txt') }}
      restore-keys: |
        ${{ runner.os }}-pip-
```

Benefits of Test Caching:

- Reduces pipeline time by skipping redundant computations.
- Speeds up incremental builds and re-runs.
- Improves developer productivity with faster feedback loops.

Job Dependency Optimization

In CI/CD pipelines, jobs are often executed in a sequence, where some jobs depend on the results of previous jobs. However, unnecessary dependencies can increase pipeline duration, as downstream jobs are forced to wait for upstream jobs even when they are not interrelated.

Techniques to Optimize Job Dependencies:

1. **Run Independent Jobs in Parallel**: Identify jobs that do not rely on each other and execute them concurrently to reduce idle time. For example, in GitHub Actions:

```
jobs:
  build:
    runs-on: ubuntu-latest
    steps:
      - run: echo "Building project"
```

```
  test:
    runs-on: ubuntu-latest
    needs: build
    steps:
      - run: echo "Running tests"

  lint:
    runs-on: ubuntu-latest
    steps:
      - run: echo "Running lint checks"
```

In this example, **`lint`** runs independently of the **`build`** job, while the **`test`** waits for the **`build`**. By removing unnecessary **`needs`** dependencies, the pipeline completes faster.

2. **Skip Unchanged Jobs/Stages**: Use conditional logic to skip jobs that do not need to run for every pipeline execution. For instance, skip deployment jobs when changes are only made to test files.
3. **Optimize Job Stages**: Combine smaller, related jobs into a single job to reduce the overhead caused by starting/stopping jobs in the pipeline.

Benefits of Job Dependency Optimization:

- Reduces idle time and pipeline duration.
- Improves pipeline efficiency by focusing only on necessary tasks.
- Minimizes wasted compute resources.

Resource Scaling and Management in Cloud-Based CI/CD Tools

Efficient resource management ensures that pipelines leverage available compute resources optimally while maintaining cost efficiency. Cloud-based CI/CD tools such as **GitHub Actions**, **Jenkins**, and **CircleCI** offer dynamic resource scaling, which can be configured to improve performance.

Techniques for Resource Scaling

Here are the techniques for resource scaling:

- **Dynamic Parallelization**: Use scalable infrastructure to dynamically allocate resources based on workload demands. Cloud-based tools can spin up additional runners or machines to handle parallel jobs.
- **Configuring Runner Types**: Choose appropriate runner types for your workloads. For example:

  - **GitHub Actions**: Use **`ubuntu-latest`** for general-purpose jobs and larger instances for resource-intensive tasks.
  - **CircleCI**: Offers configurable resource classes (for example, **`medium`**, **`large`**) to scale compute power.

  Example of configuring runner resources in GitHub Actions:

```
jobs:
  test:
    runs-on: ubuntu-latest
    container:
      image: python:3.9
      options: --cpus 2 --memory 4G
```

- **Optimizing Resource Limits**: Set limits for memory, CPU, and job duration to prevent resource overuse. Cloud providers often provide tools for monitoring resource consumption and identifying bottlenecks.
- **Clean-Up and Resource Reuse**:
  - Clean up environments and containers after each job to free resources for other tasks.
  - Use containerized environments (for example, Docker) to create reproducible and isolated test environments.

Tools for Monitoring and Scaling:

- **Kubernetes**: Enables autoscaling for CI/CD workloads.
- **AWS ECS/Fargate**: Offers on-demand resource allocation for pipeline tasks.
- **Azure DevOps**: Allows scaling of agent pools for running parallel pipelines.

Benefits of Resource Scaling and Management:

- Reduces pipeline bottlenecks by dynamically allocating resources.
- Ensures pipelines can scale efficiently as projects grow.
- Optimizes cost by scaling resources only when needed.

By implementing techniques such as test caching, job dependency optimization, and resource scaling, teams can significantly reduce CI/CD pipeline duration while ensuring efficient resource utilization. These optimizations are critical to maintaining fast and reliable pipelines in modern development workflows, enabling teams to deliver high-quality software at speed.

Advanced Test Orchestration and Management

Managing test execution across multiple layers, such as unit, API, and UI tests, is critical to optimizing CI/CD pipelines. With GitHub Actions, orchestration becomes streamlined and dynamic, offering tools for selective test execution and integration with reporting solutions like Allure Reports. This section covers strategies for advanced test orchestration, enabling you to handle complex pipelines efficiently.

Managing Test Execution Across Layers

Different layers of testing serve specific purposes and must be managed effectively:

- **Unit Tests**: Quick and low-cost tests for verifying isolated components.
- **API Tests**: Validate interactions between services or APIs, offering a mid-layer of confidence.
- **UI Tests**: High-cost, end-to-end tests simulating user interactions.

GitHub Actions provides the flexibility to manage these layers through workflows that define job dependencies and parallelism.

Example. GitHub Actions Workflow for Layered Tests

```
name: Layered Tests Workflow
on:
  push:
    branches:
      - main
jobs:
  unit-tests:
    runs-on: ubuntu-latest
    steps:
      - name: Checkout Code
        uses: actions/checkout@v3
      - name: Run Unit Tests
        run: pytest tests/unit

  api-tests:
    runs-on: ubuntu-latest
    needs: unit-tests
    steps:
      - name: Checkout Code
        uses: actions/checkout@v3
      - name: Run API Tests
        run: pytest tests/api
```

```
  ui-tests:
    runs-on: ubuntu-latest
    needs: api-tests
    steps:
      - name: Checkout Code
        uses: actions/checkout@v3
      - name: Run UI Tests
        run: pytest tests/ui
```

This configuration ensures that tests at each layer execute in sequence, with API tests running only after the successful completion of unit tests and UI tests triggered after API tests.

Conditional and Dynamic Test Execution

Running only the necessary tests based on the changes in a codebase significantly reduces execution time and resource usage.

Dynamic Execution with GitHub Actions

GitHub Actions supports dynamic workflows that use scripts to determine the specific layers of tests to run based on file changes.

Example: Dynamic Test Triggering

```
name: Dynamic Layered Test Workflow
on:
  push:
    branches:
      - main
jobs:
  dynamic-tests:
    runs-on: ubuntu-latest
    steps:
      - name: Checkout Code
        uses: actions/checkout@v3
      - name: Identify Changed Files
        id: changes
        run: |
          if git diff --name-only HEAD~1 | grep '^src/unit/'; then
            echo "RUN_UNIT=true" >> $GITHUB_ENV
          elif git diff --name-only HEAD~1 | grep '^src/api/'; then
            echo "RUN_API=true" >> $GITHUB_ENV
          elif git diff --name-only HEAD~1 | grep '^src/ui/'; then
            echo "RUN_UI=true" >> $GITHUB_ENV
```

```
      - name: Run Selected Tests
        run: |
          if [ "$RUN_UNIT" = "true" ]; then
            pytest tests/unit
          elif [ "$RUN_API" = "true" ]; then
            pytest tests/api
          elif [ "$RUN_UI" = "true" ]; then
            pytest tests/ui
          fi
```

This script dynamically checks for modified files in the repository and triggers the corresponding test suite.

Integrating Allure Reports for Test Result Aggregation

Test results visualization is essential for understanding pipeline outcomes. **Allure Reports** provides rich insights into test results, enabling developers to identify issues quickly.

Steps to Integrate Allure with GitHub Actions:

1. **Install Allure Pytest Plugin**: Add Allure support to your project:

   ```
   pip install allure-pytest
   ```

2. **Modify Test Execution to Generate Reports**: Add the **`--alluredir`** option to PyTest:

   ```
   pytest --alluredir=allure-results
   ```

3. **Add Allure to GitHub Actions Workflow**: Update the workflow to generate and publish Allure reports.

   Example: GitHub Actions Workflow with Allure Reports:

   ```
   name: Allure Test Reporting Workflow
   on:
     push:
       branches:
         - main
   jobs:
     run-tests:
       runs-on: ubuntu-latest
       steps:
         - name: Checkout Code
           uses: actions/checkout@v3
         - name: Install Dependencies
   ```

```
          run: pip install pytest allure-pytest
        - name: Run Tests with Allure
          run: pytest tests --alluredir=allure-results
        - name: Generate Allure Report
          run: |
            allure generate allure-results -o allure-report
            allure open allure-report
```

By using GitHub Actions for advanced orchestration and integrating Allure Reports for result visualization, you can design efficient, dynamic pipelines that handle diverse testing needs. These practices ensure that your CI/CD workflows remain adaptable and maintain high standards of quality and performance.

Implementing Security and Compliance in CI/CD

Incorporating security and compliance checks into CI/CD pipelines is no longer optional in modern software development. With the increasing sophistication of cyber threats and the growing emphasis on regulatory compliance, securing the software delivery lifecycle is essential to protect applications and sensitive data. This section explores the importance of embedding security into CI/CD workflows and outlines tools and techniques to ensure your pipelines are robust, compliant, and secure.

Importance of Security and Compliance in CI/CD

CI/CD pipelines often automate sensitive processes such as code building, testing, and deployment. If security is neglected, vulnerabilities could propagate to production environments, exposing systems to risks. Integrating security and compliance measures into the CI/CD pipeline offers the following benefits:

- **Early Detection of Vulnerabilities**: Identifying security issues during development reduces the cost and complexity of fixing them later.
- **Regulatory Compliance**: Ensuring compliance with standards such as GDPR, HIPAA, or PCI-DSS helps avoid legal penalties and reputational damage.
- **Safe Deployment Practices**: Enforcing security policies prevents insecure code or configurations from being deployed.

Tools and Techniques for Securing CI/CD Pipelines

Modern CI/CD workflows can incorporate various tools and techniques to achieve comprehensive security and compliance.

Static Application Security Testing (SAST)

Definition: SAST analyzes source code for vulnerabilities without executing the application, identifying issues early in the development phase.

Tool Example: Bandit for Python

Bandit scans Python codebases for security flaws.

GitHub Actions Integration:

```
name: SAST - Bandit
on:
  push:
    branches:
      - main
jobs:
  bandit-scan:
    runs-on: ubuntu-latest
    steps:
      - name: Checkout Code
        uses: actions/checkout@v3
      - name: Install Bandit
        run: pip install bandit
      - name: Run Bandit Security Scan
        run: bandit -r src/
```

Tool Example: SonarQube

SonarQube performs static code analysis for multiple languages, including Python.

Benefits:

- Identifies vulnerabilities such as SQL injection or XSS.
- Provides a dashboard to track and fix issues over time.

Dynamic Application Security Testing (DAST)

Definition: DAST examines running applications to identify vulnerabilities in real-world scenarios, such as insecure APIs or cross-site scripting.

- **Common Tools**: OWASP ZAP and Burp Suite.

GitHub Actions Example for OWASP ZAP:

```
name: DAST - OWASP ZAP
on:
  pull_request:
    branches:
      - main
```

```
jobs:
  zap-scan:
    runs-on: ubuntu-latest
    steps:
      - name: Start OWASP ZAP
        run: docker run -u zap -p 8080:8080 owasp/zap2docker-sta-
ble zap-baseline.py -t http://your-app-url
      - name: Analyze ZAP Results
        run: docker exec zap-container zap-cli report -o zap-re-
port.html
```

Vulnerability Scanning

Definition: Vulnerability scanning identifies outdated or insecure dependencies and container images.

Tool Example: OWASP Dependency-Check

A tool to detect known vulnerabilities in project dependencies.

GitHub Actions Workflow:

```
name: Dependency Check
on:
  push:
    branches:
      - main
jobs:
  dependency-scan:
    runs-on: ubuntu-latest
    steps:
      - name: Checkout Code
        uses: actions/checkout@v3
      - name: Run OWASP Dependency Check
        run: dependency-check --project MyApp --scan src/
```

Tool Example: Docker Security Scans

Scans container images for vulnerabilities.

GitHub Actions Example:

```
name: Docker Security Scan
on:
  push:
    branches:
      - main
jobs:
  security-scan:
```

```
    runs-on: ubuntu-latest
    steps:
      - name: Scan Docker Image
        run: docker scan my-docker-image
```

Enforcing Compliance Policies and Approvals

To ensure compliance and security, it is crucial to enforce checks and approvals before deployment.

Manual Approval Gates:

GitHub Actions supports manual approval steps to prevent unauthorized deployment.

Example:

```
name: Deployment Approval
jobs:
  approval:
    runs-on: ubuntu-latest
    steps:
      - name: Wait for Approval
        uses: hmarr/auto-approve-action@v2
```

Policy as Code: Using tools like Open Policy Agent (OPA), you can enforce policies on infrastructure and deployments.

By embedding security practices such as SAST, DAST, and vulnerability scanning into your GitHub Actions workflows and enforcing compliance measures such as manual approval gates, you can build robust and secure CI/CD pipelines. These strategies minimize risks, maintain compliance, and ensure the safe and reliable delivery of software.

Continuous Delivery and Deployment Strategies

Continuous Delivery (CD) and Continuous Deployment are cornerstones of modern CI/CD practices, enabling teams to deliver updates quickly, reliably, and securely. This section explores the distinctions between these two approaches, strategies for implementing safe deployments, and the tangible benefits of Continuous Deployment in fast-paced development environments.

Overview of Continuous Delivery versus Continuous Deployment

Continuous Delivery and Continuous Deployment are essential practices in modern software development pipelines. While both focus on automating the software release process, they differ in their approach to deployment, with Continuous Delivery requiring manual approval for releases and Continuous Deployment automating the entire process for seamless delivery to production. Understanding their differences helps teams choose the right strategy based on their needs and goals.

- **Continuous Delivery:**
  - Automates the process of delivering code changes to a staging or pre-production environment.
  - Requires manual approval for deploying changes to production.
  - Focuses on ensuring the code is always in a deployable state.
  - **Example Use Case:** Organizations with strict regulatory requirements or a need for rigorous quality gates before production releases.
- **Continuous Deployment:**
  - Extends Continuous Delivery by automating deployment to production without manual intervention.
  - Relies heavily on automated testing and monitoring to ensure reliability.
  - **Example Use Case:** Organizations prioritizing speed and efficiency in software delivery, such as e-commerce platforms during sales events.

Key Difference: Continuous Deployment automates production releases, while Continuous Delivery retains a manual approval step.

Strategies for Implementing Safe Deployments in CI/CD Pipelines

Implementing safe deployments ensures that changes can be delivered to users without introducing risks or disruptions. The following are the key strategies and tools for achieving this:

Feature Flagging

Definition: Feature flagging allows you to deploy changes to production while keeping them hidden or inactive for users until explicitly enabled.

- **Benefits:**
  - Enables incremental rollouts and A/B testing.
  - Reduces the risk of deploying unfinished or experimental features.
  - Allows rapid rollback by disabling the feature flag.
- **Tool Example: LaunchDarkly**
  - Supports dynamic toggling of features at runtime.

Integration with GitHub Actions:

```
name: Feature Flag Deployment
on:
  push:
    branches:
      - main
jobs:
  feature-flag:
    runs-on: ubuntu-latest
    steps:
      - name: Toggle Feature Flag
        run: launchdarkly-cli toggle-feature-flag my-feature
--state enabled
```

Automated Rollback Mechanisms

Definition: Rollback mechanisms automatically revert to a previous stable state if an issue is detected during or after deployment.

- **Strategies:**
  - Monitor production for predefined failure thresholds (for example, error rates and response times).
  - Automatically trigger rollback workflows when thresholds are exceeded.
  - Use infrastructure snapshots for restoring previous states.

GitHub Actions Example:

```
name: Automated Rollback
on:
  workflow_run:
    workflows: ["Deploy to Production"]
    types:
      - completed
jobs:
  rollback:
    if: failure()
    runs-on: ubuntu-latest
```

```
steps:
  - name: Trigger Rollback
    run: ./scripts/rollback-to-previous-version.sh
```

Progressive Delivery

Progressive delivery strategies, like blue-green and canary deployments, provide gradual exposure to new changes to minimize risk.

- **Blue-Green Deployment**: Two identical environments (blue and green) allow seamless traffic switching during deployments.
- **Canary Deployment**: Gradually routes a small percentage of traffic to the new version, increasing this percentage based on performance and user feedback.

Real-World Benefits of Continuous Deployment

Continuous Deployment enables organizations to thrive in fast-paced development environments by:

- **Accelerating Time to Market**: Updates reach users quickly, giving businesses a competitive edge.
- **Reducing Manual Effort**: Automation reduces reliance on human intervention, minimizing errors and freeing up resources for strategic tasks.
- **Improving User Feedback Loops**: Rapid delivery allows teams to collect real-world feedback and iterate faster.
- **Enhancing Developer Confidence**: Robust CI/CD pipelines with safe deployment strategies encourage frequent code changes without fear of disruption.

By adopting strategies such as feature flagging, automated rollback mechanisms, and progressive delivery, teams can ensure safe and reliable deployments while reaping the full benefits of Continuous Delivery and Continuous Deployment. These practices enable organizations to maintain quality, adaptability, and speed in their software delivery pipelines.

Blue-Green and Canary Deployments

Effective deployment strategies play a crucial role in minimizing risks and ensuring uninterrupted service during application updates. Blue-Green and Canary deployments are two widely used techniques that enhance release management by reducing downtime and allowing safe, incremental rollouts.

Blue-Green Deployment

- **Definition**: In a Blue-Green deployment, two identical environments are maintained:
  - **Blue (current environment)** serves live traffic.
  - **Green (new environment)** hosts the updated application version.
- **Process:**
  - Traffic is routed to the Blue environment during normal operations.
  - Updates are deployed to the Green environment and validated.
  - Once validated, traffic is seamlessly switched to the Green environment.
- **Benefits:**
  - Zero-downtime releases.
  - Simplified rollback by switching traffic back to the Blue environment.
  - Enables testing in a production-like environment.

Canary Deployment

- **Definition**: Canary deployments involve gradually rolling out a new version to a small subset of users or infrastructure. The rollout is expanded based on performance and feedback.
- **Process**:
  - A small percentage of traffic is routed to the updated version.
  - Monitoring systems validate the new version's stability.
  - Rollout is expanded in stages until full adoption.
- **Benefits**:
  - Minimizes risk by exposing only a small portion of users to potential issues.
  - Allows real-world feedback and incremental validation.
  - Facilitates data-driven decisions for scaling or rollback.

Step-by-Step Implementation

Let us take a look at the step-by-step implementation of blue-green deployment and canary deployment:

Blue-Green Deployment:

1. **Prepare the Environments**: Create two identical environments (Blue and Green) using Kubernetes namespaces or clusters.

2. **Deploy to Green**: Deploy the new version to the Green environment and validate it with tests.
3. **Switch Traffic**: Update the Kubernetes service to point traffic from the Blue to the Green environment using a load balancer.
4. **Monitor and Confirm**: Monitor the Green environment to ensure stability.
5. **Handle Rollback**: In case of issues, redirect traffic back to the Blue environment.

GitHub Actions Workflow Example:

```
name: Blue-Green Deployment
on:
  push:
    branches:
      - main
jobs:
  deploy:
    runs-on: ubuntu-latest
    steps:
      - name: Deploy to Green Environment
        run: kubectl apply -f green-deployment.yaml
      - name: Switch Traffic to Green
        run: kubectl apply -f green-service.yaml
      - name: Monitor Green Environment
        run: ./scripts/monitor-environment.sh
```

Canary Deployment:

1. **Prepare Canary Configuration**: Configure a subset of pods or instances in Kubernetes to handle a small percentage of traffic for the new version.
2. **Route Canary Traffic**: Use a weighted load balancer to direct a small percentage of traffic to the Canary version.
3. **Monitor Performance**: Set up automated alerts and dashboards to monitor metrics such as error rates, latency, and user feedback.
4. **Expand Rollout**: Gradually increase traffic to the Canary version based on positive feedback.
5. **Rollback if Necessary**: Quickly revert traffic to the stable version if issues arise.

GitHub Actions Workflow Example:

```
name: Canary Deployment
on:
  push:
    branches:
```

```
      - main
jobs:
  canary:
    runs-on: ubuntu-latest
    steps:
      - name: Deploy Canary Version
        run: kubectl apply -f canary-deployment.yaml
      - name: Update Traffic Weight
        run: kubectl patch service my-service --patch
'{"spec":{"trafficPolicy":{"weight":80}}}'
      - name: Monitor Canary Traffic
        run: ./scripts/monitor-metrics.sh
      - name: Expand Traffic if Successful
        run: kubectl patch service my-service --patch
'{"spec":{"trafficPolicy":{"weight":100}}}'
```

Practical Examples Using Kubernetes and GitHub Actions

- **Blue-Green Deployment Example:**
  - The Blue environment runs the stable version of an e-commerce application.
  - Deploy a new feature to the Green environment, validate it with end-to-end tests, and switch traffic upon success.
- **Canary Deployment Example:**
  - Gradually release a payment gateway update to 10% of users.
  - Monitor transaction success rates and user feedback before rolling out to all users.

Both Blue-Green and Canary deployment strategies provide robust frameworks for safe and reliable application releases. By leveraging GitHub Actions and Kubernetes, teams can automate these processes, ensuring minimal disruption while delivering high-quality updates.

Monitoring and Observability in CI/CD Pipelines

Modern CI/CD pipelines are critical for delivering software efficiently and reliably. However, as pipelines grow in complexity, monitoring and observability become essential to identify bottlenecks, detect failures, and maintain optimal performance. This section focuses on the importance of monitoring CI/CD pipelines, the tools used for effective observability, and the best practices for tracking pipeline health and performance.

Importance of Monitoring CI/CD Pipelines

Monitoring CI/CD pipelines provides valuable insights into the development process, enabling teams to:

- **Detect Failures Early**: Identify issues in test cases, deployments, or builds before they escalate.
- **Optimize Performance**: Highlight bottlenecks, such as slow-running tests or resource constraints.
- **Ensure Resource Efficiency**: Track resource usage to prevent overutilization or underutilization of infrastructure.
- **Improve Reliability**: Monitor critical metrics and alerts to ensure the pipeline is resilient and responsive to failures.
- **Facilitate Continuous Feedback**: Provide actionable insights to developers for iterative improvement.

Without robust monitoring, teams risk delayed issue detection and reduced confidence in the pipeline's reliability.

Tools for Effective Observability

Here is a list of tools that can be utilized for effective observability:

- **Prometheus for Metrics Collection**
  - **Purpose**: Collects and stores real-time metrics such as build durations, CPU usage, memory consumption, and test execution times.
  - **Usage**:
    - Set up exporters to gather metrics from CI/CD tools such as GitHub Actions or Kubernetes.
    - Define alerting rules for key thresholds (for example, build duration exceeds 10 minutes).
  - **Example**: Monitor pipeline stages with Prometheus queries to identify long-running steps.
- **Grafana for Visualization**
  - **Purpose**: Provides dashboards to visualize metrics collected by Prometheus or other tools.

- **Usage**:
  - Create dashboards for build durations, test failure trends, and resource utilization.
  - Configure alerts to notify teams about pipeline anomalies.
- **Example**: A Grafana dashboard that displays pipeline success rates and failure causes in real-time.

- **Logging Tools (for example, ELK Stack)**
  - **Purpose**: Collects, processes, and analyzes logs from various CI/CD stages.
    - Elasticsearch, Logstash, and Kibana (**ELK Stack**) is a popular logging solution.
  - **Usage**:
    - Use Logstash to aggregate logs from CI/CD workflows.
    - Analyze logs in Elasticsearch and visualize trends in Kibana.
  - **Example**: Investigate frequent test failures by filtering logs in Kibana for error patterns.

Best Practices for Monitoring CI/CD Pipelines

- **Track Test Failures**
  - Categorize test failures into transient (for example, flaky tests) and persistent (for example, bugs in code).
  - Integrate failure trends into dashboards to identify recurring issues.
- **Monitor Pipeline Performance**
  - Analyze, build, and test execution times to pinpoint bottlenecks.
  - Use tools such as Prometheus to track stage-wise durations.
- **Measure Resource Usage**
  - Monitor CPU, memory, and storage usage during pipeline execution.
  - Scale resources dynamically based on demand using cloud-native tools such as Kubernetes autoscaling.
- **Set Alerts and Notifications**
  - Configure alerts for critical events, such as build failures or high resource usage.
  - Use email, Slack, or other communication channels for timely notifications.
- **Centralize Logs and Metrics**
  - Consolidate logs from all stages of the pipeline into a single observability platform.

- Ensure logs are searchable and tagged with contextual metadata (for example, build ID).

Example: Monitoring CI/CD with Prometheus and Grafana

Integrating Prometheus for metrics collection and Grafana for visualization provides actionable insights into pipeline performance and health.

1. **Set Up Prometheus**: Install Prometheus in a Kubernetes cluster to monitor GitHub Actions metrics.
2. **Define Metrics**: Collect metrics such as pipeline success rates, stage durations, and resource usage.
3. **Visualize in Grafana**: Create a Grafana dashboard showing build trends, resource utilization, and error rates.
4. **Configure Alerts**: Set alerts for anomalies, such as a sudden spike in test failures.

By implementing robust monitoring and observability practices, teams can ensure their CI/CD pipelines operate smoothly, remain reliable, and adapt to the demands of modern software delivery. Tools such as Prometheus, Grafana, and the ELK Stack empower teams to gain actionable insights, reducing downtime and fostering continuous improvement.

Best Practices and Common Pitfalls in Advanced CI/CD

As CI/CD pipelines become more advanced, adhering to best practices and avoiding common pitfalls is crucial for maintaining efficiency, reliability, and scalability. This section highlights key best practices and potential challenges that teams often encounter in implementing advanced CI/CD strategies.

Best Practices

1. **Optimizing Test Execution Time and Pipeline Efficiency**

    a. Implement **parallel test execution** to reduce overall pipeline duration while maintaining thorough test coverage.

    b. Use **test caching** to avoid redundant test runs, leveraging tools such as pytest-cov or native GitHub Actions caching.

   c. Minimize **job dependencies** by designing independent pipeline stages that can be executed concurrently.

2. **Incorporating Security and Compliance Checks**
   a. Integrate **Static Application Security Testing (SAST)** and **Dynamic Application Security Testing (DAST)** into the pipeline to catch vulnerabilities early.
   b. Automate **compliance checks** using pre-deployment approval gates to enforce organizational policies.
3. **Ensuring Visibility with Monitoring Tools**
   a. Use observability tools such as **Prometheus**, **Grafana**, or **ELK Stack** to track pipeline performance and detect bottlenecks.
   b. Set up **alerts and notifications** for key failure scenarios to ensure quick remediation.
   c. Maintain a centralized dashboard for visibility into test results, resource usage, and deployment statuses.
4. **Scaling CI/CD Pipelines Effectively**
   a. Use **Infrastructure as Code (IaC)** tools such as Terraform to provision and manage scalable resources.
   b. Implement **dynamic scaling** in cloud environments to handle peak workloads without over-provisioning.
   c. Regularly review and refine pipeline configurations to accommodate growing project requirements.

Common Pitfalls

- **Neglecting Flaky Tests During Parallel Execution**
  - Flaky tests can undermine the reliability of CI/CD pipelines, leading to false negatives or intermittent failures.
  - Regularly review test stability and isolate or refactor flaky tests to maintain trust in pipeline results.
- **Overloading Pipelines with Unnecessary Jobs**
  - Including excessive or redundant jobs in the pipeline increases execution time and resource consumption.
  - Audit pipeline workflows periodically to remove obsolete or non-critical jobs.

- **Ignoring Monitoring and Reporting**
  - Lack of monitoring leads to undetected issues, such as performance bottlenecks or resource constraints.
  - Ensure monitoring and reporting are integral to the pipeline, with clear visibility into critical metrics.

By adopting these best practices and addressing common pitfalls, teams can create CI/CD pipelines that are efficient, secure, and scalable. These practices not only improve delivery speed and quality but also foster a proactive approach to managing pipeline challenges.

Conclusion

In this chapter, we delved into advanced strategies for designing and optimizing CI/CD pipelines, emphasizing their transformative role in achieving efficient, secure, and reliable software delivery. Starting with scaling workflows to meet modern challenges such as speed and reliability, we explored techniques such as parallel test execution, pipeline optimization, and advanced security integration.

Deployment strategies such as blue-green and canary deployments, combined with monitoring and observability practices, were highlighted to ensure seamless and efficient releases. These discussions equip you with the knowledge to build scalable and secure CI/CD pipelines, setting the stage for future innovations in software delivery.

In the next chapter, we will explore the future of test automation, focusing on emerging technologies such as AI/ML, evolving practices such as shift-left and shift-right testing, and their impact on modern testing landscapes. We will also examine the role of test automation engineers in adapting to these advancements, ensuring you are prepared to leverage cutting-edge tools and methodologies in your testing journey.

Key Takeaways

- **Scaling CI/CD Pipelines:** Advanced strategies, such as parallel execution and pipeline optimization, address challenges of speed, reliability, and observability.
- **Parallel Test Execution:** Configuring parallel execution reduces pipeline duration with techniques such as matrix builds in GitHub Actions. Handling flaky tests and managing dependencies are crucial for success.
- **Pipeline Optimization:** Techniques such as test caching, optimizing job dependencies, and resource scaling improve pipeline efficiency without compromising quality.

- **Security and Compliance Integration:** Incorporating SAST, DAST, and vulnerability scans into CI/CD workflows ensures secure and compliant software delivery.
- **Deployment Strategies:** Techniques such as blue-green and canary deployments reduce risks during production rollouts, offering flexibility and control over releases.
- **Monitoring and Observability:** Tools such as Prometheus, Grafana, and ELK Stack provide visibility into pipeline performance, enabling proactive issue detection and resolution.
- **Best Practices:** Optimizing execution times, leveraging caching, incorporating security checks, and ensuring visibility with monitoring tools are essential for efficient CI/CD pipelines.
- **Avoiding Pitfalls:** Addressing flaky tests, avoiding unnecessary jobs, and implementing robust monitoring practices ensure reliable and trustworthy pipelines.

This chapter has prepared you to implement and refine advanced CI/CD strategies, ensuring that your pipelines are optimized for performance, security, and reliability.

CHAPTER 10
Future of Test Automation

Introduction

In this chapter, we explore the rapidly evolving landscape of test automation and its role in shaping the future of software quality assurance. As technologies such as Artificial Intelligence (AI), Machine Learning (ML), and cloud computing revolutionize the software development lifecycle, test automation must evolve to keep pace with these innovations. Understanding and adapting to these changes is crucial for maintaining the effectiveness and relevance of testing practices.

We will examine emerging technologies and methodologies that are poised to redefine how testing is performed. From AI-driven testing solutions and self-healing scripts to the integration of DevOps and testing workflows, this chapter covers the tools, strategies, and trends that will shape the field in the coming years. Additionally, the shift-left and shift-right testing approaches will be explored to demonstrate how testing can be integrated into earlier and later stages of the software development process.

The future of test automation is also deeply tied to advancements in cloud computing, enabling scalable and cost-effective testing solutions, and in Agile and Continuous Delivery models, which demand faster feedback cycles and seamless integration. By staying informed about these trends, test automation engineers can adapt their skills and embrace new opportunities, ensuring they remain indispensable contributors to software quality.

By the end of this chapter, you will have a clear understanding of the challenges, opportunities, and tools shaping the future of test automation, empowering you to proactively navigate and leverage these changes in your own projects.

Structure

This chapter explores the future of test automation by addressing its evolving technologies, methodologies, and challenges. Here is what we will cover:

- Introduction to the Future of Test Automation
- Shift-Left and Shift-Right Testing Approaches
- Integration of DevOps and Testing
- Impact of Cloud Computing on Test Automation
- Test Automation in Agile and Continuous Delivery
- Future Role of Test Automation Engineers
- Predictions and Speculations for the Future of Test Automation

Introduction to the Future of Test Automation

In the ever-evolving world of software development, test automation has emerged as a cornerstone of ensuring quality and reliability. However, as technology advances, staying ahead in the testing landscape is no longer optional–it is imperative. Organizations that fail to adapt risk falling behind competitors, delivering subpar software, or encountering critical failures in production.

Test automation is not just about efficiency; it is about enabling agility, scalability, and resilience in an increasingly fast-paced environment. By staying updated with advancements, testers and organizations can unlock new possibilities to enhance software quality, optimize workflows, and reduce time-to-market.

Factors Driving Change in Test Automation

The future of test automation is shaped by a variety of factors, including technological advancements, evolving development practices, and market demands.

- **Technological Advancements:** Emerging technologies such as Artificial Intelligence (AI), Machine Learning (ML), and the Internet of Things (IoT) are transforming the capabilities of test automation. For instance, AI-powered tools can intelligently prioritize test cases, while ML algorithms predict potential failure points based on historical data. Similarly, IoT-driven testing has introduced the need to validate complex integrations across connected devices.
- **Evolving Development Practices:** Agile methodologies and DevOps have redefined how software is developed and delivered. The adoption of Shift-Left

and Shift-Right testing approaches ensures quality across every stage of the software lifecycle. Continuous Integration/Continuous Deployment (CI/CD) pipelines now demand automation frameworks that are adaptable, scalable, and capable of running diverse tests efficiently.

- **Market Demands and User Expectations:** Modern users demand seamless, secure, and high-performance applications. This expectation drives the need for comprehensive testing that covers functionality, performance, security, and usability. Market demands also push organizations to adopt rapid delivery models, emphasizing the importance of reliable, automated testing solutions to meet these tight deadlines without compromising quality.

Looking Ahead

As the testing landscape evolves, so does the role of test automation engineers. They must not only master traditional testing methodologies but also adapt to emerging technologies and practices. By embracing innovation and understanding market dynamics, engineers can contribute significantly to shaping the future of test automation, ensuring that software remains robust, reliable, and ready to meet the demands of the digital age.

In the following sections, we will delve deeper into these transformative factors, exploring how they influence the tools, strategies, and roles in test automation. Together, these insights will equip you to navigate and excel in the dynamic world of modern software testing.

Evolution of Test Automation

Test automation has undergone a remarkable transformation since its inception, adapting to technological advancements and evolving development methodologies. From its rudimentary beginnings to the sophisticated frameworks of today, understanding the historical progression of test automation reveals valuable insights into its current state and future trajectory.

Historical Progression of Test Automation Practices

Let us dive into the historical progression of test automation practices:

- **Early Days: Functional Testing and Basic Automation:** In the early stages of software development, functional testing was the primary means of ensuring quality. Automation emerged as a necessity to reduce repetitive tasks and improve efficiency. The earliest automation tools focused on recording and replaying user actions, enabling testers to simulate interactions without writing code. These tools, however, were limited by their inability to adapt to dynamic changes in applications.

- **The Rise of Record-Playback Tools:** Tools such as Mercury WinRunner and QuickTest Professional (now Micro Focus UFT) marked a significant step forward. These tools introduced record-playback functionality, allowing testers to create automated scripts by recording user actions and playing them back. While revolutionary at the time, these tools had significant limitations:
    - Lack of flexibility to handle dynamic and complex applications.
    - High maintenance costs due to fragile scripts that broke with minor UI changes.
- **Transition to Keyword-Driven and Data-Driven Testing:** To address the shortcomings of record-playback tools, keyword-driven and data-driven testing methodologies emerged. Tools such as Selenium IDE and frameworks built around keyword-driven testing empowered testers to design test cases using reusable keywords or actions. Similarly, data-driven testing allowed the execution of the same test logic across different data sets. This era marked a shift towards making automation more modular and reusable.
- **Advent of Code-Based Frameworks:** As applications grew more complex, the limitations of script-based and keyword-driven approaches became apparent. This led to the rise of code-based automation frameworks such as Selenium WebDriver and Playwright, which offered developers and testers greater flexibility and control. These frameworks introduced the concept of writing tests as code, allowing for:
    - Enhanced adaptability to complex workflows and dynamic applications.
    - Integration with development workflows such as version control and CI/CD pipelines.
    - Use of programming languages to implement custom logic and extend framework capabilities.
- **Modern Practices: Shift-Left, Shift-Right, and Continuous Testing:** Today, test automation is deeply embedded in Agile and DevOps practices, with testing starting early (Shift-Left) and continuing throughout the software lifecycle (Shift-Right). Continuous testing, integrated into CI/CD pipelines, ensures that every code change is validated for quality. Modern frameworks and tools support API testing, performance testing, and even AI-driven automation, significantly expanding the scope of automated testing.

Key Milestones in Test Automation

The following are the key milestones in test automation:

- **Record-Playback Tools**: These marked the beginning of automation but lacked scalability and flexibility.

- **Keyword-Driven Testing**: Introduced modularization and reusable components for test design.
- **Selenium WebDriver**: Revolutionized test automation with open-source accessibility and flexibility.
- **CI/CD Integration**: Enabled automation to become a continuous and seamless part of development workflows.
- **AI and ML in Testing**: Current innovations use AI to optimize test case selection, predict failures, and identify flaky tests.

Lessons Learned from Past Trends and Practices

Let us take a look at the lessons learned from past trends and practices:

- **Flexibility Is Crucial:** Automation strategies must accommodate dynamic and complex applications. Code-based frameworks emerged as a solution to the rigidity of record-playback tools, teaching us the importance of adaptability.
- **Maintenance Is a Continuous Effort:** Fragile scripts and outdated frameworks have consistently proven costly. The shift to modular and reusable components in keyword-driven testing underscored the value of maintainability in automation.
- **Collaboration Enhances Success:** The integration of testing into CI/CD pipelines highlights the importance of collaboration between developers, testers, and operations teams. Test automation is no longer a standalone effort but a shared responsibility.
- **Automation Alone Is Not Enough:** While automation improves efficiency, it must be combined with exploratory testing and continuous monitoring to ensure comprehensive quality assurance.
- **Innovation Drives Growth:** The evolution from record-playback tools to AI-driven frameworks illustrates that staying ahead of technological advancements is key to meeting the demands of modern software development.

Understanding the evolution of test automation helps us appreciate its current capabilities and provides valuable insights into future trends. As automation continues to evolve, these lessons will guide us in building more resilient, scalable, and effective testing strategies.

Emerging Technologies in Test Automation

As the complexity of software applications grows, so does the need for innovative technologies to enhance test automation. Emerging technologies such as Artificial Intelligence (AI), Machine Learning (ML), Internet of Things (IoT), and blockchain are reshaping how testing is conducted, ensuring greater efficiency, accuracy, and scalability. This section explores these advancements and the tools enabling them, highlighting their potential to redefine the testing landscape.

AI and ML Advancements

Let us discuss AI and ML advancements in depth:

- **AI-Driven Test Case Generation:** Traditional test case generation relies heavily on manual effort, requiring testers to identify edge cases, design scenarios, and write scripts. AI is transforming this process by:
  - **Analyzing Application Behavior**: Tools such as Testim and Functionize use AI to learn application workflows and generate relevant test cases automatically.
  - **Predictive Analytics**: AI identifies high-risk areas based on historical defect data, ensuring targeted and efficient testing.
  - **Coverage Optimization**: Machine Learning algorithms assess test coverage gaps and recommend additional tests to maximize coverage.
- **Intelligent Test Maintenance:** One of the biggest challenges in test automation is maintaining scripts as applications evolve. AI and ML provide solutions by:
  - **Self-Healing Scripts**: AI-powered frameworks such as Mabl and Katalon Studio can automatically update tests when locators change, minimizing script breakages.
  - **Flaky Test Detection**: ML models identify flaky tests by analyzing historical execution patterns and reducing false positives.
  - **Dynamic Element Handling**: AI can dynamically adapt to changes in UI elements, eliminating the need for frequent manual intervention.
- **Defect Prediction and Root Cause Analysis:** Advanced ML algorithms predict potential defects before they occur by analyzing code changes, user behaviors, and historical data. They also assist in pinpointing the root causes of failures, accelerating debugging efforts.

Impact of IoT Testing and Automation for Connected Devices

The impact of IoT testing and automation for connected devices is as follows:

- **Complexity of IoT Ecosystems:** The Internet of Things (IoT) connects a wide array of devices, sensors, and platforms, making testing a challenging task. Key challenges include:
  - Diverse hardware and software configurations.

- Real-time communication protocols and latency issues.
- Scalability to handle billions of devices.

- **Automation in IoT Testing:** IoT testing requires a mix of traditional and specialized approaches. Emerging automation solutions focus on:
  - **Protocol Testing**: Tools such as Wireshark automate the validation of communication protocols such as MQTT, CoAP, and Bluetooth.
  - **Emulators and Simulators**: Platforms such as AWS IoT Device Simulator mimic device behavior, reducing the need for physical hardware.
  - **End-to-End Testing**: Tools such as IoTIFY and Selenium IoT Extensions enable the testing of complete IoT workflows, from device inputs to cloud processing and user interfaces.
- **Security Testing in IoT:** Automation tools such as OWASP IoT Security Testing Framework help identify vulnerabilities in IoT devices and ecosystems, ensuring robust security measures.

Blockchain and Distributed Systems Testing

Here is a brief explanation of the blockchain and distributed systems testing:

- **Unique Testing Challenges in Blockchain:** Blockchain systems rely on decentralized architectures, cryptographic protocols, and consensus mechanisms, posing unique testing challenges such as:
  - Validating smart contracts for security and functionality.
  - Ensuring data immutability and transaction integrity.
  - Scalability testing under high transaction loads.
- **Automation in Blockchain Testing:** Automation plays a pivotal role in addressing these challenges:
  - **Smart Contract Testing**: Tools such as Truffle and Hardhat automate the testing of smart contracts, ensuring their correctness and security.
  - **Load and Performance Testing**: Platforms such as Hyperledger Caliper evaluate blockchain network performance under various conditions.
  - **Integration Testing**: Tools such as Ganache provide a simulated blockchain environment for testing integration with applications.
- **Testing Distributed Systems:** Distributed systems, such as microservices-based architectures, benefit from automation tools such as Chaos Monkey (for resilience testing) and Locust (for load testing). These tools help ensure fault tolerance and performance in complex, interconnected environments.

Overview of Emerging Tools and Platforms for the Future

Let us delve into the emerging tools and platforms for the future:

- **AI-Powered Automation Tools:** Tools such as Applitools Eyes and Percy leverage AI for visual testing, detecting even subtle UI inconsistencies across devices and resolutions. AI is also being used in tools such as TestRigor and Subject7 for automating complex workflows with minimal coding.
- **Cloud-Based Testing Platforms:** Cloud platforms such as BrowserStack, Sauce Labs, and LambdaTest provide scalable environments for testing across diverse configurations. These platforms are now integrating advanced analytics and AI-driven insights to enhance testing efficiency.
- **DevOps and CI/CD Integration Tools:** Emerging tools such as Harness, GitHub Actions, and GitLab Pipelines automate the integration of testing into CI/CD workflows, enabling faster feedback loops and seamless deployment processes.
- **IoT-Specific Platforms:** Tools such as ThingWorx and Azure IoT provide comprehensive solutions for automating IoT application testing, focusing on device interaction, data validation, and cloud integration.
- **Blockchain Testing Frameworks:** Frameworks such as Ethereum Testnet and Corda Testing Kit facilitate testing decentralized applications (dApps) and blockchain infrastructures, ensuring robustness and scalability.

Emerging technologies in test automation are shaping a future where testing is smarter, faster, and more reliable. By leveraging advancements in AI, IoT, blockchain, and cloud-based tools, testers can address modern challenges with innovative solutions. These technologies not only enhance efficiency but also pave the way for a more adaptive and resilient testing ecosystem, preparing us for the demands of tomorrow.

AI and Machine Learning in Test Automation

Artificial Intelligence (AI) and Machine Learning (ML) are at the forefront of technological advancements, and their integration into test automation is revolutionizing how testing is conducted. By automating complex tasks, improving test reliability, and enhancing efficiency, AI/ML is transforming testing workflows. In this section, we will delve into the role of AI/ML in test automation, explore its practical use cases, review key tools, and address the limitations and challenges of adopting these technologies.

Role of AI/ML in Improving Test Efficiency and Reliability

- **Automating Repetitive Tasks:** AI simplifies repetitive testing tasks such as test case generation, data population, and test execution. This automation reduces manual effort and accelerates testing cycles, allowing teams to focus on higher-value tasks.
- **Enhanced Test Coverage:** AI-driven algorithms identify edge cases and scenarios that might be missed by manual efforts. By analyzing patterns in application usage, AI ensures comprehensive test coverage.
- **Improved Reliability:** Traditional test scripts often break due to application changes. AI introduces self-healing capabilities to adjust tests dynamically, reducing false positives and negatives.
- **Real-Time Feedback:** ML models process large volumes of test data in real-time, providing actionable insights on application performance, bottlenecks, and potential risks.

Use Cases: Self-Healing Tests, Predictive Analytics, and Anomaly Detection

- **Self-Healing Tests**
  - **Problem**: UI element changes (for example, updated locators or altered DOM structures) frequently cause automated test failures.
  - **Solution**: AI-powered tools such as Mabl and Testim identify these changes and dynamically update test scripts to accommodate them. This reduces script maintenance and enhances reliability.
  - **Example**: If a button's identifier changes from **`btnSubmit`** to **`submitButton`**, the AI framework detects the change and updates the locator without manual intervention.
- **Predictive Analytics**
  - **Problem**: Anticipating test failures and defects in large-scale systems can be time-consuming and error-prone.
  - **Solution**: ML models analyze historical defect data, code changes, and testing trends to predict potential failure points.
  - **Example**: AI can prioritize tests based on areas of the codebase with a high likelihood of introducing bugs, optimizing resource allocation.
- **Anomaly Detection**
  - **Problem**: Detecting subtle anomalies in performance metrics or application behavior often requires deep domain expertise and manual effort.

- **Solution**: AI detects deviations in expected application behavior during testing, even for patterns that are not explicitly predefined.
- **Example**: Tools such as Dynatrace leverage AI to monitor performance metrics and flag anomalies such as memory leaks or unusual latency spikes.

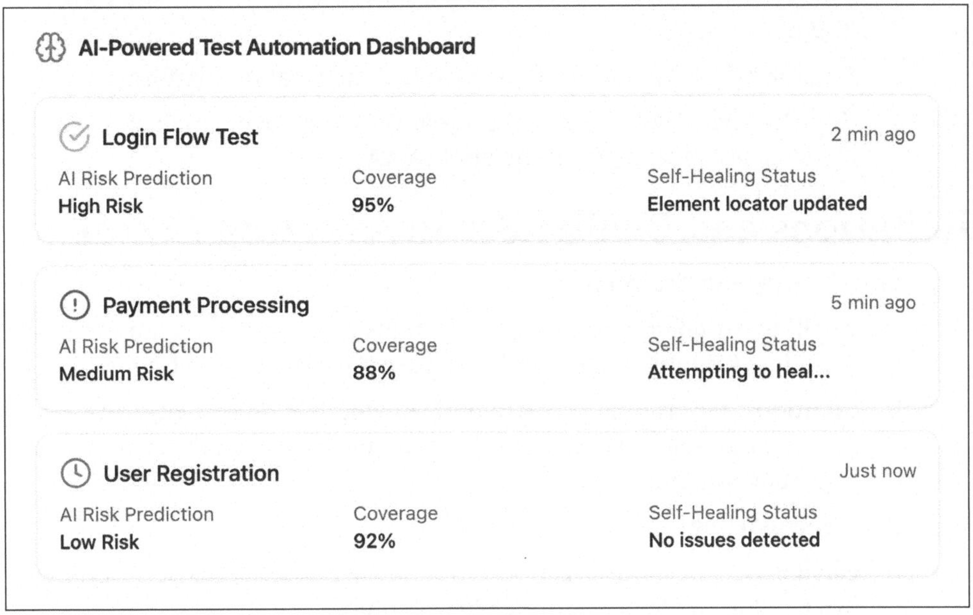

***Figure 10.1**: AI-Powered Test Automation Dashboard Example*

Key Tools Leveraging AI/ML in Testing

- **Applitools Eyes**
  - **Functionality**: Visual testing powered by AI to detect UI changes.
  - **Key Feature**: AI algorithms identify visual bugs across various devices and resolutions, ensuring pixel-perfect UI consistency.
- **Testim**
  - **Functionality**: AI-driven end-to-end test automation for web applications.
  - **Key Feature**: Self-healing tests and adaptive execution to handle application changes with minimal intervention.
- **Mabl**
  - **Functionality**: Low-code test automation using AI for web and API testing.
  - **Key Feature**: Continuous monitoring and self-healing capabilities to maintain test reliability.

- **Functionize**
  - **Functionality**: AI-powered test case creation and execution.
  - **Key Feature**: Automatically adapts to application changes and generates detailed insights into test outcomes.
- **TestRigor**
  - **Functionality**: AI-powered no-code test automation platform.
  - **Key Feature**: Allows test case creation using plain English and adapts dynamically to changes in the application.

Limitations and Challenges in Adopting AI/ML

- **Initial Setup and Training**
  - **Challenge**: Implementing AI/ML systems requires significant initial setup, including training models and integrating tools with existing workflows.
  - **Solution**: Leveraging pre-trained AI models and platforms reduces complexity, but organizations need to invest in skilled professionals to fine-tune systems.
- **Data Dependency**
  - **Challenge**: ML models rely heavily on high-quality data. Incomplete or biased data can lead to unreliable outcomes.
  - **Solution**: Establishing robust data pipelines and cleaning mechanisms is critical to ensure model accuracy.
- **Complexity and Cost**
  - **Challenge**: Advanced AI/ML tools can be expensive, both in terms of licensing and operational overhead.
  - **Solution**: Organizations should start with smaller use cases and gradually scale AI/ML adoption as they realize its benefits.
- **Interpretability of Results**
  - **Challenge**: ML algorithms often function as "*black boxes*," making it challenging to interpret why certain decisions or predictions are made.
  - **Solution**: Tools that provide explainable AI (XAI) frameworks can help teams understand and trust AI-driven insights.
- **Resistance to Change**
  - **Challenge**: Team members accustomed to traditional testing methods may resist adopting AI/ML technologies.
  - **Solution**: Training programs and showcasing tangible benefits can help overcome resistance and build confidence in new tools.

- **Scalability Concerns**
  - **Challenge**: Integrating AI/ML into large-scale projects can lead to scalability issues, especially if models need frequent retraining.
  - **Solution**: Using cloud-based platforms and modular frameworks ensures that AI/ML systems scale effectively with growing requirements.

AI and ML are revolutionizing test automation by enabling smarter, faster, and more reliable testing processes. While the benefits are substantial, organizations must carefully navigate the associated challenges to maximize their potential. By adopting the right tools, fostering a culture of innovation, and addressing limitations, testers can harness AI/ML to build future-ready testing ecosystems.

Shift-Left and Shift-Right Testing Approaches

Shift-Left and Shift-Right testing approaches are integral to modern software testing strategies. These methodologies emphasize testing earlier in the development lifecycle (Shift-Left) and extending testing activities to post-deployment phases (Shift-Right). By adopting these practices, teams ensure software quality throughout the development lifecycle, leading to faster feedback, enhanced reliability, and better alignment with user expectations.

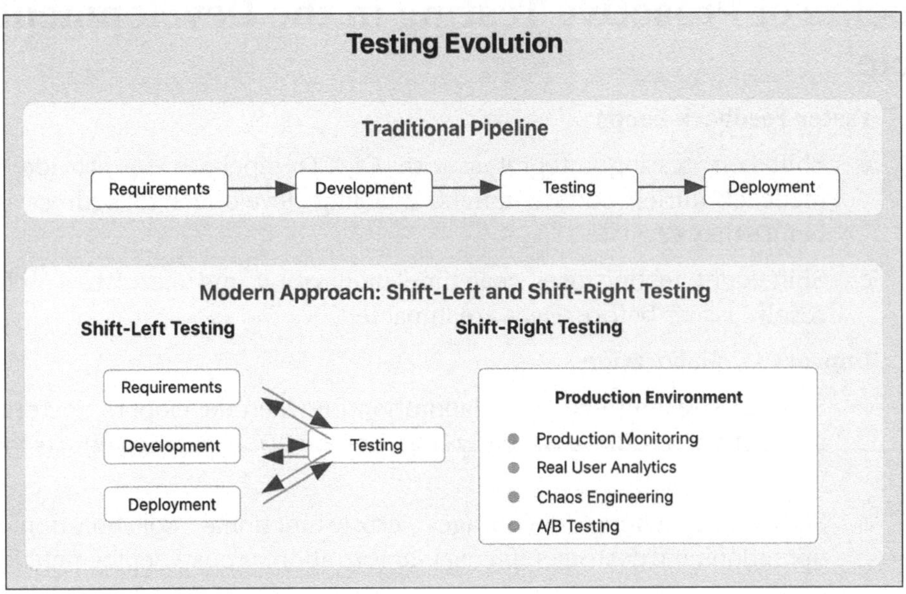

Figure 10.2: *Testing Evolution: Traditional versus Modern Approaches*

Definitions and Importance of Shift-Left and Shift-Right Testing

- **Shift-Left Testing**
    - **Definition**: Shift-Left testing involves moving testing activities earlier in the Software Development Life Cycle (SDLC), focusing on identifying and addressing defects during the requirements, design, and development phases.
    - **Importance**: By addressing issues at their source, teams reduce the cost and effort of fixing defects, ensuring higher-quality outcomes. Early testing improves collaboration between developers and testers and shortens development cycles.
- **Shift-Right Testing**
    - **Definition**: Shift-Right testing emphasizes validating software quality in the production environment by leveraging post-deployment testing practices such as monitoring, observability, and real-user feedback.
    - **Importance**: By testing in production, teams gain insights into real-world performance, scalability, and user behavior. It ensures that the software continues to meet user expectations after deployment.

Benefits of Proactive Testing in the Development Cycle

- **Faster Feedback Loops**
    - Shift-Left testing integrates with CI/CD pipelines to provide rapid feedback during code commits, enabling developers to address issues before they escalate.
    - Shift-Right testing uses real-time monitoring and alerts to catch and resolve issues before users are impacted.
- **Improved Collaboration**
    - Shift-Left testing fosters collaboration between developers, testers, and product teams during the early stages of the SDLC, aligning efforts toward quality goals.
    - Shift-Right testing encourages cross-functional collaboration with operations and customer-facing teams to address post-deployment issues.
- **Cost Efficiency**
    - Identifying and fixing defects earlier in the SDLC (Shift-Left) is significantly cheaper than resolving them in production.

- Shift-Right testing reduces long-term maintenance costs by uncovering and addressing latent issues that might affect user experience.

- **Enhanced Product Quality**
  - Proactive testing leads to more robust software by uncovering design flaws and bottlenecks early while ensuring production resilience.
  - Real-world testing under Shift-Right practices provides insights into application performance, helping teams fine-tune their systems.

Techniques and Tools to Implement These Approaches Effectively

This section explores the essential techniques and tools that empower teams to implement these approaches effectively.

Shift-Left Testing Techniques and Tools

- **Behavior-Driven Development (BDD)**
  - **Technique**: BDD encourages collaboration between stakeholders to define acceptance criteria in plain language, ensuring clarity in requirements.
  - **Tool Example**: Cucumber, SpecFlow
- **Static Code Analysis**
  - **Technique**: Analyzing code for errors, vulnerabilities, and performance issues during development ensures adherence to coding standards.
  - **Tool Example**: SonarQube, ESLint
- **Unit Testing**
  - **Technique**: Writing unit tests alongside development helps validate the correctness of individual components early.
  - **Tool Example**: PyTest, JUnit
- **Continuous Integration (CI)**
  - **Technique**: Automating builds and running test suites after each code commit ensures early defect detection.
  - **Tool Example**: Jenkins, GitHub Actions

Shift-Right Testing Techniques and Tools

- **Chaos Engineering**
  - **Technique**: Intentionally introducing failures in production to assess system resilience and recoverability.

  - **Tool Example**: Gremlin, Chaos Monkey
- **Synthetic Monitoring**
  - **Technique**: Simulating user interactions in production to ensure key functionalities are working as expected.
  - **Tool Example**: New Relic, Dynatrace
- **Real-User Monitoring (RUM)**
  - **Technique**: Collecting data from real users to understand application performance and user experience in production.
  - **Tool Example**: Google Lighthouse, AppDynamics
- **Canary and Blue-Green Deployments**
  - **Technique**: Gradual or parallel deployment strategies to test new features in production environments with minimal user impact.
  - **Tool Example**: Kubernetes, Spinnaker

Integration of Shift-Left and Shift-Right Approaches

While Shift-Left and Shift-Right testing are often discussed as separate practices, the most effective testing strategies integrate both. For example:

- **End-to-End CI/CD Pipelines**: Start with static code analysis, unit tests, and integration tests during development (Shift-Left), and conclude with real-user monitoring, chaos testing, and feedback analysis in production (Shift-Right).
- **AI-Driven Testing**: Leveraging AI tools enables seamless integration of early defect detection and real-time production monitoring, creating a unified testing workflow.

By embracing both approaches, organizations can achieve a balanced testing strategy that ensures software quality across the entire lifecycle. This not only improves user satisfaction but also builds confidence in delivering reliable and high-performing applications.

Integration of DevOps and Testing

DevOps, with its emphasis on collaboration, automation, and continuous improvement, has profoundly reshaped software development and testing practices. The integration of testing into DevOps pipelines ensures that quality is embedded throughout the development lifecycle rather than being treated as a separate phase. Key aspects include:

- **Automation and Speed**: DevOps relies heavily on automated processes to maintain fast and frequent deployments. Automated testing ensures that code changes are validated quickly without manual bottlenecks.

- **Shift-Left Testing**: Testing earlier in the development lifecycle aligns with DevOps principles, reducing the time and cost of defect resolution.
- **Shift-Right Testing**: Post-deployment testing and monitoring help teams capture real-world issues, ensuring continuous quality improvement.

By embedding testing into every stage of the DevOps lifecycle, teams deliver robust and reliable software more efficiently.

Continuous Testing Within CI/CD Pipelines

Continuous testing is the practice of executing automated tests at every stage of the CI/CD pipeline to validate changes quickly and consistently. It plays a pivotal role in maintaining the speed and quality of DevOps workflows.

- **Stages of Continuous Testing**:
  - **Build Stage**: Unit and static code analysis tests verify individual components' functionality.
  - **Integration Stage**: API and integration tests ensure that modules work together seamlessly.
  - **Pre-Deployment Stage**: End-to-end and performance tests validate the application before deployment.
  - **Post-Deployment Stage**: Monitoring and observability tools identify production issues.
- **Benefits**:
  - Faster feedback loops reduce time-to-market.
  - Increased test coverage leads to fewer production defects.
  - Early detection of issues minimizes rollback frequency.
- **Popular Tools**:
  - **Jenkins** and **GitHub Actions** for CI/CD.
  - **Selenium**, **PyTest**, and **Cypress** for automated testing.
  - **Dynatrace** and **New Relic** for post-deployment monitoring.

Collaboration between Development, Operations, and Testing Teams

The collaboration between the development, operations, and testing teams appears as follows:

- **Unified Objectives**: DevOps fosters a culture of shared responsibility, where quality is everyone's concern. Testers work closely with developers and operations teams to ensure a seamless delivery process.

- **Tools for Collaboration**:
    - **Communication**: Platforms such as Slack and Microsoft Teams for real-time collaboration.
    - **Source Control**: Git repositories enable version control for code and test scripts.
    - **Shared Dashboards**: Tools such as Grafana provide visibility into testing and production metrics.
- **Blurring of Roles**: Testers adopt skills in coding and infrastructure, developers learn testing practices, and operations teams focus on observability, ensuring cross-functional expertise.

By breaking silos and encouraging collaboration, DevOps creates a testing ecosystem that is fast, adaptive, and reliable, driving the future of test automation.

Impact of Cloud Computing on Test Automation

Cloud computing has transformed test automation by offering platforms that are scalable, accessible, and easy to integrate into development workflows. The rise of cloud-based testing platforms such as BrowserStack, Sauce Labs, and LambdaTest demonstrates how teams can leverage the cloud to simplify testing operations.

- **Demand for Scalability**: Cloud platforms provide on-demand resources, enabling teams to run large-scale test suites without the need for costly infrastructure.
- **Global Accessibility**: Distributed teams can collaborate seamlessly using cloud platforms, ensuring efficient testing workflows regardless of location.

Advantages of Scalability, Cost Efficiency, and Flexibility in Cloud Testing

- **Scalability:**
    - Run hundreds of parallel tests to reduce execution time.
    - Scale resources up or down based on project needs.
- **Cost Efficiency**:
    - Pay-as-you-go models reduce upfront investment in hardware.
    - Cloud services eliminate maintenance costs for physical infrastructure.
- **Flexibility**:
    - Test across diverse environments, including different operating systems, browsers, and devices.

    - Quickly spin up and tear down environments using pre-configured templates.
- **Improved Collaboration**:
    - Centralized dashboards and real-time reporting enhance transparency and decision-making.

Popular Tools and Services for Cloud-Based Test Automation

- **BrowserStack:**
    - Provides real device and browser testing on a cloud platform.
    - Supports Selenium, Appium, and other frameworks.
- **Sauce Labs:**
    - Offers cross-browser and cross-device testing capabilities.
    - Integrates with CI/CD tools for seamless workflows.
- **AWS Device Farm**:
    - Enables testing of mobile and web applications across a wide range of devices.
    - Scales automatically based on testing demand.
- **Google Cloud Testing Tools**:
    - Integrates with Kubernetes and CI/CD pipelines for scalable testing.
- **Azure DevTest Labs**:
    - Simplifies environment provisioning and integrates with Azure Pipelines for test automation.

Cloud computing has become an indispensable part of modern test automation, enabling teams to deliver quality software faster and more efficiently. As cloud platforms evolve, their role in enhancing flexibility, scalability, and cost-effectiveness will continue to grow, solidifying their position as a cornerstone of the future of test automation.

Test Automation in Agile and Continuous Delivery

Agile and DevOps methodologies prioritize rapid, iterative development cycles and frequent deliveries, making test automation a critical component of the software development lifecycle. Automation enables teams to meet the demands of shorter sprint cycles and continuous delivery pipelines by ensuring high-quality outputs without compromising speed.

- **Supporting Agile Principles**:
  - **Quick Feedback Loops**: Automated tests provide immediate feedback on code changes, helping developers address issues early.
  - **Frequent Regression Testing**: Automation ensures that new features do not break existing functionality, enabling seamless additions during sprints.
  - **Consistency**: Automated tests eliminate the variability of manual testing, ensuring reliable results across iterations.
- **Enhancing DevOps Workflows**:
  - **Integration with CI/CD**: Automated tests are integrated into CI/CD pipelines, enabling continuous testing across all stages of development and deployment.
  - **Shift-Left Testing**: Automation allows teams to identify defects early in the development cycle, reducing the cost of fixing issues.
  - **Shift-Right Testing**: Automation supports post-deployment testing by monitoring applications in production environments, ensuring continued reliability.

Automation acts as the backbone of Agile and DevOps practices by ensuring rapid development cycles without compromising quality.

Techniques to Align Test Automation with Rapid Delivery Cycles

To keep up with the fast pace of Agile and continuous delivery workflows, test automation strategies must be highly adaptive and efficient.

- **Modular Test Design**:
  - Break test cases into reusable modules to reduce maintenance efforts and adapt quickly to changing requirements.
- **Parallel Test Execution**:
  - Leverage tools and frameworks such as Selenium Grid, PyTest-xdist, or TestNG to run multiple tests simultaneously, reducing execution time.
- **Continuous Test Automation**:
  - Automate as much as possible, from unit tests to performance tests, ensuring that testing is embedded in every stage of the pipeline.

- **Incremental Automation**:
  - Start by automating high-priority test cases, such as smoke and regression tests, and gradually expand coverage to include other scenarios.
- **Dynamic Test Selection**:
  - Use techniques such as test impact analysis to run only relevant test cases based on recent code changes, optimizing execution time.
- **Integration with Tools**:
  - Use CI/CD platforms such as Jenkins, GitHub Actions, or GitLab to trigger automated test suites on every commit or pull request.
  - Integrate test management tools such as JIRA or TestRail to maintain seamless communication between teams.

Aligning test automation with rapid delivery cycles ensures that quality remains a priority, even under the pressures of shorter timelines.

Challenges and Solutions for Continuous Test Integration

Despite its benefits, integrating continuous testing into Agile and DevOps workflows comes with challenges. Here is a look at common obstacles and how to address them:

- **Challenge: Flaky Tests**
  - Automated tests may produce inconsistent results due to environmental issues or timing dependencies.
  - **Solution**: Use retries with tools such as PyTest-rerunfailures, adopt robust test frameworks, and ensure test environments are isolated and stable.
- **Challenge: High Maintenance Costs**
  - Rapid changes in application features can lead to frequent updates in test scripts.
  - **Solution**: Adopt practices such as self-healing tests that automatically adjust to UI changes and use page-object models to reduce script dependencies.
- **Challenge: Limited Test Coverage in Short Cycles**
  - Achieving high test coverage can be difficult within short sprint cycles.
  - **Solution**: Focus on risk-based testing to prioritize critical paths and use automated tools for exploratory testing to identify issues quickly.
- **Challenge: Environment and Data Management**
  - Managing consistent test environments and datasets can be complex in dynamic workflows.

  - **Solution**: Use Infrastructure as Code (IaC) tools such as Terraform for environment provisioning and data virtualization to create reusable datasets.
- **Challenge: Integration Complexity**
  - Incorporating various tools and frameworks into a single pipeline can be overwhelming.
  - **Solution**: Use orchestration tools such as Jenkins or Azure Pipelines to create cohesive workflows and establish clear integration standards.
- **Challenge: Resistance to Change**
  - Teams accustomed to traditional methods may resist adopting automation in Agile and DevOps workflows.
  - **Solution**: Promote a culture of collaboration and continuous learning through training programs and hands-on workshops.

By addressing these challenges, teams can successfully implement continuous test integration and maximize the benefits of Agile and DevOps practices.

Test automation is indispensable in Agile and continuous delivery environments. By leveraging advanced techniques, overcoming challenges, and adopting best practices, teams can ensure that their development cycles are efficient, reliable, and scalable. This proactive approach equips organizations to meet the ever-increasing demands of modern software delivery.

Future Role of Test Automation Engineers

The rapid evolution of test automation demands that engineers continually adapt their skills to remain valuable in a competitive market. As testing practices and technologies shift, automation engineers must embrace a combination of technical expertise, analytical abilities, and soft skills.

- **Advanced Technical Proficiency:**
  - **Programming and Scripting**: Mastery of languages such as Python, JavaScript, or Java is essential for designing robust test scripts and frameworks.
  - **AI and Machine Learning**: Familiarity with AI/ML concepts enables engineers to implement predictive testing models, anomaly detection, and self-healing tests.
  - **Cloud Technologies**: Understanding cloud platforms such as AWS, Azure, or Google Cloud is crucial for leveraging cloud-based testing solutions.
  - **DevOps and CI/CD**: Knowledge of continuous integration and deployment pipelines, as well as tools such as Jenkins, GitHub Actions, or

GitLab CI/CD, ensures seamless integration of testing with development workflows.

- **Analytical and Problem-Solving Skills**:
  - Engineers must analyze complex systems, identify potential failure points, and design comprehensive testing strategies.
- **Soft Skills**:
  - **Collaboration**: Working closely with developers, product managers, and operations teams is vital for success in Agile and DevOps environments.
  - **Adaptability**: Staying open to learning and adapting to new tools, technologies, and methodologies is essential in a rapidly changing landscape.

By developing a diverse skill set, test automation engineers can maintain their relevance and become indispensable assets in the software development lifecycle.

Evolving Responsibilities: From Scriptwriting to Strategic Automation

The role of test automation engineers has shifted significantly over the years. Initially focused on scriptwriting and basic test execution, the scope of responsibilities has now expanded to encompass strategic contributions to the software development process.

- **Beyond Scriptwriting:**
  - Engineers are now expected to design comprehensive test frameworks that accommodate scalability and flexibility.
  - Automation efforts extend beyond functional testing to include performance, security, and compliance testing.
- **Strategic Involvement:**
  - Test automation engineers actively participate in defining quality metrics and setting benchmarks for success.
  - They collaborate with teams to integrate testing seamlessly into CI/CD pipelines, ensuring continuous quality.
- **Innovation and Experimentation:**
  - Engineers are tasked with exploring new tools and technologies to improve efficiency and reliability.
  - This includes adopting AI-driven testing solutions, dynamic test case generation, and advanced monitoring systems.

- **Coaching and Mentorship:**
  - Senior automation engineers often take on roles as mentors, guiding junior team members and sharing best practices to foster a culture of quality.

This evolution emphasizes the strategic importance of automation engineers in ensuring robust, scalable, and efficient testing practices.

Importance of Cross-Disciplinary Knowledge

In the future, test automation engineers will need to bridge the gap between various disciplines, combining their expertise with knowledge from fields such as DevOps, AI, and system architecture.

- **DevOps Integration**:
  - Engineers must understand DevOps principles to create testing strategies that align with development and operations workflows.
  - Automation engineers play a critical role in continuous testing, helping to maintain rapid feedback loops within CI/CD pipelines.
- **Artificial Intelligence and Machine Learning**:
  - Familiarity with AI/ML concepts allows engineers to harness tools that enhance testing efficiency, such as predictive analytics, intelligent test generation, and self-healing scripts.
  - This cross-disciplinary knowledge also enables engineers to evaluate and implement cutting-edge solutions tailored to specific testing needs.
- **Domain Knowledge**:
  - Gaining a deeper understanding of the domain under test (for example, finance, healthcare, or IoT) helps engineers design test cases that address industry-specific requirements and challenges.
- **Security and Compliance**:
  - Engineers are increasingly involved in ensuring that applications meet security standards and comply with regulations, requiring knowledge of security testing frameworks and compliance tools.
- **Collaboration Across Teams**:
  - The ability to communicate and work effectively with developers, operations teams, and business stakeholders is crucial. Engineers must act as a bridge, ensuring testing aligns with broader business goals.

By embracing cross-disciplinary knowledge, test automation engineers can expand their influence and impact within organizations, shaping the future of quality assurance in the software development lifecycle.

The role of test automation engineers is evolving from a purely technical focus to a strategic position that bridges multiple disciplines. Engineers who adapt to these changes by cultivating diverse skills, embracing innovation, and collaborating across teams will play a pivotal role in shaping the future of software testing. This transformation not only enhances the value of individual engineers but also drives the quality and efficiency of software development at large.

Predictions and Speculations for the Future of Test Automation

The field of test automation is undergoing a profound transformation, influenced by advancements in technology and evolving software development practices. Several trends are poised to shape the future, driving innovation and redefining testing workflows:

- **AI-Driven Testing**:
  - **Predictive Testing**: AI will analyze historical data to predict potential vulnerabilities and optimize test coverage.
  - **Self-Healing Automation**: Test scripts will dynamically adapt to changes in the application under test, reducing maintenance overhead.
- **Hyperautomation**:
  - Combining test automation with business process automation to create end-to-end automated workflows that go beyond traditional testing boundaries.
  - Tools powered by AI and Robotic Process Automation (RPA) will facilitate seamless integration between different systems.
- **Test Automation for Edge and IoT**:
  - With the rise of edge computing and IoT, automation will expand to include connected devices, requiring robust tools for handling complex data streams and edge-case scenarios.
- **Low-Code/No-Code Automation**:
  - Tools enabling non-technical users to design and execute automated tests will grow in popularity, democratizing access to testing capabilities.
- **Blockchain Testing**:
  - As blockchain adoption increases, testing tools will evolve to ensure the integrity, security, and scalability of decentralized systems.

These trends will not only enhance the efficiency of testing processes but also elevate the strategic importance of test automation in delivering reliable and innovative software solutions.

Speculations on the Role of Automation in the Next Decade

As software systems grow in complexity and scale, test automation is expected to assume an even more central role in software development. The following are some of the speculations about its trajectory:

- **Automation as a Service (AaaS)**: Cloud platforms will provide modular and scalable test automation solutions, allowing teams to access pre-built testing frameworks and on-demand resources.
- **Full Lifecycle Integration**: Automation will span the entire software lifecycle, from requirements validation to deployment monitoring, enabling a continuous quality pipeline.
- **Cognitive Automation**: Automation tools will incorporate cognitive capabilities, such as Natural Language Processing (NLP) and decision-making, to understand test requirements and generate cases automatically.
- **Human-AI Collaboration**: Engineers will work alongside intelligent systems to design, execute, and interpret complex test scenarios, blending human insight with machine precision.
- **Ubiquitous Testing**: Testing will be embedded across all phases of development and operations, ensuring that every aspect of the software lifecycle is monitored and validated in real time.

These shifts indicate a future where automation transcends its current role, becoming a cornerstone of innovation and quality assurance across industries.

Vision for the Integration of Cutting-Edge Technology with Testing

The future of test automation is intrinsically linked to the adoption of cutting-edge technologies that amplify its capabilities and scope. Here is a vision of how these integrations may unfold:

- **AI-Enhanced Test Orchestration**: AI will enable the intelligent orchestration of tests, automatically prioritizing high-risk areas and optimizing execution sequences to maximize efficiency.
- **Quantum Computing and Testing**: As quantum computing becomes more accessible, test automation tools will evolve to validate quantum algorithms and systems, unlocking new dimensions of computational testing.
- **5G and Real-Time Automation**: With the proliferation of 5G networks, real-time testing of applications across distributed environments will become a reality, ensuring performance and reliability at unprecedented speeds.

- **Virtual Reality (VR) and Augmented Reality (AR)**: Automation frameworks will incorporate VR/AR testing capabilities to validate immersive user experiences and interface interactions in next-generation applications.
- **Sustainability and Green Testing**: The integration of environmental considerations into testing practices will lead to the development of eco-friendly automation frameworks, optimizing energy consumption and resource usage.
- **Holistic Observability**: Automation will leverage observability tools to provide end-to-end insights, enabling proactive issue resolution and continuous improvement.

By embracing these advancements, test automation will not only evolve to meet the demands of future technologies but also redefine how software quality is ensured in a rapidly changing world.

The future of test automation is brimming with possibilities, driven by emerging technologies and a growing focus on innovation. By anticipating these changes and preparing for them, professionals in the field can ensure that they remain at the forefront of this transformative journey. As automation continues to evolve, its role will expand beyond testing, becoming a pivotal enabler of reliable, efficient, and groundbreaking software solutions.

Conclusion

As we conclude this book, it is clear that the world of test automation is more dynamic and promising than ever. The evolution of testing practices–from early manual approaches to modern, AI-driven, and cloud-powered solutions–highlights the relentless pursuit of efficiency, quality, and innovation in software development.

Throughout this chapter, we explored the exciting possibilities of test automation's future, driven by advancements in AI, ML, IoT, and blockchain, as well as the integration of DevOps and agile methodologies. These trends underscore that staying ahead in the testing landscape requires not only technical proficiency but also adaptability and a vision for the long-term impact of cutting-edge technologies.

A Glimpse into the Future

The journey does not end here. Test automation will continue to evolve, shaping the software development lifecycle in ways we can only imagine today. By embracing innovation, fostering collaboration across disciplines, and honing critical skills, test automation engineers have the opportunity to lead the way in building faster, more reliable, and transformative digital solutions.

As you move forward, may the insights from this book empower you to embrace the challenges and opportunities that lie ahead, positioning yourself as a pioneer in the ever-changing realm of software testing and automation. The future is full of potential, and the role you play in shaping it is as important as the tools and technologies that define it.

As a special addition, we have included a bonus chapter exploring the transformative potential of Generative AI in automation testing. As the testing landscape evolves, Generative AI emerges as a transformative force, revolutionizing test case generation, data creation, and coverage enhancement. This bonus chapter dives into the potential of GenAI to redefine automation testing, offering practical insights and future possibilities.

Key Takeaways

- **The Ever-Changing Landscape of Test Automation:** Test automation continues to evolve, driven by advancements in AI, machine learning, IoT, blockchain, and cloud technologies. Staying ahead requires continuous learning and adaptation to emerging trends.
- **AI and ML Revolutionizing Testing**: AI and ML enable innovations such as self-healing tests, predictive analytics, and anomaly detection, making test automation smarter, faster, and more reliable. However, challenges such as adoption complexity and trust must be addressed.
- **Shift-Left and Shift-Right Testing**: Proactive testing in earlier stages (Shift-Left) and monitoring in production (Shift-Right) ensure better quality and faster feedback. Techniques such as test-driven development, real-time analytics, and chaos testing are critical to these approaches.
- **Integration of DevOps and Agile Practices**: Continuous testing within CI/CD pipelines and seamless collaboration between development, operations, and testing teams enable streamlined workflows, faster delivery, and higher software quality.
- **Cloud Computing's Impact**: Cloud-based testing platforms offer unparalleled scalability, cost efficiency, and flexibility, transforming how testing environments are managed and enabling global collaboration.
- **The Evolving Role of Test Automation Engineers**: Test automation engineers must adapt to shifting responsibilities, including strategic decision-making, leveraging AI and DevOps practices, and gaining cross-disciplinary knowledge to remain relevant in the future landscape.

- **Predictions for the Future**: Emerging trends such as hyper-automation, the rise of autonomous testing systems, and the deeper integration of AI/ML into testing processes will define the next decade of software development.
- **The Road Ahead**: Test automation will play a pivotal role in bridging innovation and quality in software development. Engineers equipped with technical expertise and strategic foresight will be instrumental in shaping this future.

These takeaways encapsulate the key learnings from the chapter and provide actionable insights to navigate the evolving field of test automation confidently.

CHAPTER 11
Leveraging Generative AI in Testing

Introduction

Generative AI (GenAI) is transforming software testing by introducing intelligent automation that goes beyond traditional scripted approaches. With models such as ChatGPT, Claude, and Gemini, testers can now generate test cases, create diverse test data, and even enhance test coverage with minimal manual intervention. This shift is redefining how test automation is implemented, making it more adaptive, efficient, and capable of handling complex testing scenarios.

In this chapter, we will explore how GenAI can be leveraged to streamline various aspects of test automation. We will discuss its role in test case generation, dynamic test data creation, and improving overall test coverage. Additionally, we will examine the practical applications of integrating GenAI into existing workflows, along with real-world use cases showcasing its effectiveness.

While GenAI brings significant advantages, it also introduces challenges, such as maintaining accuracy, ensuring security, and addressing ethical concerns. We will delve into these considerations and discuss how to balance the power of AI-driven automation with responsible testing practices. By the end of this chapter, you will have a deep understanding of how to harness GenAI to enhance test automation and prepare for the next wave of AI-driven testing innovations.

Structure

This chapter explores the impact of Generative AI (GenAI) on software testing, focusing on its capabilities, applications, and challenges. Here is what we will cover:

- Introduction to Generative AI in Testing
- Benefits of Using GenAI for Automation Testing
- Using GenAI in Testing

- Integrating GenAI Tools into Existing Workflows
- Challenges and Ethical Considerations
- Future Directions for AI in Testing

Introduction to Generative AI in Testing

The rapid advancement of Artificial Intelligence (AI) has significantly influenced various domains, including software testing. Among these advancements, Generative AI (GenAI) stands out as a groundbreaking technology capable of transforming the way tests are designed, executed, and maintained. By leveraging Large Language Models (LLMs) such as ChatGPT, Claude, and Gemini, Generative AI introduces a new paradigm in test automation, helping testers generate test cases, test data, and even predict potential failures with greater efficiency and accuracy.

Overview

Generative AI refers to a subset of AI that can create new content, including text, images, and code, based on patterns learned from vast amounts of training data. Unlike traditional AI models that primarily classify or analyze data, GenAI is designed to generate human-like responses, making it particularly useful in software testing.

Key capabilities of GenAI include:

- **Natural Language Understanding (NLU):** Interpreting and generating human-like test scenarios.
- **Code Generation:** Writing test scripts based on user prompts.
- **Pattern Recognition:** Identifying common bugs and suggesting improvements in test automation strategies.

In the context of test automation, these capabilities enable testers to automate various aspects of the software testing lifecycle, from writing test scripts to identifying defects, thus reducing manual effort and increasing test coverage.

Application of Generative AI in Software Testing

The application of Generative AI in software testing primarily revolves around automation, intelligence, and efficiency. Here are some key ways it enhances testing workflows:

- **Automated Test Case Generation:**
    - GenAI can generate test cases based on functional requirements or user stories.

  - It can cover a wide range of scenarios, including edge cases that might be overlooked in manual test creation.
- **Test Data Generation:**
  - GenAI models can create diverse, realistic test datasets, ensuring better coverage for different input conditions.
  - AI-generated data helps in performance, security, and boundary testing.
- **Self-Healing Tests:**
  - One of the biggest challenges in test automation is maintaining test scripts as the application evolves.
  - GenAI-powered frameworks can analyze UI changes and self-heal automation scripts by dynamically adapting to modifications.
- **Code Optimization and Debugging:**
  - AI can assist testers in identifying inefficiencies in test scripts and suggesting optimizations.
  - It can also debug failing test cases by analyzing logs and pinpointing errors.
- **Predictive Analysis and Test Optimization:**
  - AI models can predict flaky tests and suggest more stable alternatives.
  - They can analyze past failures to identify recurring patterns and improve test strategy.

Evolution of AI-Driven Testing

AI-driven testing has evolved significantly over the past decade, with Generative AI marking the latest leap in automation. The journey can be divided into three major phases:

- **Rule-Based Automation (Pre-2010s):**
  - Early automation relied on predefined rules and scripts.
  - Lacked intelligence to adapt to changes, making maintenance costly.
- **AI-Powered Test Automation (2010s – Early 2020s):**
  - Introduction of Machine Learning (ML) models for test execution and defect prediction.
  - AI-assisted test frameworks (for example, self-healing automation) gained popularity.
- **Generative AI in Testing (Present and Beyond):**
  - AI can now generate test cases, scripts, and reports without human intervention.

- Continuous learning models improve accuracy and efficiency over time.
- Integration with DevOps and CI/CD pipelines enables real-time, AI-driven test execution.

As Generative AI continues to evolve, its role in test automation will only grow, making testing more intelligent, efficient, and scalable. The following sections will explore its benefits, practical applications, and future possibilities in greater detail.

Benefits of Using GenAI for Automation Testing

Generative AI is transforming the landscape of automation testing by introducing intelligence, adaptability, and efficiency into traditional testing workflows. By leveraging advanced AI models such as **ChatGPT, Claude, and Gemini**, testers can generate test cases, optimize automation scripts, and even predict failures with minimal manual intervention. This section explores the key benefits of integrating Generative AI into automation testing.

Improved Test Coverage and Efficiency

One of the biggest advantages of Generative AI in testing is its ability to expand test coverage while maintaining efficiency. AI-powered models can generate diverse test cases covering multiple scenarios that might be overlooked in manual test creation.

How GenAI Improves Test Coverage:

- **Automated Generation of Edge Cases:** AI can analyze application logic and create test cases for boundary values, negative scenarios, and rare conditions that testers might miss.
- **Comprehensive UI and API Testing:** GenAI can assist in both UI and API testing by generating meaningful interactions and validating responses across different environments.
- **Multi-Browser and Multi-Device Testing:** AI can create test scenarios that ensure cross-browser and cross-platform compatibility, reducing the risk of missing critical bugs.

Efficiency Gains with GenAI:

- AI significantly reduces the time required to create and execute test cases, improving test execution speed in CI/CD pipelines.
- It enables faster feedback loops, helping teams detect and resolve issues early in the development cycle.

- AI-powered tools can prioritize test execution based on risk analysis, ensuring that critical test cases run first.

By automating repetitive tasks and generating high-quality test cases, Generative AI ensures comprehensive test coverage with minimal human effort, making the testing process faster and more reliable.

Reduced Manual Effort in Test Generation

Traditionally, writing test cases requires significant time and expertise, often leading to bottlenecks in fast-paced development environments. Generative AI addresses this challenge by automating test creation, reducing the need for manual intervention.

How GenAI Reduces Manual Effort:

- **Test Case Generation from Requirements:** AI models can interpret natural language specifications and convert them into structured test cases.
- **Automated Test Script Writing:** AI can generate Selenium, Playwright, or API test scripts in Python, Java, or JavaScript-based on high-level test descriptions.
- **Instant Test Scenario Expansion:** AI can take a single user story and generate multiple test cases covering different functional flows, reducing the time spent on manual test design.

Example Use Case: A QA team receives a new feature description. Instead of manually writing test cases, they provide the feature details to an AI model, such as ChatGPT, which automatically generates a full test suite, including functional, edge, and regression tests. This accelerates the test creation process and ensures consistency across test cases.

By leveraging AI-driven automation, testers can focus on high-value activities such as test strategy, exploratory testing, and analyzing test results instead of spending time on repetitive test case creation.

Adaptive and Self-Healing Automation

One of the most frustrating challenges in automation testing is test script maintenance. Automated tests often break due to minor UI changes, leading to false positives and unnecessary debugging efforts. Generative AI helps overcome this issue with self-healing automation capabilities.

How GenAI Enables Self-Healing Tests:

- **Dynamic Element Identification:** AI-powered test frameworks can detect UI changes (for example, renamed buttons, modified layouts) and automatically update test scripts instead of failing.

- **Adaptive Locators:** Instead of relying on hardcoded element locators, AI dynamically adjusts XPath, CSS selectors, or test identifiers based on page structure changes.
- **Smart Failure Analysis:** AI models can analyze test failures and suggest fixes, helping teams quickly resolve issues.

Example Use Case: A login page undergoes a minor update, changing the "`Sign In`" button to "`Login`." Traditional automation scripts would fail, requiring manual intervention. However, a GenAI-enhanced automation framework can detect this UI modification and adjust the test script automatically, preventing test failures.

Additional Benefits of Self-Healing Automation:

- Reduces test flakiness, leading to more stable CI/CD pipelines.
- Minimizes maintenance overhead, allowing testers to focus on new test development.
- Improves test execution reliability, making automation a more robust part of the SDLC.

The integration of Generative AI in automation testing brings several key benefits, including:

- **Improved test coverage** through automated edge-case generation.
- **Faster test creation** with reduced manual effort.
- **Self-healing automation** minimizes maintenance efforts and enhances test stability.

By adopting GenAI-driven testing, teams can accelerate development cycles, improve software quality, and reduce the time spent on repetitive tasks, making testing more efficient, adaptive, and scalable.

Using GenAI in Testing

Generative AI is revolutionizing the way test cases, test data, and test coverage are managed in automation testing. By leveraging Large Language Models (LLMs) such as ChatGPT, Claude, and Gemini, testers can automate critical parts of their workflow, making testing more efficient, scalable, and intelligent. This section explores three key areas where GenAI enhances automation testing:

- Generating Test Cases with AI
- Creating AI-Generated Test Data
- Enhancing Test Coverage

Generating Test Cases with GenAI

Traditionally, test case creation requires manual effort, domain expertise, and extensive documentation. Generative AI simplifies this by analyzing application code, user behavior, and system logs to automatically generate functional, regression, and edge test cases.

How AI Generates Test Cases:

- **Code Analysis for Test Case Generation**
    - GenAI models can scan application code, detect critical functions, and suggest relevant test cases.
    - AI can identify untested code paths, ensuring better code coverage.
    - **Example**: Given a Python Flask API, AI can generate API test cases covering valid, invalid, and edge inputs.
- **User Behavior Analysis for Test Generation**
    - AI models can analyze real-world user interactions from logs, analytics, or heatmaps to generate realistic test scenarios.
    - Helps in automating frequently used workflows and detecting common failure patterns.
    - **Example**: AI identifies that 80% of users abandon checkout due to a slow payment gateway and generates performance and UI tests targeting that flow.
- **Natural Language Processing (NLP) for Test Scenarios**
    - AI can convert user stories or requirements into structured test cases.
    - Given a feature description, AI can create test cases covering positive, negative, and boundary conditions.
    - **Example**: "A *user should be able to reset their password.*" AI generates:
        i. Verify a valid password reset request.
        ii. Test invalid email input handling.
        ii. Ensure expired reset links are rejected.

By automating test case generation, AI reduces manual effort, improves efficiency, and ensures more comprehensive test coverage.

Creating Test Data with GenAI

Test data plays a crucial role in validating application behavior, but generating diverse and realistic test data is often time-consuming. Generative AI can automate test data generation, ensuring that testing scenarios reflect real-world use cases.

AI-Generated Synthetic Data for Testing

AI models can create **synthetic test data** for:

- **Functional Testing:** Generating valid and invalid input combinations.
- **Performance Testing:** Creating large datasets to simulate high user loads.
- **Security Testing:** Crafting malicious payloads to test injection vulnerabilities.
- **Compliance Testing:** Ensuring GDPR-compliant masked data for regulated industries.

Example: Generating API Test Data

A banking application needs test data for loan applications. AI can generate:

- **Valid scenarios:** Age > 21, credit score > 700, or stable income.
- **Edge cases:** Age = 18, credit score = 699, or missing income details.
- **Negative cases:** Empty fields, invalid formats, or duplicate records.

By automating test data creation, AI eliminates manual data entry, reducing errors while ensuring full test coverage.

Ensuring Diverse and Realistic Test Data

Generating high-quality test data is essential for comprehensive testing, but manually creating diverse and realistic datasets can be time-consuming and error-prone. AI-driven test data generation simplifies this process by producing varied, compliant, and edge-case data, ensuring robust test coverage across multiple scenarios.

- **AI-Based Data Variability**
    - AI generates data variations covering different demographics, device types, and transaction patterns.
    - Helps in localization testing by producing names, addresses, and currencies from different countries.
- **Masking and Anonymization for Compliance**
    - AI can generate synthetic personal data that mimics real-world information without exposing sensitive user data.
    - Useful for healthcare, finance, and e-commerce applications that require GDPR and HIPAA compliance.
- **Generating Edge Case Data**
    - AI can stress-test applications by creating extreme data scenarios (for

example, usernames with 100+ characters, numeric overflow, missing fields).

- Ensures applications handle rare but possible conditions effectively.

By leveraging AI-generated test data, testers save time, improve test reliability, and enhance security compliance.

Enhancing Test Coverage with GenAI

Achieving high test coverage is a major challenge in software testing. Generative AI expands coverage by generating tests that explore edge cases, unexpected behaviors, and hidden risks.

How AI Improves Exploratory Testing and Edge Case Identification:

- **AI-Driven Exploratory Testing**
    - AI analyzes application behavior in real time and suggests new test cases dynamically.
    - Identifies unexpected user behaviors or system responses that manual testers might overlook.
    - **Example**: The AI notices that users repeatedly abandon checkout when switching payment methods and generates new test scenarios to validate multi-payment flows.
- **Edge Case Identification**
    - AI can automatically detect missing scenarios by simulating:
        - Unusual input values (for example, emojis in text fields, special characters in usernames).
        - Concurrent user interactions (for example, two users editing the same document at the same time).
        - Extreme load conditions (for example, processing 1 million transactions in a second).
- **Auto-Generated Regression Tests**
    - AI monitors previous test executions and identifies critical areas that require automated regression tests.
    - Helps teams quickly adjust to application changes without rewriting test scripts.

Example Use Cases in Complex Applications:

- **E-commerce Platform Testing**
    - AI automatically generates checkout flow test cases based on real-world purchase behaviors.

    - Identifies edge cases such as discount stacking, invalid promo codes, and abandoned cart scenarios.
- **Healthcare Application Validation**
    - AI creates synthetic patient data that mimics real-world medical records without violating privacy laws.
    - Generates edge cases such as overlapping medication schedules or incorrect dosage alerts.
- **Banking and Finance Security Testing**
    - AI generates fraud detection test cases by simulating money laundering attempts or duplicate transactions.
    - Creates stress-test scenarios with millions of concurrent banking transactions to validate system robustness.

Generative AI is transforming software testing by:

- Generating test cases dynamically based on code and user interactions.
- Creating high-quality test data for diverse and compliant test scenarios.
- Enhancing test coverage through AI-driven exploratory and edge case testing.

By integrating GenAI-powered tools such as ChatGPT, Claude, and Gemini, testers can improve efficiency, expand test coverage, and automate critical testing processes, ensuring robust software quality.

Integrating GenAI Tools into Existing Workflows

Generative AI can significantly enhance test automation, but to fully realize its benefits, it must be seamlessly integrated into existing testing workflows and CI/CD pipelines. This section explores:

- Incorporating AI-based tools into CI/CD pipelines
- Challenges in AI integration and overcoming them

Incorporating AI-Based Tools into CI/CD Pipelines

Modern software development relies on Continuous Integration and Continuous Deployment (CI/CD) to ensure rapid, high-quality releases. Integrating GenAI-powered testing tools into CI/CD pipelines can improve test automation, defect detection, and regression testing without adding manual overhead.

Automating Test Generation in CI/CD

GenAI can generate test cases dynamically based on code changes, pull requests, and system logs.

Integration Steps:

1. Set up an AI-powered test generator (for example, ChatGPT API) within your CI/CD pipeline.
2. Configure it to analyze commits and suggest new test cases dynamically.
3. Automatically run AI-generated test cases using pytest, JUnit, or other testing frameworks.
4. Integrate with test management tools (for example, TestRail, Zephyr) for better tracking.

Example:

A **GitHub Actions pipeline** triggers AI-based test generation whenever a developer pushes new code. The pipeline dynamically creates and executes test cases using **pytest**, ensuring that new functionality is adequately tested.

Enhancing Test Data Generation in CI/CD

AI models can generate synthetic test data on demand, eliminating the need for static datasets.

Integration Steps:

1. Configure an AI data generator (for example, OpenAI API, Faker with AI extensions) in your pipeline.
2. Automate test data creation for unit, integration, and performance testing.
3. Use AI-generated data to test edge cases, security vulnerabilities, and performance bottlenecks.

Example: A Jenkins pipeline uses an AI-powered tool to generate realistic banking transaction data, allowing QA teams to test fraud detection algorithms at scale.

AI-Driven Test Optimization and Self-Healing Automation

AI can monitor test execution results, detect flaky tests, and auto-correct failing scripts.

Integration Steps:

1. Use GenAI-powered self-healing test frameworks (for example, Mabl, TestRigor) to detect UI and API changes.
2. Set up auto-healing scripts that update locators and API endpoints dynamically.
3. Integrate AI-driven defect analysis tools to identify patterns in test failures.

Example: A CircleCI pipeline integrates with AI-based test automation tools that detect changes in web elements (for example, CSS selectors, XPath) and automatically update test scripts, reducing flaky test failures.

Overcoming Integration Challenges

Despite its advantages, integrating GenAI into existing testing pipelines poses certain challenges. Here is how to tackle them:

Ensuring AI Model Accuracy and Reliability

AI-generated test cases and data must be **relevant, reliable, and free from bias.**

Solution:

- Continuously validate AI-generated tests against real user workflows.
- Train AI models using historical test execution results for better accuracy.
- Implement human-in-the-loop validation where testers review AI suggestions before execution.

Managing Security and Compliance Risks

AI-generated data may expose sensitive information or violate compliance requirements.

Solution:

- Use data anonymization and masking techniques for compliance (for example, GDPR, HIPAA).
- Limit AI model access to sensitive data using role-based security policies.
- Regularly audit AI outputs to ensure compliance with security standards.

Addressing AI Integration Complexity

Many existing CI/CD tools are not AI-native, requiring additional effort to integrate AI functionalities.

Solution:

- Use AI-powered testing platforms (for example, TestCraft, Functionize) that integrate with CI/CD tools such as Jenkins, GitHub Actions, and GitLab CI.
- Leverage AI APIs (for example, OpenAI, Gemini, Claude) to create custom AI-powered testing workflows.
- Start with pilot projects before fully rolling out AI-driven automation.

Handling AI Resource Constraints and Execution Time

AI-based test generation and execution can slow down CI/CD pipelines if not optimized.

Solution:

- Use parallel test execution to distribute AI-generated test cases across multiple test environments.
- Optimize AI model calls by caching frequently used responses to reduce processing time.
- Implement smart AI triggers that selectively generate tests only when critical changes occur.

By integrating GenAI-based tools such as ChatGPT, Claude, and Gemini into CI/CD pipelines, teams can:

- Automate test case generation and execution.
- Improve test coverage with AI-generated data and self-healing automation.
- Reduce manual effort while enhancing test reliability and scalability.

With proper validation, security, and performance optimizations, AI-powered testing can seamlessly integrate into existing workflows, making test automation more efficient and adaptive.

Challenges and Ethical Considerations

While Generative AI introduces significant advancements in software testing, it also brings several challenges and ethical concerns. AI-generated tests must be reliable, unbiased, and aligned with ethical guidelines to ensure fairness, security, and trustworthiness in automation. This section explores key challenges, including bias in AI-generated tests, reliability issues, and the ethical implications of using AI in testing.

Bias and Reliability Concerns in AI-Generated Tests

AI models are trained on vast amounts of data, but the quality of their outputs depends on the training data and the model's ability to generalize across different scenarios. Bias and reliability are two major concerns when using AI-generated tests.

- **Bias in Test Case Generation:** AI models may introduce biases if they are trained on imbalanced datasets. For example, an AI-powered testing tool that generates test cases based on historical data may fail to cover edge cases that were not frequently encountered in the past. This can lead to an overrepresentation of common test scenarios while missing critical failure points. To mitigate bias, it is crucial to train AI models on diverse datasets that include a wide range of user behaviors, system configurations, and edge cases. Regular audits of AI-generated test cases can help identify gaps in coverage.
- **False Positives and False Negatives:** AI-driven test automation may generate test cases that incorrectly flag valid functionality as a failure (false positives) or overlook actual defects (false negatives). This can lead to unnecessary debugging efforts or undetected issues slipping into production. Improving AI model accuracy requires continuous feedback loops where human testers validate AI-generated tests and refine test strategies based on real-world results. Hybrid approaches that combine AI-generated tests with traditional scripted tests can also improve reliability.
- **Context Awareness and Logical Understanding:** AI-generated test cases often lack deep contextual understanding, which can lead to irrelevant or incorrect test scenarios. Unlike human testers who apply domain knowledge to test design, AI models rely solely on pattern recognition. This can result in tests that do not align with actual business requirements or user workflows.

  To address this challenge, AI-generated test cases should be reviewed by experienced testers who can validate their relevance and correctness before they are integrated into automation suites.

Ethical Considerations of AI-Driven Testing

As AI becomes more integrated into testing, ethical considerations must be addressed to ensure transparency, accountability, and fairness.

- **Transparency and Explainability:** AI models operate as black boxes, making it difficult to understand why a particular test case was generated or why a certain test outcome occurred. This lack of transparency can create challenges in debugging and decision-making.

Organizations should adopt AI models that offer explainability features, providing insights into how test cases are generated and why specific failures are detected. This helps build trust in AI-driven testing and allows testers to make informed decisions.

- **Accountability for AI-Generated Outcomes:** When AI-driven tests fail or produce incorrect results, it is essential to determine responsibility. If a faulty AI-generated test leads to a critical production defect, who should be held accountable–the AI system, the development team, or the testing team?

  To ensure accountability, AI-generated tests should be continuously monitored and reviewed by human testers. Establishing clear guidelines on AI decision-making and assigning human oversight can help mitigate risks associated with automation failures.

- **Security and Privacy Risks:** AI-generated test data may inadvertently expose sensitive information, especially when working with real-world datasets. If an AI tool generates test scenarios based on production data, there is a risk of violating data privacy regulations. Organizations should enforce strict data anonymization and access control policies when using AI-generated test data. Ensuring compliance with data protection regulations such as GDPR and HIPAA is essential when leveraging AI in testing.

- **Job Displacement and Ethical Workforce Impact:** The adoption of AI-driven testing tools raises concerns about job displacement within the software testing industry. While AI can automate many aspects of test generation and execution, human testers remain critical for test planning, validation, and exploratory testing.

  Rather than replacing testers, AI should be seen as an augmentation tool that enhances productivity. Organizations should invest in reskilling programs to help testers adapt to AI-driven workflows, focusing on higher-level testing strategies and AI oversight rather than repetitive test execution.

Balancing AI Automation with Ethical and Reliable Testing

To ensure responsible AI adoption in testing, organizations must establish ethical guidelines that prioritize fairness, accuracy, and transparency. AI should be used as a complement to human expertise rather than a complete replacement. By continuously validating AI-generated tests, addressing bias, and maintaining accountability, teams can leverage the benefits of AI while mitigating potential risks.

Future Directions for AI in Testing

The role of AI in software testing is evolving rapidly, with new advancements reshaping how teams approach automation, test generation, and quality assurance. As Generative AI continues to mature, it will play a more significant role in optimizing testing processes, reducing human effort, and improving software reliability. This section explores emerging trends in AI-driven test automation, predictions for the next decade, and the potential of AI agents in testing workflows.

Emerging Trends in AI and Test Automation

As AI continues to evolve, its impact on test automation is becoming increasingly profound. From AI agents that autonomously manage test execution to advanced generative models that assist in test creation, the future of testing is moving toward greater intelligence and efficiency. These emerging trends are shaping a new era where AI-driven tools not only optimize testing processes but also collaborate with human testers to enhance software quality.

- **AI Agents for Autonomous Testing:** AI agents—autonomous software programs that can analyze, learn, and make decisions—are set to revolutionize test automation. Unlike traditional AI-based test automation tools, AI agents can dynamically adapt to changes in applications, create and execute test cases, and self-heal broken tests without human intervention. These agents leverage reinforcement learning, knowledge graphs, and reasoning capabilities to perform exploratory testing, detect UI changes, and optimize test coverage.

  In the near future, AI agents will be able to collaborate with human testers, providing intelligent recommendations and automating routine testing tasks while allowing testers to focus on complex scenarios that require critical thinking.

- **Self-Healing Test Automation:** One of the biggest challenges in automation testing is test script maintenance. AI-driven self-healing test automation enables test scripts to automatically adjust to UI or API changes without requiring manual intervention. By analyzing historical execution patterns and real-time application updates, AI can modify locators, test assertions, and workflows to prevent test failures caused by minor UI changes.

- **Generative AI for Code and Test Case Creation:** AI models such as ChatGPT, Claude, and Gemini are already being used to generate code snippets, documentation, and test cases. In the coming years, these models will become even more refined, allowing testers to generate end-to-end automation scripts using natural language prompts. This will democratize test automation, enabling non-programmers to write and execute automated tests with minimal coding knowledge.

- **AI-Augmented Exploratory Testing:** While automation testing primarily focuses on predefined scripts, exploratory testing relies on human intuition to uncover unexpected issues. AI-driven exploratory testing tools will analyze user interactions, application logs, and past defect trends to suggest high-risk areas that need manual testing. This hybrid approach will enhance software quality by combining AI's analytical power with human creativity.
- **Advanced AI-Driven Test Data Generation:** AI-generated synthetic test data will become more sophisticated, allowing teams to create diverse and privacy-compliant datasets for testing. Future AI models will be able to generate realistic user behaviors, simulate different geographic locations, and even predict edge-case scenarios to ensure robust software performance under various conditions.
- **Automated Root Cause Analysis and Debugging:** AI models will not only detect software defects but also assist in debugging by analyzing logs, stack traces, and historical defect patterns. This will significantly reduce the time required for defect triage, helping developers and testers identify the root cause of issues faster.

Predictions for the Next Decade in GenAI Testing

With rapid advancements in AI, the next decade will bring transformative changes to software testing. AI-powered autonomous testing, natural language-driven automation, and hyper-personalized AI agents will redefine how teams approach test strategy and execution. As AI continues to mature, the collaboration between human testers and intelligent systems will unlock new levels of efficiency, reliability, and scalability in software testing.

- **Fully Autonomous Testing Pipelines:** By 2035, AI-powered autonomous testing systems will handle the entire testing lifecycle, from test planning and execution to defect analysis and reporting. These systems will integrate seamlessly with DevOps pipelines, continuously learning from application changes to improve test efficiency.
- **AI-Driven Continuous Testing in CI/CD Pipelines:** AI will play a pivotal role in Continuous Testing by automatically identifying critical areas that need frequent testing, optimizing test execution times, and dynamically prioritizing tests based on recent code changes. This will lead to faster software releases with higher confidence in quality.
- **Natural Language Testing with AI Assistants:** The gap between testers and automation engineers will narrow as AI-powered assistants allow testers to write and execute test cases using plain English. For example, testers will be

able to input commands such as "`Validate login functionality across different devices`," and AI agents will generate and execute the corresponding automation scripts.

- **Hyper-Personalized AI Agents for Test Strategy and Execution:** AI agents will evolve to act as personalized virtual test strategists, recommending optimal test coverage, risk-based testing strategies, and real-time performance insights. These AI-driven assistants will analyze historical project data and industry trends to help teams make informed decisions about test planning.
- **AI-Powered Security and Compliance Testing:** With increasing concerns around cybersecurity and data privacy, AI will enhance security testing by simulating cyberattacks, identifying vulnerabilities, and ensuring compliance with global regulations. AI-driven compliance testing will continuously validate software against regulatory frameworks, reducing the risk of legal and financial repercussions.
- **Human-AI Collaboration in Testing:** AI will not replace human testers but will serve as an augmentation tool, enabling testers to focus on high-value tasks such as exploratory testing, usability evaluation, and strategic test planning. The future of AI in testing will be defined by a strong partnership between AI-driven automation and human expertise.

The Future of AI in Software Testing

Generative AI is set to transform software testing by making automation more adaptive, intelligent, and scalable. With advancements in AI agents, self-healing tests, and AI-assisted exploratory testing, the next decade will see a significant shift in how software quality is ensured. By embracing AI-driven testing strategies, organizations can improve test efficiency, reduce costs, and accelerate software delivery, all while maintaining high-quality standards.

Conclusion

As we conclude this chapter on Generative AI in automation testing, it is evident that AI is not just an enhancement but a transformative force in the world of software quality assurance. The adoption of AI-driven test automation, from intelligent test case generation to self-healing scripts and AI-powered exploratory testing, marks a significant shift toward efficiency, reliability, and adaptability in modern software development.

Throughout this chapter, we have explored how AI is revolutionizing test automation by improving test coverage, generating diverse and realistic test data, and seamlessly integrating into CI/CD pipelines. The rise of AI agents further demonstrates the potential for autonomous, self-learning testing systems that reduce manual effort and increase test accuracy. However, this evolution is not without challenges. Ethical considerations, biases in AI-generated tests, and the complexities of integration must be carefully managed to ensure that AI-driven testing remains reliable, fair, and effective.

Looking ahead, AI in testing will continue to evolve, with trends such as fully autonomous testing pipelines, AI-driven security testing, and natural language-based automation defining the next decade. AI agents will play a more prominent role, working alongside human testers to optimize testing strategies, analyze real-time data, and uncover defects with unprecedented speed.

For software testers, developers, and automation engineers, the key to success in this AI-driven era lies in adaptability, continuous learning, and a deep understanding of both AI capabilities and testing fundamentals. By embracing these advancements, professionals can position themselves at the forefront of innovation, contributing to the development of high-quality, resilient software systems.

Key Takeaways

- **GenAI is Transforming Test Automation:** AI-driven automation enhances test case generation, data creation, and test execution efficiency, reducing human effort and improving overall test coverage.
- **AI Enhances Test Coverage and Exploratory Testing:** AI-powered tools identify edge cases, simulate real-world user behavior, and expand testing beyond predefined scenarios, leading to more comprehensive test coverage.
- **AI-Generated Test Data is More Diverse and Realistic:** AI enables the creation of synthetic yet realistic test data, ensuring better coverage of different user conditions while maintaining compliance with data privacy regulations.
- **AI Agents are the Future of Testing:** Autonomous AI agents can dynamically adapt to changes in the application, perform self-healing automation, and assist testers in exploratory testing, reducing maintenance overhead.
- **Seamless AI Integration into CI/CD Pipelines:** AI-driven tools enhance DevOps workflows by enabling continuous testing, prioritizing test execution, and automatically adjusting test suites based on recent changes in the codebase.
- **Challenges in AI Testing Must Be Addressed:** AI-generated test scripts and predictions must be monitored for bias, reliability, and ethical implications to ensure fairness and effectiveness in test automation.

- **The Role of Testers is Evolving:** Testers and automation engineers must shift toward leveraging AI as a collaborative tool rather than a replacement, focusing on strategy, validation, and test optimization.
- **Future Trends in AI Testing:** The next decade will witness hyper-automation, fully autonomous testing pipelines, AI-driven security testing, and natural language-based test automation, reshaping the landscape of software quality assurance.

By embracing Generative AI and its capabilities, testing professionals can stay ahead in an evolving industry, driving efficiency, innovation, and reliability in software testing.

Index

B

C

D

E

F

G

H

M

T

U

W

Z